LIBRARY
LYNDON STATE COLLEGE
LYNDONVILLE, VT   05851

The Enduring Effects of Prenatal Alcohol Exposure on Child Development

Birth Through Seven Years, a Partial Least Squares Solution

Ann P. Streissguth, Ph.D.
Professor and Director, Fetal Alcohol and Drug Unit
Department of Psychiatry and Behavioral Sciences
University of Washington Medical School

Fred L. Bookstein, Ph.D.
Distinguished Research Scientist, Center for Human Growth
    and Development and the Institute for Gerontology
University of Michigan

Paul D. Sampson, Ph.D.
Associate Professor, Department of Statistics,
College of Arts and Sciences, University of Washington

Helen M. Barr, M.A., M.S.
Research Scientist, Fetal Alcohol and Drug Unit
Department of Psychiatry and Behavioral Sciences
University of Washington Medical School

**International Academy for Research in Learning Disabilities
Monograph Series, Number 10**

Ann Arbor

THE UNIVERSITY OF MICHIGAN PRESS

618.92
En 25

Copyright © by the University of Michigan 1993
All rights reserved
Published in the United States of America by
The University of Michigan Press
Manufactured in the United States of America

1996   1995   1994   1993   4 3 2 1

Library of Congress Cataloging-in-Publication Data

The Enduring effects of prenatal alcohol exposure on child development
  : birth through seven years, a partial least squares solution / Ann
  P. Streissguth ... [et al.].
      p.   cm. — (International Academy for Research in Learning
  Disabilities monograph series ; no. 8)
    Includes bibliographical references and index.
    ISBN 0-472-10455-1 (alk. paper)
    1. Children of prenatal alcohol abuse—Development—Longitudinal
  studies.   2. Learning disabilities—Etiology—Longitudinal studies.
  3. Children of prenatal alcohol abuse—Psychology—Longitudinal
  studies.   4. Behavioral toxicology.   5. Least squares.
  I. Streissguth, Ann Pytkowicz.   II. Series.
  RJ496.L4E53   1993
  618.92'861—dc20   93-38280
                                                             CIP

This series of monographs published under the sponsorship of the International Academy for Research in Learning Disabilities is dedicated to the recognition of Professor Alexander Romanovich Luria, Ph.D., a world-class professional whose work underscores a major development in an understanding of the neurophysiological development of learning disabled children and adults.

International Academy for Research in Learning Disabilities Monograph Series

This monograph is dedicated, with deep appreciation, to the 500 children and their parents who have participated so loyally in this study over the past 18 years. Without their commitment, this research, which should help future children, would have been impossible.

Contents

Acknowledgments

This book would not have been possible without the continuing support of the National Institute on Alcohol Abuse and Alcoholism, now a branch of the National Institutes of Health. The continuing emergence of new deficits not predicted by earlier measurements was a surprise not envisioned in the original project design, begun in 1974 for 36 months of support and now entering its eighteenth year. Without such sustained funding, it would have been impossible to carry out and extend our original mission.

The encouragement and support of three NIAAA staff has been particularly appreciated in carrying out the work on grant number AA01455-01-18: Kenneth Warren, Ph.D., Director of Scientific Affairs, and Tina Vanderveen, Ph.D. and Laurie Foudin, Ph.D., past and current project officers. Additional funding has been obtained from the National Council on Alcoholism, the University of Washington Alcoholism and Drug Abuse Institute, the University of Washington Medical Student Training Program, the Foundations Fund for Research in Psychiatry, and from anonymous donors through the Seattle Foundation, as well as from the National Institute of General Medical Sciences (through GM37251 to Dr. Bookstein, University of Michigan).

We thank the Obstetrics and Nursing Services of the University of Washington Hospital and the Group Health Cooperative of Puget Sound where the prenatal and neonatal components were carried out and the approximately 400 teachers who provided school information on the children in their second grade classrooms.

We gratefully acknowledge the generous collaboration of all those who helped in the original study design, the collection of the sample, the waves of data gathering over and over since 1975, and the earlier publications in this series: the late David W. Smith, M.D. for his original conceptualization of alcohol teratogenesis; Joan C. Martin, Ph.D. and Donald C. Martin, Ph.D.: original Co-Investigators for their important contributions to study design;

Ruth E. Little, Sc. D.: original Epidemiology consultant for her invaluable assistance in measuring alcohol use during pregnancy; Thomas H. Shepard, M.D., consultant on Embryology; Kathryn Barnard, Ph.D. and Francis Degen Horowitz, Ph.D.: consultants on the Brazelton Scale; James W. Hanson, M.D., John Graham, and Sterling K. Clarren, M.D.: Dysmorphologists; Sharon Landesman Ramey, Ph.D., Charles A. Lund, Ph.D., Veronica Buffington, Ph.D., Cynthia Herman Ervin, Ph.D., Arlene Ragozin, Ph.D., Betty L. Darby, Ph.D., and Grace Kirchner, Ph.D.: Psychologists; Donna Burgess, Ph.D. and Doris J. Johnson, Ph.D.: Educational Specialists; Bonnie Worthington-Roberts, Ph.D. and Nathan J. Smith, M.D.: Nutrition Consultants; Thomas Horst, M.D., James C. Parrish-Johnson, M.D., Jeanne Larsen, M.D., and Tanya Sorenson, M.D.: Medical Students; Carol Mullin, Bonny Young, Debra Clark, Linda McEcheren: Interviewers; Virginia Williams, Mary Jane Lambert, Helen Bergen Carlson: Sample Selection and Scheduling; Vicki Long, Madeline Parashar, Linda Brakke, and Susan Vlahakis: Medical Records Technicians; Sara Barbee, Stephanie Zimmerman, Jean Bretherton, Gudrun Geibel, Allison Arsove, Aimee Sodetani, Judy Furukawa, Lise Arsove, Laurel Menois, Mona Zuill, Jane Gaston, Pat Krehbiel and Heidi Grady: Neonatal Examiners; Joan Rocheleau, Nancy Mathews, Heather Carmichael Olson, Lisa Buenaventura, Joanne Ito, and Kris Box: Psychometrists; Mary Ann McCabe, Abigail Halperin, and Janet Gillespie: Outreach Workers; Peter Mills, Lauren Harris, Ann Garing: Research Assistants; Kelly Landreth, Susan Woodell, Beth MacGregor-Sandman, Sue Brimmer, Donna Stock, Therese Grant, Robert Treder, Deborah Donnell, Sylvia Vega-Gonzales, Teree Gilbert and Jed Dennis: Statistical Assistants; Khanh Phi Bui, Mgi Woo, Randy Carr, Nouanta Yansana, and Xinh Trong: Work Study Students; Virginia Williams, Marion Sturm, Sheila Quinn, Marlene Leaman Blessing, Nydia Fabian, Maryann Luse, and Pam Phipps: Program Assistants. Manuscript preparation was ably directed by Cara C. Ernst with the assistance of Kim Carson, Jeanne Kim Gray, Pamela Swanborn and James Hochstein. Sue Lippek typeset the manuscript. Translations of the Abstract were provided by Patricia Barron, M.A. (Spanish), Stanislav Dehaene, Ph.D. (French) and Elisabeth Scheuer-Sturgeon of German Language Services, Seattle, Washington (German). Many additional students, colleagues and volunteers have contributed to this research effort over the years; we thank them all.

We are especially grateful to Donald E. Hutchings, Ph.D., editor of Neurobehavioral Toxicology and Teratology, who encouraged us to publish our initial Partial Least Squares analyses in 1989 as a trilogy of 120 manuscript pages. This effort led to our extension of PLS into the longitudinal analyses of the present book.

Finally, to Daniel Streissguth, Edith Bookstein, Sandy Sanford and Timothy Barr, we express our gratitude for all the nights, early mornings, and weekends they left us undisturbed to develop this book, which represented, for each of us, a type of scientific writing for which our training left us unprepared.

Ann P. Streissguth
Fred L. Bookstein
Paul D. Sampson
Helen M. Barr

Abstract

In 1974/75, the Seattle Longitudinal Prospective Study on Alcohol and Pregnancy interviewed 1529 women in their fifth month of pregnancy regarding their alcohol consumption and many other pregnancy risk factors. A subsample of some 500 of these women was selected, of whom half represented an oversampling of the heavier drinkers and smokers from the 1529, and their offspring were studied intensively as neonates and at ages 8 and 18 months and 4 and 7 years. This monograph is a summary of the effects of prenatal alcohol exposure upon a total of 474 outcome measures spanning those ages. The measures of alcohol dose included average intake per day and various measures of peak dose both early in pregnancy and at the time of the interview. The high end of these measures in our sample rarely exceeds what might be called "heavy social drinking." Neurobehavioral outcome measures, many known to be abnormal in cases of Fetal Alcohol Syndrome, include the Brazelton and other neonatal scales, Bayley scores at 8 and 18 months, tests of intellectual, attentional, cognitive/neurological, and motor performance at ages 4 and 7 years, diverse parents', psychometrists', and teachers' ratings, and a variety of academic indicators of "learning disability."

Analyses are by the method of Partial Least Squares, a relatively new multivariate statistical method combining themes from factor analysis, multiple regression and nonlinear scaling.

Our principal findings are as follows. (1) Effects of prenatal alcohol exposure are manifest at all ages from birth to seven years; they are manifest on a variety of behavioral measures; and they do not attenuate with time. (2) Among the most salient sequelae of exposure are neonatal habituation to light, time in error from the Wisconsin Motor Steadiness Battery at age 4, standardized WISC-R and WRAT-R arithmetic subtests at age 7 years, and academic adjustment as rated by the second-grade teacher. (3) For most of the outcomes, binge drinking has more serious consequences than the same amount of steady drinking, and drinking early in pregnancy has more serious consequences than the same reported pattern of drinking in mid-pregnancy. (4) There is no statistical evidence for a "risk-free" or threshold level of prenatal drinking. (5) These alcohol effects cannot be "explained away" by any of 150 covariates we considered, including parents´ education, prenatal nutrition, and prenatal exposure to nicotine. (6) Profiles of alcohol-related scholastic and neurobehavioral deficit strikingly independent of the usual covariates are manifest by the second grade in school. These show promise for the characterization of individual children as fetal-alcohol-affected based on neurobehavioral criteria.

Abstrakt

In den Jaren 1974/75 wurden in einer Langzeitstudie zu Alkohol und Schwangerschaft in Seattle 1529 Frauen im fünften Schwangerschaftsmonat über ihren Alkoholkonsum und eine Anzehl anderer Risikofaktoren in der Schwangerschaft befragt. Eine Teilstichprobe von ca. 500 dieser Frauen wurde ausgewählt, von denen die Hälfte überdurchschnittlich hohes Trink- und Rauchverhalten innerhalb der 1529 Teilnehmerinnen aufwies. Ihre Kinder wurden als Neugeborene, im Alter von 8 bzw. 18 Monaten und 4 bzw. 7 Jahren intensiv beobachtet. Mit 474 Ergebniswerten, die diese Altersgruppen umspannen, gibt diese Monographie einen Überblick über die Auswirkungen von pränataler Exposition zu Alkohol. Die Bestimmung der Alkoholmenge schloß die durchschnittliche tägliche Einnahme und verschiedene höchste Dosen sowohl in der Frühschwangerschaft als auch zum Zeitpunkt der Befragung ein. Das obere Ende der Meßwerte dieser Stichprobe geht nur selten über das hinaus, was man als "starkes soziales Trinken" bezeichnet. Zu den neurobehavioralen Ergebnismaßen, welche anomal sind in Fällen der Alkoholem-bryopathie (fötales Alkoholsyndrom), gehören die Brazelton-Skala und andere neonatale Skalen, die Bagley-Skalen im 8. und 18. Lebensmonat, Tests zu intellektuellen, kognitiven/neurologischen und motorischen Leistungen und zur Aufmerksamkeitsspanne im 4. und 7. Lebensjahr, verschiedene Beurteilungen durch Eltern und Lehrer sowie durch Psychometrie und eine Vielzahl wissenschaftlicher Indikatoren der "Lernbehinderung".

Die Analysen erfolgen anhand der Methode der partiellen kleinsten Quadrate (Partial Least Square), einer relativ neuen multivariaten statistischen Methode, die mehrere Elemente der Faktorenanalyse, multiplen Regression und nicht-linearen Skalierung kombiniert.

Es ergeben sich folgende Hauptbefunde: (1) Auswirkungen pränataler Alkolexposition manifestieren sich in allen

Altersstufen von der Geburt bis zum 7. Lebensjahr; sie
manifestieren sich in einer Vielfalt von Verhaltensmaßen und
schwächen sich auch mit der Zeit nicht ab. (2) Zu den
hervorstechendsten Folgeerscheinungen der Exposition gehören
neonatale Gewöhnung an Licht, Verzögerung in der Wisconsin
Motor Steadiness Battery im 4. Lebensjahr, in den standardisierten
arithmetischen WISC-R (Wechsler -Intelligenztest für Kinder, vgl.
Hamburg-Wechsler-Intelligenztest für Kinder HAWIK) und
WRAT-R Untertests im 7. Lebensjahr und auch Verzögerung in der
schulischen Anpassung nach Einschätzung von Zweitklaßlehrern.
(3) Für die meisten Ergebnisse gilt, daß einmaliges exzessives
Trinken schwerwiegendere Konsequenzen hat als die gleiche Menge
Alkohol bei regelmäßigem Trinken, und daß Trinken in der
Frühschwangerschaft schwerwiegendere Folgen hat als berichtetes
gleiches Trinkverhalten im mittleren Teil der Schwangerschaft. (4)
Es gibt keinen statistischen Beweis für "risikoloses" pränatales
Trinken oder einen bestimmten Schwellenwert dafür. (5) Die
Alkoholauswirkungen lassen sich nicht "wegdiskutieren" durch
irgendeine der 150 in Betracht gezogen Kovariaten, Bildungsstand
der Eltern, pränatale Ernährung und pränatale Exposition gegenüber
Nikotin eingeschlossen. (6) Die Profile von alkoholbedingten
schulischen und neurobehavioralen Defiziten, die bemerkenswert
unabhängig von den gewöhnlichen Kovariaten sind, manifestieren
sich bis zum zweiten Schuljahr .
Die Befunde sind vielversprechend, soweit es gilt, auf der Grundlage
von neurobehavioralen Kriterien die Alkoholembryopathie (fötales
Alkoholsyndrom) einzelner Kinder zu charakterisieren.

Résumé

En 1974/75, dans le cadre de l'Etude Longitudinale Prospective de Seattle sur l'Alcool et la Grossesse, 1529 femmes enceintes de cinq mois ont été interrogées sur leur consommation alcoolique ainsi que d'autres facteurs de risque pour la grossesse. Un sous-ensemble de 500 de ces femmes a été sélectionné, dont la moitié parmi les plus grandes consommatrices d'alcool et de tabac de l'échantillon initial, et leurs enfants ont été attentivement étudiés en période néonatale, puis à 8 mois, 18 mois, 4 ans et 7 ans. Cette monographie résume les effets d'une exposition anténatale à l'alcool sur près de 474 indices recueillis à ces divers âges. Les mesures de consommation alcoolique comprenaient la quantité moyenne absorbée par jour ainsi que diverses appréciations du pic d'alcoolémie tant en début de grossesse qu'au moment de l'interview. Les plus grandes consommations observées dans notre échantillon dépassaient rarement le cadre de ce que l'on pourrait appeler: "l'alcoolisation lourde en société". Nos indices de développement neurologique, dont beaucoup sont affectés dans le Syndrome d'Alcoolisme Foetal, comprenaient le test de Brazelton et d'autres échelles néonatales, les scores de Bayley à 8 et 18 mois, divers tests des performances intellectuelles, attentionnelles, cognitives/-neurologiques et motrices à 4 et 7 ans, diverses appréciations des parents, des psychologues et des enseignants, et de nombreuses indicateurs d'échec scolaire et de troubles de l'apprentissage. Les données ont été analysées par la méthode des moindres carrés partiels, une statistique multivariée relativement nouvelle qui combine certains aspects de l'analyse factorielle. de la régression multiple et des transformations non-linéaires.

Nos principaux résultats sont les suivants. (1) Les effets de l'exposition anténatale à l'alcool sont visibles à tous les âges, de la naissance jusqu'à sept ans; ils s'observent dans de nombreuses mesures comportementales, et ne s'atténuent pas au cours du temps. (2) Parmi les séquelles les plus marquantes figurent l'habituation néonatale à la lumière, la durée des persévérations dans la Batterie de Coordination Manuelle de Wisconsin à 4 ans, les épreuves standardisées d'arithmétique du WISC-R et du WRAT-R à 7 ans, et l'adaptation scolaire estimée par l'enseignant du cours élémentaire. (3) Sur la plupart des indices, l'alcoolisation aigu massive a des conséquences plus sévères, a dose égale, que l'alcoolisation réguliere, et la même alcoolisation est plus dangereuse en tout début qu'en milieu de grossesse, (4) Il n'existe aucune preuve statistique de l'existence d'un seuil d'alcoolisation en deça duquel une consommation prénatale d'alcool serait sans risque. (5) Aucune des 150 variables covariantes que nous avons considérées, y compris le niveau scolaire des parents, la diététique maternelle au cours de la grossesse, ou l'exposition prénatale à la nicotine, ne peuvent expliquer ces effets de l'alcool. (6) Un profil de déficits scolaires et neurologiques imputables à l'alcool et étonnamment indépendants des variables covariantes habituelles est perceptible à l'école dès le cours élémentaire. Il pourrait peut-être permettre de diagnostiquer des cas individuels d'"effet d'alcoolisme foetal" sur la base de critères comportementaux.

Sumarío

En 1974/75, se realizó en Seattle por primera vez un estudio longitudinal sobre alcohol y embarazo para lo cual se entrevistaron 1529 mujeres en su quinto mes de embarazo de acuerdo a su consumo de alcohol y a muchos otros factores de riesgo. Una submuestra de 500 de esas mujeres fue seleccionada, la mitad de las cuales eran bebedoras y fumadoras consuetudinarias, y sus hijos fueron estudiados intensivamente al nacimiento, de los 8 a 18 meses y a los 4 y 7 años de edad. Esta monografía tiene un sumario de los efectos que se presentan por una exposición al alcohol en la etapa prenatal, aproximadamente un total de 474 medidas fueron tomadas en el trascurso de esas edades. Las medidas en las dósis de alcohol incluyen un promedio de toma por dia y varias medidas de la dósis mas altas tomadas tanto al principio del embarazo como en el momento en que fue efectuada la entrevista. El extremo mas alto de estas medidas en nuestra muestra raramente excede lo que podria ser llamado "beber en exceso en reuniones sociales." Las medidas de neuro-comportamiento mas sobresalientes, muchas conocidas como anormales en el caso del síndrome del alcoholismo fetal, incluyen las escalas de Brazelton y otras escalas neonatales, escores de Bayley a los 8 y 18 meses, pruebas de inteligencia, atención, cognocitivas/neurologicas y de actividad motríz a los 4 y 7 años, las clasificaciones de diversos padres, psicometristas, maestros y una variedad de indicadores academicos los consideran como "incapacidades del aprendizaje"

El análisis se hizo por el método de los mínimos cuadrados parciales, un método relativamente nuevo de multivariables estadísticas combinado temas de análisis factorial, regresion múltiple y escalas no lineales.

Nuestros principales hallazgos son los siguientes: (1) Los efectos de la exposicíon al alcohol en etapas prenatales en nuestra muestra se presentan en todas las edades desde el nacimiento hasta los siete años; estas se manifiestan en una variedad de medidas del comportamiento; y no se atenuan con la edad. (2) Entre las secuelas mas sobresalientes estan la habituación a la lúz, error en tiempo de la prueba de estabilidad motríz de Wisconsin a la edad de 4 años, exámenes estandarizados de WISC-R (Escala de inteligencia para niños de Wechsler) y WRAT-R (Exámen de amplio rango de mejoramiento-revisado) asi como subexámenes de aritmética a los 7 años, y el ajuste academico es proporcionado por el maestro de segundo año escolar. (3) Por la mayoría de nuestros resultados vemos que, el beber ocasionalmente en exceso tiene consecuencias mas serias que las que se presentan bebiendo la misma cantidad pero en pequenas dósis y el beber en etapas tempranas del embarazo tiene consecuencias mas severas que el beber con el mismo patrón a la mitad del embarazo. (4) No hay evidencia estadística de que no exista "riesgo alguno" o un nivel permitido o tolerado de ingestión de alcohol durante el embarazo. (5) Estos efectos del alcohol no pueden ser "explicados" por ninguna de las 150 covariables que nosotros consideramos como son: padres, educación, nutrición prenatal y exposición a la nicotina en etapas prenatales. (6) Los perfiles de las deficiencias en la escolaridad y el neuro-comportamiento presentadas por los efectos de la ingestión del alcohol son mas notorias y se apartan de las covariables normales que se tienen para el segundo año escolar. Esto es muy promisorio para la caracterizacion individual de los niños afectados por el alcohol en etapas fetales basadose en un criterio del neuro-comportamiento.

Introduction and Guide to Using This Monograph

This monograph describes what we believe to be the first long-term human behavioral teratology study. Teratology is the study of "birth defects": undesirable modifications of normal embryonic development. From its origins in ancient times through at least 1960, the birth defects field was primarily concerned with gross physical malformations (such as cleft palate) that could be detected at birth and that typically required immediate surgical intervention and/or long-term management for the well-being of the child. Basic research in the field of teratology typically involved exposing laboratory vertebrates to toxic substances that proved capable of modifying normal pathways of embryologic or fetal development. Clinical work on birth defects involved the identification of recognizable patterns of human malformation and efforts to establish their putative causes, whether genetic or environmental.

The epidemiology of "poor pregnancy outcome" was likewise advancing rapidly by the 1970s. We knew, for instance, that smoking during pregnancy was one cause of low birthweight in babies, and that maternal malnutrition could deter normal development. Epidemiologic studies of poor pregnancy outcome generally focused on the immediately observable condition of the baby at birth (low birthweight, anoxia, low apgar scores, etc.) and the investiga-tion of risk factors for discrete end points.

Meanwhile, behavioral teratology was growing up in the animal laboratory in the 1960s and 1970s, examining the effects of prenatal-ly administered X-ray, vitamin A, and drugs. A new methodology of animal behavioral testing was developed to provide a better means of detecting new and more subtle forms of early offspring damage, particularly to the brain. Animal models of behavioral dysfunctions were thought to be analogous to mental retardation, learning disabili-ties and emotional disturbances in children. It was hoped that through these models, the prenatal causes and mechanisms of these functional disabilities could be understood and ultimately prevented in children. Some of the most important contributions of these traditional behavioral teratology studies have involved their use by governmental regulatory agencies for safety evaluations of new pharmaceutical products. Knowledge that neurobehavioral effects of drugs and other teratogens can occur at lower levels than the more traditional teratogenic end points has made these subtle long-term neurobehavioral outcomes of great utility in protecting the health of future generations. Ironically, it was through research on alcohol, the legal drug, that behavioral teratology made such astounding progress in the past 20 years. This book goes to press on the twentieth anniversary of the first diagnostic labeling of children as having "fetal alcohol syndrome" and on the thirtieth anniversary of the first published use of the term "behavioral teratology."

The discovery of Fetal Alcohol Syndrome (FAS) by the early 1970s represented an unprecedented opportunity for a blending of these forms of investigation. Here was the first hard evidence that a substance that had been in constant use for thousands of years might itself be a "risk factor" carrying a computable weight of responsibility for clear offspring deficits. Unfortunately for millennia of children but fortunately for study design, the role of alcohol in causing these defects was "officially unknown." The Collaborative Perinatal Project and other federally funded investigations of the 1960s on prenatal causes of neurological disorders considered maternal alcohol use irrelevant, and did not record it; alcohol drips were used to prevent premature delivery; government advisory pamphlets stated that the placenta protected the fetus from any adverse consequences of alcohol use during pregnancy. In fact, until FAS was discovered, there was no research evidence in common knowledge suggesting that prenatal exposure to alcohol carried any risk at all. Only in retrospect have we assembled the centuries of anecdotal evidence, folk wisdom, and early studies on the problems, appearance and behavior of children of alcoholic mothers.

Once FAS was recognized as a syndrome, however, it became an urgent matter of public health to explore the possibility of milder forms of the syndrome corresponding to milder exposures. The window of the middle 1970s was a propitious time for establishing such a study. Except among experts, there was little general knowledge that drinking during pregnancy could have any effect on offspring, and while cigarette labelling was "in the air," the labelling of containers for alcoholic beverages was still 15 years in the future.

Perhaps only around 1973, then, could a study be designed that would combine the best of teratologic and epidemiologic methods: a study specifically to evaluate the long-term implications of prenatal alcohol exposure set in a context of other risks to the child and em-ploying the subtle long-term neurobehavioral outcomes of behavioral teratology. Our sample was not a study of an impacted subpopula-tion, but a carefully calibrated cohort representative of women pregnant in the Seattle/King County (Washington) area in 1974. The mothers and children of our sample are typical of the fabric of this community. In 1974, one did not need to be ignorant, misinformed, stubborn, complacent, or self-destructive to drink during pregnancy. Levels of alcohol use were distributed without large imbalances over the myriad of other determinants of child outcome in a fashion likely never to be seen again.

Of course, it is not enough merely to construct an appropriately stratified sample making possible an estimate of the effects of alcohol exposure separate from simultaneously acting effects of nicotine and other teratogens. To investigate long-term implications, we needed to follow our sample for a long time. To calibrate the consequences of alcohol with sufficient power, we needed a wide range of measures of exposure, an enormously wide range of outcome measures that might show offspring damage, and an equally wide range of measures of other determinants of those outcome measures.

Eighteen years of arduous sample measurement, instrument design, and data collection and analysis have culminated in the one coherent finding, the main theme of this book: There is an enduring effect of prenatal alcohol exposure on children's neurobehavioral development discernible across levels well below those leading to the appearance of the Fetal Alcohol Syndrome itself.

In this book, we only briefly review the voluminous literatures of the last 20 years on alcohol and pregnancy, FAS, and the detailed mechanisms of alcohol teratogenesis. Likewise, we review only briefly the 106 scientific papers already written in the course of this study, papers listed in Appendix I. (Some of these papers have progressed beyond the first eight years of study data reviewed here, to explore continuing manifestations of prenatal dose at 11 and even 14 years of age; others discuss clinical work on FAS.) Readers interested in work from our Unit on the clinical manifestations of fetal alcohol syndrome and/or suggestions for patient management may wish to consult the papers identified by an '‡' in Appendix I. Those interested in public policy and prevention issues deriving from the prevention research on our Unit may find papers marked '†' in Appendix I to be helpful. This book is essentially a report on new longitudinal analyses from the Seattle Longitudinal Prospective Study on Alcohol and Pregnancy — work not covered in previous publications. This book is not the equivalent of a collection of scientific papers in any sense. Instead, we present the form of scientific argument—the "rhetoric," if you will—by which we organize the tremendously rich and varied tapestry of neurobehavioral findings that had accrued in our study of five hundred children across the first eight years of their lives. The enduring effects of prenatal alcohol exposure are best presented not one finding at a time, but all together, across ages, across levels of exposure, and across channels of response. We best understand the effects of alcohol by considering its consequences for hundreds of outcomes at once, both those outcomes that are affected and those that are not. When we began our synthesis, there were no methods for truly longitudinal analysis of the impact of one single teratogen on the developing child. Over the last six years of our writing for this book, we think we have developed such a method, one that is sturdy, reliable, and sensitive. The medium of the single scientific paper is too constrained for a proper explanation of what this method is about; this book, then, represents our best effort at describing and justifying this new methodology for longitudinal studies in behavioral teratology.

We hope this method will be useful to other researchers involved in similar investigations. Seemingly modest decisions about sampling, measurement, and computation interact with powerful consequences for the cogency of the recommendations that ultimately emerge from studies like ours, studies too urgent to wait for the laboratory-driven understanding of mechanisms.

Our book incorporates the degree of statistical explication necessary for the imitation of our computations in other contexts. But our fundamental concern here is always epidemiologic and teratologic: our concern is public health, not statistical method. Throughout our argument we return again and again to the linkage between science and public policy. Studies of widespread teratogens, however cogent their biochemistry, are not complete until they can be turned persuasively to improve the common health.

A Guide to Using this Monograph

The first three chapters review study rationale, design, and methodology. In these we emphasize the specific procedures we used to intercept many of the pitfalls and biases that can arise in longitudinal research in general, and specifically in human behavioral teratology. (In Chapter 9 we evaluate the successes and failures of our design considerations.)

Chapter 2 describes sample selection and retention, measurement of alcohol and covariates. We describe the subjects in the interview sample and the stratification procedures by which we selected the follow-up cohort. Appendix II outlines the prenatal interview, and lists the QFV (quantity-frequency-variability) and Supplemental Alcohol questions. Table 2.3 decodes and describes the 13 Alcohol predictor variables.

Chapter 3 is a survey of our full roster of 474 neurobehavioral outcomes measured in cohort children from 1 day through 7 years of age. This chapter is supplemented by Appendix III-a and b aggregating these measures into "blocks" representing "mental," "neuro-motor," or "attention" measures, age by age, and a 7-year learning disabilities block. Appendices III-a and b decode and describe the 474 outcome variables and list their sources.

Chapter 4 is more narrowly statistical in its language. It intro-duces the primary technique we exploit here for analysis of alcohol effects on whole blocks of variables: Wold's method of Partial Least Squares. The chapter begins with a tutorial on two-block PLS analysis, analyzing the Alcohol Block (containing the 13 prenatal alcohol predictors) against the 11 WISC-R subtest scores. Figure 4.2 diagrams the two-block Latent Variable model; Table 4.4 is our standard format for presentation of the results of two-block analyses. This analysis shows not only the overall strength of the relationship between alcohol and IQ subtests, but also the relative salience of each of the alcohol predictors for the 11 subtests and the relative salience of each of the subtests for alcohol. Chapter 4 goes on to develop a version of PLS appropriate for the analysis of more than two blocks and demonstrates it in an analysis of prenatal alcohol by mental development assessed at four ages.

Chapter 5 uses two-block PLS analysis to examine the effect of prenatal alcohol on the full spectrum of 474 neurobehavioral out-comes obtained across all five waves of data collection. The standard PLS analysis (Table 5.1) now yields two alcohol latent variables, each with many associated outcomes. Figure 5.2 and 5.3 portray the alcohol dose on a "map" of prenatal exposure-patterns together with clusters of outcomes most salient for them. We survey the entire diagram to see which outcomes are associated with each prenatal alcohol pattern. Chapter 5 also presents a longitudinal PLS path analysis for the effect of prenatal alcohol on the four domains of behavior (mental, neuromotor, attentional, and learning disabilities) across all the ages at which they were examined in this study.

Chapter 5 deals with properties of individual variables (measures of dose or of outcome), but not with scores for individual subjects. Taking for granted the two dimensions of alcohol dose as reported there, the remaining three chapters of data analysis dig into more detailed aspects of the alcohol dose-response relationship that can be studied only when we consider subject-by-subject scores as well. Section 6.1 shows the relation between dose score and the principal outcome latent variable scores as scatterplots over all 581 subjects (Figure 6.1). The appearance of these justifies the care we took in stratifying the sample and in constructing the latent variables: just as we had hoped, the scatters have the appearance of a smooth dose-response relationship. Of course, epidemiological studies like ours must verify that the claimed dose-response relationship is not instead expressing the effect of covariates of dose. The later sections of Chapter 6 explore several versions of this essential verification. Even though our outcome scores are indubitably affected by some of the usual covariates (for instance, parental education) as well as by alcohol, the alcohol-outcome relation we uncovered in Chapter 5 is not due to covariates (Section 6.2). In fact, "new" alcohol effects "drip" into the outcome LV at every new wave of outcome measurement (Section 6.3).

Chapter 7 combines the concern for saliences from Chapter 5 with the concern for scores from Chapter 6. Section 7.1 compares the analyses of two particularly interesting outcome blocks, learning disabilities and neuromotor function, from the 7-year exam. We show how analysis of saliences and analysis of scores can lead to different kinds of findings, some stronger, some weaker. More tightly defined subblocks, such as the subscales of the WISC IQ test, support a better mode of covariate adjustment that relies on the existence of general factors for those blocks. Sections 7.2 and 7.3 shows how PLS analyses of such blocks can be directly interpreted as "profiles" that simplify the reporting of the alcohol effect by stripping away most of the effects of covariates in advance.

In Chapter 8 is the culmination of all this data analysis: our first attempt to see if, using all the data collected through age 7 years, we can identify some of these 581 subjects not merely as "damaged" but specifically as having been damaged by *alcohol exposure*. Of all our blocks of outcome measures, wave by wave, the highest dose-response correlation is for the 7-year neuromotor block. The subjects in the highest percentiles of latent variable score for this block were very often subnormal in performance at all other waves of measurement and also were very often highly exposed to alcohol. We find thirteen subjects that appear to meet all three criteria. Two of these were already called FAS; the remaining eleven, we submit, are appropriately described as *truly alcohol-affected*. Their scores for dose and for outcomes are shown explicitly in Figure 8.2.

Chapter 9 includes a critique of the study design, a summary of the main findings, and a discussion of some of their implications.

Appendix I is a chronological listing of the 106 publications and technical reports from this study. These are referenced by number in the text. Other papers cited in the text are referenced by author names and year of publication and listed alphabetically in the Reference List. Appendix I also contains publications from research on our Unit pertaining to clnical aspects of fetal alcohol syndrome (identified by a '‡') and our research on prevention and public policy (identified by a '†').

Appendix II describes the original maternal questionnaire in greater detail, in particular, the assessment of maternal alcohol use.

Appendix III-a contains a list of the 474 outcomes evaluated in this monograph from birth through 7 years, and some useful descriptive statistics. The outcomes are listed chronologically according to the outcome block to which they have been assigned and the test situation from which they derived. Appendix III-b is an alphabetical listing of the 474 computer names or acronyms for all the outcome variables, keyed to Appendix III-a for easy access.

Appendix IV-a is a graphic representation of the 99 outcomes most salient for *some* alcohol pattern, and Appendix IV-b lists the computer names or acronyms and verbal definitions of these same 99 outcomes (to permit cross-referencing to Appendix III-a and III-b). This latter Appendix also shows the saliences of each of these 99 best outcomes for the two Alcohol LVs as well as their net correlation with these two dimensions of exposure.

Appendix V compiles all of the findings from the Partial Least Squares analyses of our many blocks at up to four ages.

The reference list (Literature Cited) includes full citations on all papers cited in the monograph *except* those deriving from our

Unit, identified in the text by a numerical listing, which keys to the full citation in Appendix I.

Readers with specific needs may find these suggestions helpful:

1. To decode a computer name, go to Appendix II-b to find its index number, then go to Appendix II-a to see what block it's in. The Footnote to Appendix II-a identifies the names of the tests from which the items derive and appropriate references; also see Chapter 3.

2. To see how any single outcome item relates to alcohol, there are several choices:

    A. Appendix II-a gives the mean scores of each item on the dichotomous Binge/No Binge score. Remember that some items relate primarily to non-binge scores—these would go undetected here.

    B. Figure 5.2 shows the salience of all 474 outcomes for *some* alcohol pattern, with the 24 most salient identified by their computer names.

    C. Appendix IV-a shows 99 items most salient for *some* pattern of alcohol exposure. The companion Appendix IV-b decodes these 99 "best" outcomes, the salience for each of the two Alcohol LVs, and their overall relationship to alcohol as shown in Appendix III-a.

    D. Figure 5.4 portrays the "best" outcomes in terms of their block membership so that one can see at which ages and in which domains the alcohol effects are best measured.

2. To see how any single alcohol pattern relates to the outcome items most highly related to it, see Figure 5.3.

This monograph has been designed for three types of readers. Those who are interested in learning what *are* the enduring effects of alcohol on child development through 7 years may focus on Chapters 1 through 3 and Chapter 9. Those interested in the actual measures and in details of the findings may want to add Appendix V and the Introductions and Summaries of Chapters 4 through 8.

Those interested in learning our PLS analytic technique will want to read all of Chapters 4 through 8.

To duplicate these analyses for your own data sets, software for the "S-Plus" system is available through Dr. Sampson, Department of Statistics, University of Washington.

## CHAPTER 1

Theoretical Background, Historical Context, Study Aims, and a Glimpse of the Findings

This monograph is primarily a description of the first 7 years of the Seattle Longitudinal Prospective Study on Alcohol and Pregnancy and new longitudinal analysis of this data. In this chapter, we present the theoretical framework in which the research is set, describe briefly the historical context in which the discovery of Fetal Alcohol Syndrome (FAS) led to the recognition of alcohol as a teratogen, and review the Seattle Study in the context of other epidemiologic studies. Finally, we discuss the objectives of the Seattle Study and present a first glimpse at the enduring effects of prenatal alcohol, as measured in this monograph.

1.1 Theoretical Background

Alcohol is a teratogenic drug: exposure during gestation can damage the embryo and fetus. Alcohol readily crosses the placenta; fetal blood alcohol levels approximate those of the mother within minutes of consumption. Alcohol can alter the development of the central nervous system (CNS) *in utero* in a fashion dependent on the dose, timing, and conditions of exposure (Vorhees & Mollnow, 1987; West, 1986; Meyer & Riley, 1986).

Because alcohol is the most commonly ingested neurobehavioral teratogen (Hutchings, 1980), the study of the long-term effects of prenatal alcohol exposure is an important field of investigation. While some teratogenic drugs, such as thalidomide, cause gross physical malformations, the most devastating and pervasive effects of alcohol are seen in central nervous system (CNS) dysfunction. In human studies, then, behavioral dysfunction and poor or atypical performance are the outcomes of interest. We call this field of endeavor human neurobehavioral teratology, reflecting that the primary assault occurs prenatally and that the neurologic consequences of the assault are reflected in behavior. The theoretical context of the Seattle Study on Alcohol and Pregnancy lies within the field of behavioral teratology (Riley & Vorhees, 1986), a subspecialty of the field of teratology.

The principles of teratology were laid down in the mid 1970s by James G. Wilson. The final manifestations of teratogenesis are death, malformation, growth deficiency and functional disorder. Some of the principles include the following: The manifestations of deviant development increase in degree as dosage increases. Susceptibility to teratogenic agents varies with the developmental stage at the time of exposure, with the genotype, and with the manner in which the genotype interacts with the environment (Wilson, 1973, 1977).

In the early 1980s the field of teratology was formally expanded to behavioral outcomes by Hutchings (1980), Vorhees and Butcher (1982), and Riley and Vorhees (1986). The manifestations of behavioral teratogenesis include impaired cognitive, affective, social, arousal, reproductive and sensorimotor behavior; delayed behavioral maturation of these capacities; and other indices of compromised behavioral competence. Behavioral teratogens alter development of the central nervous system (CNS). The type and magnitude of effects depend on the dose and the developmental stage of the nervous system. Behavioral teratogenic effects are demonstrable at doses below those causing malformations. The CNS is vulnerable to behavioral teratogenic effects during all stages of its development; maximum susceptibility of the CNS to structural injury is during the period of neurogenesis (Vorhees, 1986).

The fields of teratology and behavioral teratology have most usually been pursued in animal laboratories where the conditions of exposure are under experimental control.

Studies of laboratory animals in the late 1970s and 1980s directly demonstrated a variety of neurobehavioral, structural, and biochemical effects of gestational alcohol exposure on the CNS (Abel, 1980, 1981; Porter, O'Connor, & Whelan, 1984; West, 1986). Summaries of more recent animal studies on alcohol teratogenesis describe alcohol-induced disruption of cell proliferation, neuronal migration, and morphogenesis (Miller, 1992; Pentney & Miller, 1992), delays in glial cell and myelin development (Phillips, 1992), and the relationship of these and other neuroanatomic correlates to offspring behavior (Goodlett, Bonthius, Wasserman, & West, 1992; Goodlett & West, 1992; Riley, 1990; West, Goodlett, Bonthius & Pierce, 1989).

Animal models, carried out after the Seattle Study began, have demonstrated that CNS and behavioral effects are produced at exposure levels that are lower than those needed to produce effects on growth and/or malformations, that effects are more closely associated with blood alcohol level than with administered dose, and that a massed pattern of dosing is more predictive of some outcomes than a lower steady dose. Dosing levels in some animal studies are well within the extrapolation range to those consumed by women (e.g., 70; Clarren et al., 1990; Goodlett et al., 1990; Goodlett & West, 1992; Savage, Montano, Paxton, & Kasarskis, 1989).

This monograph describes the systematic examination of the effects of prenatal alcohol exposure upon a variety of neurobehavioral measures in a carefully controlled study of some 500 children followed from gestation for seven years. We show how the conscientious pursuit of redundancy of outcome, measured over a great breadth of neurobehavioral scores, compensates for the imprecision that is unavoidable when "dose" is measured by verbal reports instead of physiological assessment, as are necessary in large-sample teratogenic studies in humans. To our knowledge this is the first major longitudinal prospective study designed within the framework of human behavioral teratology.

1.2 Historical Context and the Fetal Alcohol Syndrome (FAS)

At the time this study began in 1974, the field of behavioral teratology was in its infancy and confined to the animal laboratory, and the first papers on FAS had just appeared. Drs. Kenneth L. Jones and David W. Smith and colleagues in Seattle had just identified a specific pattern of malformations, growth deficiency, and CNS dysfunction observable in some offspring of alcoholic mothers (Jones, Smith, Ulleland & Streissguth, 1973), a pattern that they named Fetal Alcohol Syndrome (Jones & Smith, 1973).

Identification of this new birth defect kindled interest in the teratogenic effects of alcohol (22; Abel, 1979; Randall & Taylor, 1979; Riley, Lochry & Shapiro, 1979), brought to light previous reports from France of a similar clinical picture in affected children of alcoholic mothers (Lemoine, Harousseau, Borteyru & Menuet, 1968; Rouquette, 1957), and stimulated historical study of the dangers of drinking during pregnancy (Warner & Rosett, 1975). In the decade that followed, more than 2,000 scientific papers were published on alcohol teratogenicity; most were research reports on laboratory animals, short-term epidemiologic studies of pregnancy outcome, or case reports of children with FAS.

Early estimates of FAS prevalence from France, Sweden, and the United States indicated the rate might be 1 per 600 to 750 live births (10; Dehaene et al., 1977a & b; Olegård et al., 1979). One of these earliest prevalence studies was, in fact, from a substudy of the Seattle Study on Alcohol and Pregnancy, in which a dysmorphologist carried out blind examinations of a subset of the heaviest exposed and most lightly exposed babies from the current Seattle cohort (10).

By the late 1970s, FAS was recognized as one of the three leading causes of mental retardation with a known etiology, having a prevalence comparable to Down Syndrome and spina bifida (Smith, 1980). Of the three, FAS is the only known cause of mental retardation that is entirely preventable.

It was also recognized by this time that the birth defect known as Fetal Alcohol Syndrome was only the "tip of the iceberg" of prenatal alcohol-related disabilities. Clinicians observed that a *spectrum* of offspring effects was found in the presence of prenatal alcohol exposure. While a specific phenotype characterized FAS, partial manifestations were often described as Fetal Alcohol Effects (Clarren & Smith, 1978). Fetal Alcohol Effects (FAE) is a term commonly used in the clinical context to describe children who have some of the characteristics of FAS but lack the full complement of features necessary for a diagnosis of the syndrome. As one of the three component characteristics of FAS is CNS dysfunction, the term FAE is often used quite broadly; but in proper usage it should be restricted to those patients with a clear history of significant prenatal alcohol exposure. "Fetal alcohol effects" is also used for the broad gamut of findings detected in epidemiologic studies that relate to prenatal alcohol exposure. In this sense, this monograph is a longitudinal study of fetal alcohol effects.

In human teratology, the tie between exposure and damage is not perfect. Clinical studies of heavily exposed children, for instance, indicate that not all are physically affected by prenatal alcohol. An early study from Germany (Seidenberg & Majewski, 1978; Majewski, 1981) reported that one-third of the chronically alcoholic mothers drinking during pregnancy had children with clear FAS. Studies from northern France (Dehaene et al., 1977a) had similar findings. Whereas many children without FAS are born to alcoholic mothers, no children with FAS have been reported who have *not* had alcoholic mothers. In animal studies, genetic differences among mothers and fetuses account for some of this lack of concordance (Chernoff, 1980). Differential outcomes in dizygotic twins born to alcoholic mothers demonstrate the genetic modulation of the teratogenic effects of alcohol (103).

For alcohol, as with other teratogens, the more severe effects are associated with heavier exposure. Children of alcoholic mothers generally are more severely affected than children of moderate drinkers. Children with the most severe physical manifestations of FAS tend to be the most mentally handicapped (14; Steinhausen, Nestler & Spohr, 1982). Although the average IQ of patients with FAS is around 68 to 70, the range of IQ scores is very broad (14, 83). We found that when we classified patients according to the severity of their physical symptoms (degree of growth deficiency and number and severity of physical anomalies) (14) there were still large differences in average IQ by category (average IQ for those classified as "severe" was 55; moderately severe, 58; moderate, 68; and mild or very mild, 82). Since these early studies, we have seen many patients with the full FAS who have IQ scores in the normal range. The highest IQ to date, in our lab, is 116 in an adolescent patient with the full FAS, tested on the WISC-R.

Several studies have demonstrated that children of alcoholic mothers drinking during pregnancy have IQ and achievement scores significantly lower than those of carefully matched non-alcoholic controls, even in the absence of physical stigmata (1; Jones, Smith, Streissguth & Myrianthopoulos, 1974; Aronson, Kyllerman, Sabel, Sandin & Olegård, 1985; Horowitz, 1984). In an important early clinical study, Shaywitz, Cohen & Shaywitz (1980) reported behavioral and learning problems in children of "normal intelligence" born to alcoholic mothers.

Although the early studies on children with FAS focused on intelligence testing, interest is now growing in assessing a broader range of abilities and functions across a wider range of ages. Problems with arithmetic and mathematics have long been known to characterize many patients with FAS/FAE and children of alcoholics (1, 83; Horowitz, 1984). These may relate to difficulties with abstract thinking and poor judgement so frequently observed in older patients with FAS, especially those who are not diagnosable as retarded.

A recent follow-up study of patients with FAS into adolescence and adulthood found the following cluster of behaviors to characterize even those who were not mentally retarded: failure to consider consequences of action, lack of appropriate initiative, unresponsiveness to social cues, and lack of reciprocal friendships (83). We speculate that the roots of these behavior problems lie in prenatal brain damage from alcohol reflected in attentional, memory and learning problems: the kinds of deficits that several decades ago were called "minimal brain damage" before we even knew that prenatal alcohol could be a contributing factor. Abnormal MRI scans in three patients with FAS have just been reported (Mattson et al, 1992), complementing earlier reports of neuropathology in patients with FAS (Clarren, 1986).

The CNS effects are not necessarily ameliorated by a good environment (43; Aronson et al., 1985; Steinhausen et al., 1982), but longer duration in a chaotic alcoholic environment can contribute to additional behavioral problems (Aronson, Sandin, Sabel, Kyllerman & Olegård, 1984).   Furthermore, the primary CNS dysfunction associated with FAS/FAE does not appear to diminish with increasing age (83, 84).   However, the growth deficiency and characteristic pattern of malformation often becomes less pronounced after puberty (43, 83; Lemoine & Lemoine, 1992).   This contributes to considerably greater difficulty in making the diagnosis in adolescents and adults. As larger groups of patients with FAS/FAE have been examined, it has become clear that not all persons with FAS are mentally retarded. Many have normal IQ scores, although their behavior may reflect attentional, memory, and/or learning problems.

Case/control studies of children with FAS or children of alcoholic mothers have shown a wide range of early developmental and CNS problems to be characteristic, including early problems with sucking, failure to thrive, retarded motor development and speech, problems with sleeping, eating, peer relations, hyperactivity, distractibility, concentration, neuropsychological function and learning, and lowered IQ (Aronson et al., 1985; Conry, 1990; Jones et al., 1974; Kyllerman et al., 1985; Nanson & Hiscock, 1990; Steinhausen et al., 1982).

It is now absolutely clear that a teratogen like alcohol is associated with a broad range of outcomes that reflect the rich diversity of exposures, in terms of timing, duration, and quantity, and the broad array of individual differences in maternal and fetal genetic vulnerability to prenatal alcohol effects.

This rich clinical picture of the devastating life-long influences of heavy prenatal alcohol exposure has guided our epidemiologic study through each wave of data collection, helping us focus our hypotheses and select our outcomes.

1.3 Epidemiologic Studies on Alcohol and Pregnancy

The observation that mental retardation was associated with maternal alcoholism immediately suggested questions about possible adverse effects of lower levels of prenatal alcohol exposure. To address them, three large federally-funded projects were initiated in 1974 by the National Institute on Alcohol Abuse and Alcoholism (NIAAA) (see 22 for details). The Seattle Longitudinal Prospective Study on Alcohol and Pregnancy, the subject of this monograph, is the only one still in progress.

In designing our study of the enduring effects of alcohol on child development, we were able to draw on our early clinical experience in working with young children and infants with FAS, and those without FAS also born to alcohol-abusing mothers (1, 2, 14, 15, 28; Jones et al., 1973; Jones et al., 1974). Our association with the late David W. Smith (Smith, 1970, 1976, 1982) and his Dysmorphology Unit at the University of Washington Medical School made this possible, as well as our continuing association with his successor Sterling K. Clarren and his Craniofacial and Fetal Risks Clinic. These associations were enhanced by our own fetal alcohol follow-up studies through the Fetal Alcohol and Drug Unit in the Department of Psychiatry and Behavioral Sciences, University of Washington Medical School. From our clinical experience with hundreds of patients with FAS across many years of their lives (83), we have been able to derive specific hypotheses about the outcomes to be targeted in our social drinking study.

In this study we use the term "social drinking" (in accordance with current usage [NIAAA, 1990]) to refer to the alcohol use patterns of persons who do not themselves report major alcohol-related problems. Our population of study mothers were all in prenatal care by the 5th month of pregnancy. This distinguishes them from populations selected from alcohol and drug treatment programs and from that subgroup of high-risk alcohol- and drug-abusing mothers who deliver babies without adequate prenatal care. This primarily middle-class group of women were drinking what women in our community normally drank during pregnancy, before awareness of the risks associated with prenatal alcohol exposure was widespread. We found a broad distribution of alcohol use patterns. The fortuitous timing of the onset of this study in 1974 placed it right in that small window of time when middle-class women knew they shouldn't smoke during pregnancy, but didn't know they shouldn't drink. There resulted a unique and ideal sample in which to study the long-term consequences of prenatal alcohol exposure.

Today, as we write this monograph in year 18 of our longitudinal prospective study, we could cite thousands of reports of alcohol teratogenesis, many showing alcohol-related decrements of developmental indices in both animals and humans. At the time this study began there were none except those from the University of Washington (Jones et al., 1973; Jones & Smith, 1973; Jones et al., 1974) and the early study from France by Lemoine et al. (1968).

Amid the wealth of clinical case studies published on Fetal Alcohol Syndrome in the mid-to-late 1970s, four important population-based studies (one from France, one from Boston, and two from Seattle) began reporting data indicating that alcohol was related to adverse pregnancy outcomes not accounted for by smoking, other drug use, or socioeconomic factors. Kaminski, Rumeau-Rouquette & Schwartz (1976) associated alcohol use at three or more drinks per day with a significantly increased rate of stillbirths and with decreased placental weight and decreased birth weight. Little (1977) reported an association between intake of two or more drinks of wine, beer, and/or liquor per day and significantly decreased infant birth weight. Ouellette, Rosett, Rosman, & Wiener (1977) reported an association between use of 45 drinks or more per month and sometimes five drinks or more per occasion, and an increased rate of minor physical anomalies, jitteriness, and lower birth weight in offspring.

Three papers published between 1977 and 1979 from our study reported other neonatal outcomes significantly related to moderate drinking during pregnancy: neonatal operant learning deficits (5), "fetal alcohol effects" (defined as growth deficiency plus some of a specific group of minor malformations and/or microcephaly) (10), and neonatal sucking deficits (decreased pressure and increased latency to suck) (18). An additional paper involving autopsy reports from our study plus other clinical material (9) indicated early gestational embryonic and fetal damage in aborted and stillborn offspring of moderate-drinking mothers. These early papers anticipated the wealth of published literature forthcoming on the human behavioral teratology of alcohol, much of which has continued to come from this study (see Appendix I for a full listing).

In addition to our project, several other prospective studies are now underway on the effects of prenatal alcohol exposure on child development. These include one study out of Pittsburgh (Nancy L. Day and colleagues), one out of Atlanta (Claire D. Coles and colleagues), one out of Cleveland (Robert J. Sokol, Claire Ernhardt and colleagues), one out of Ottawa (Peter Fried and colleagues), and one out of Detroit (Robert J. Sokol, Joseph and Sandra Jacobson, and colleagues).

There are now many findings of alcohol-related decrements in infant developmental indices (for example, 20; Golden, Sokol, Kuhnert & Bottoms, 1982; Gusella & Fried, 1984; Aronson et al., 1985; O'Connor, Brill & Sigman, 1986). Some alcohol-related performance and electrophysiologic decrements are detectable as early as day 1 or 2 of life (5, 11, 18, 35, 37, 41; Chernick, Childiaeva & Ioffe, 1983; Coles et al., 1985; Coles et al., 1987; Rosett et al., 1979; Scher, Richardson, Coble, Day & Stoffer, 1988; Stoffer et al., 1988; Ioffe & Chernick, 1988). Two reports failed to find prenatal alcohol effects on neonatal Brazelton scores; one of these (Richardson, Day & Taylor, 1989) did find alcohol effects on more sensitive sleep and EEG measures (Scher et al., 1988; Stoffer et al., 1988), while the other (Ernhardt et al., 1985) has not found prenatal alcohol effects on later behavioral outcomes either (Boyd et al., 1990; Green et al., 1990 & 1991). Another study reporting prenatal alcohol effects within the first 13 months of life (Gusella & Fried, 1984) failed to find effects at 3 to 6 years (Fried & Watkinson, 1990; Fried, Watkinson & Grey, 1992). Many methodologic factors can contribute to inconsistent findings, including the constituency of the sample, the measurement techniques for both the alcohol and the outcome variables, the degree of confounding of alcohol with other important covariates, and the success of follow-up. Prenatal alcohol effects on preschool and early school age cognitive, attentional, and/or motor performance have now been shown in four different cohorts of children, in addition to our own (e.g. 37; 38; 49; 63; 65-67; 69; 76; Landesman-Dwyer, Ragozin & Little, 1981; Coles et al., 1991; Brown et al., 1991; Russell et al., 1991.) Our most recent reports have shown classroom and laboratory attention/memory effects of prenatal effects at 11 and 14 years, respectively (95; 104). For recent reviews of the literature on children with FAS, children of alcoholic mothers, and children of mothers drinking moderately during pregnancy, see (48; 92; Day, 1992).

1.4   The Seattle Longitudinal Prospective Study on Alcohol and Pregnancy: Study Design and Specific Aims for Analyses in This Monograph

In designing a study of the behavioral teratology of alcohol in accordance with the principles described earlier, one must study the offspring from birth well through ages at which learning can be evaluated. One must measure alcohol and other exposures as carefully and fully as possible during the prenatal period. One must measure multiple aspects of the prenatal and postnatal environment that also affect neuropsychological development. Finally, to detect effects if they exist, one must have many sufficiently exposed offspring. An adequate sample size is necessary for appropriate statistical control of the many potentially intervening variables. Yet the sample must be small enough for administration of the laboratory tests which, child by child, best detect the more subtle effects of moderate levels of exposure. Careful sample maintenance is required if the children most at risk are not to be lost to follow-up. Multiple teratogenic endpoints must be assessed in light of different patterns and conditions of exposure. The study design we developed accorded with all of these requirements. Although it is characterized within the framework of human behavioral teratology, it proved capable of supporting the powerful inferences about the effects of doses upon multiple outcomes commonly found primarily in animal studies.

The Seattle Study explores the range of functional effects of prenatal alcohol exposure from infancy through the early school-age years, with particular emphasis on effects of "social" levels of drinking. The study is longitudinal, prospective, and population-based. We measured prenatal alcohol exposure by interviewing a large group of women during the fifth month of pregnancy; we subsequently followed a cohort of approximately 500 offspring of these mothers, oversampled for higher levels of drinking, at six ages from the first day of life through 7 years. In this monograph we examine the enduring effects of prenatal alcohol on these children; we consider the relevance of many prenatal and postnatal covariates in modifying these effects; and we introduce Partial Least Squares methods for longitudinal analyses across the full seven years for which data is available.

The goal of the study, as it applies to this monograph, is to examine the long-term consequences of prenatal alcohol exposure for the neurobehavioral development of children from birth to 7 years. The relevant study aims can be summarized in four basic questions:

1. What domains of children's neurobehavioral development are affected by prenatal alcohol exposure?

2. What patterns of prenatal alcohol exposure are the most detrimental?

3. Is there longitudinal structure in these relationships across time?

4. Who are the individual children most affected by prenatal alcohol, and how do we detect them?

The first two questions are the easiest. They have been addressed in previous publications from this study and are re-addressed here in a global fashion across all neurobehavioral outcomes assessed in the first 7 years of the children's lives. Answers to these questions are extremely important to society from the standpoint of public health and prevention efforts. If we want to prevent fetal alcohol effects in the population, then we have to know what they are and what patterns of exposure cause them. We address these questions in Chapters 5 and 7.

The third question, which is more difficult, is of theoretical interest in understanding the predictive validity of early outcome measures and the antecedents of later deficit. We address this question with longitudinal path models in Chapter 6. The fourth question bears the most clinical relevance to individual children and is also extremely important to society from the standpoint of intervention. If we want to help, remediate, or plan for the needs of individual children who are themselves affected by prenatal alcohol exposure, then we need to know how to identify them individually and what characteristic profiles of deficit they have across their young lives. Answers to questions 1, 2, and 3 do not, unfortunately, provide direct insight into question 4. Chapter 8 in this monograph reports on our first approach to this latter question using the present database.

The rationale for the study design and the selection of outcome variables have been discussed in previous publications (26, 46, 50). Results from prior examinations have been summarized previously (26, 37, 46, 50, 64, 70, 94, 101). This monograph does not include analyses of physical growth and morphology, or of traditional medical records outcomes from this study. These other outcomes are part of the original study design, and have been presented elsewhere (9, 10, 32, 40, 52, 60, 71, 106).

1.5 The Seattle Study: A Preliminary Glimpse of the Findings from Analyses in This Monograph

1. Functional outcomes showing effects of prenatal alcohol exposure are manifest across all ages from birth to 7 years. We discovered that these effects do not diminish with age and that they are manifested in a great variety of behavioral dimensions across time. Among the most salient individual consequences of prenatal alcohol exposure are habituation to light from the Brazelton Neonatal Assessment Scale on day 1, time in error from the Wisconsin Motor Steadiness Battery at age 4 years, standardized WISC-R and WRAT-R arithmetic subtests at age 7 years, and academic adjustment as rated by the second-grade teacher. (Chapter 5.)

2. Particular profiles of alcohol dose (timing, quantity, frequency, and variability of consumption) are associated with particular sorts of deficit. For the majority of our outcome measures, binge drinking has more serious consequences than the same amount of spaced drinking, and drinking early in pregnancy (prior to pregnancy recognition) has more serious consequences than the same reported pattern of drinking in mid-pregnancy. (Chapter 5.)

3. There is no evidence for a "risk-free" level of prenatal drinking. Each of our 13 indicators of prenatal alcohol dose is substantially correlated with at least some of our outcome scores, and the relationships cannot be shown to have "thresholds" or "safe levels." (Chapter 5.)

4. The effects of alcohol cannot be "explained away" by attribution to any of 150 covariates examined, including smoking, other drug use, parental education, other measures of socioeconomic status and so forth. (Chapters 6 and 7.)

5. Longitudinal analyses reveal substantially new effects of prenatal alcohol exposure at each exam wave. These are neither explained by prior environmental factors nor expressed in terms of deficits measured at earlier ages. Some of the long-term effects of prenatal alcohol exposure are simply not measurable until ages at which more complex learning processes can be observed. (Chapter 6.)

6. Alcohol-related learning problems, particularly in the areas of arithmetic, self-regulation, and conduct problems, are already manifest by the second grade in school. (Chapter 7.)

7. Centered profiles of deficit on common measures of learning disabilities (such as the battery of 11 WISC-R subtests, and the 24 items on the Myklebust Pupil Rating Scale) are useful for identifying alcohol effects that are strikingly independent of the usual important environmental factors such as parent education, family structure, and mother-child interaction. (Chapter 7.)

8. Neuromotor deficits measured at 7 years were strongly enough related to prenatal alcohol that they could be used to describe a profile of alcohol-related neuromotor deficits in individual children. (Chapter 8.)

A summary of all these findings, a discussion of their import for public health and a preview of things to come appear in the final chapter. (Chapter 9.)

## CHAPTER 2

Study Design: The Seattle Longitudinal Prospective Study on Alcohol and Pregnancy, Antenatal Through Seven Years

The study design of the Seattle Longitudinal Prospective Study on Alcohol and Pregnancy is diagrammed in Figure 2.1. 1529 women in the fifth month of pregnancy were interviewed regarding alcohol, smoking, and other pertinent aspects of the prenatal environment. A follow-up cohort of about 500 was selected at delivery, over-sampled for heavier drinkers and smokers. We have added additional subjects from the original screening sample from time to time to keep the total cohort size around 500. As Figure 2.1 depicts, the cohort was examined on 1 and 2 days of age, at 8 and 18 months, and at 4 and 7 years. The follow-up sample size of 582 reported in the tables of this chapter represents all cases with a valid neonatal Brazelton exam together with all cases seen at any postnatal follow-up exam (8 months, 18 months, 4 years, 7 years).

2.1 Sample Selection and the Maternal Interview

Of the pregnant women receiving prenatal care during a one-year period (1974-75) at two large Seattle hospitals, all those were approached for interview who were in prenatal care by the fifth month of pregnancy and who lived within a 20-mile radius of Seattle. One of the hospitals was a prepaid medical cooperative, the other a university hospital; together they produced a sample demographically representative of the Seattle area (see Section 2.4).

Our recruitment procedures maximized participation and avoided selection bias. The study was referred to as a Pregnancy and Health Study and the focus throughout was on understanding the relationship of prenatal health practices to pregnancy outcome and child development. We sent eligible women a letter describing the study, and followed it up with a phone call for those with phones and a clinic contact for those without phones. A home interview administered during the fifth month of pregnancy followed for the 85% of the women who gave informed consent and could participate in the follow-up study.

Beyond the obvious desirability of standardization, there were two reasons that we set the interview for the fifth gestational month: (1) to interview as early in pregnancy as possible, so as to improve recall of drinking during embryogenesis, and (2) to exclude the multi-risk alcohol-abusing women who often come for prenatal care only late in pregnancy. In order to reduce anxiety about revealing personal habits, all interviews were conducted in the women's own homes (or a place of their choice) without husbands or children present. The interviewer was one of six personable young women explicitly identified as not representing the prenatal clinic or hospital and highly trained in interviewing skills. In addition to being shown the usual human subjects guidelines regarding confidentiality, the women were assured that their responses would be used only for research and would not be entered into their medical records.

The 30-35 minute maternal interview was designed to assess the primary independent variables (see Appendix II-a). Questions about alcohol use were embedded in a general health interview with questions on pregnancy history, occupation, education, race, smoking history, use of caffeine, other drugs and medications, and nutritional intake. Beverage questions utilized the Quantity-Frequency-Variability (QFV) interview developed by Mulford & Miller (1960). These were asked twice for each beverage, first for the "during" pregnancy period and once for the month or so "prior" to pregnancy or prior to pregnancy recognition (see Appendix II-b). For each beverage, women were asked how frequently they drank (with forced-choice answers ranging from "never" to "three or more times a day") and how often they drank each of the quantities ("five or more," "three or four," or "one or two" glasses). Forced choice answers ranged from "never" to "nearly every time." At the time this study began, the QFV interview

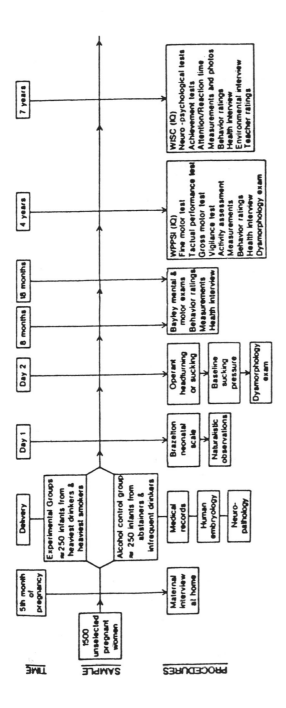

Figure 2.1. Study design for the Seattle Longitudinal Prospective Study on Alcohol and Pregnancy. Sample size included: Brazelton, N=469; naturalistic observations, N=469; operant head turning, N=124; operant sucking, N=225; baseline sucking, N=80; neonatal dysmorphology, N=165; 8-month exam, N=468; 18-month exam, N=469; 4-year exam, N=465; 7-year exam, N=486.

was considered to be the "state of the art" in alcohol interviews. A similar format had been used successfully with nearly 1000 pregnant women from one of these same hospitals (Little, 1977; Little, Schultz & Mandell, 1976, 1977). The mothers and interviewers sat side by side and the mother was given colored cards with the different forced-choice responses appropriate for each question. Questions and answers were given verbally and an easy rhythmical flow developed as the different beverages were discussed, first coffee and tea, then wine, beer, and liquor, and finally cola beverages. In addition to the QFV questions, four additional types of information on alcohol were obtained through the "Reasons for Drinking Scale" (Mulford & Miller, 1960) not used in the present analyses; the Number of Intoxications; the Supplemental Questions (Appendix II-c); and the Alcohol Problems Scale, which derives from Rimmer, Pitts, Reich & Winokur (1971) but was modified for this study. For the Intoxication Scale, women were asked "Have you ever been drunk or intoxicated since you have been pregnant?". Subjects responding affirmatively were asked to recall each occasion of intoxication, and to report the amount and type of alcohol consumed, the duration of drinking on each occasion, and when during the pregnancy the intoxication (or intoxications) occurred. For the Alcohol Problems Scale, subjects were asked four questions considered at that time to reflect serious alcohol-related problems in the areas of marriage and family, job, trouble with the law, and hospitalization (Rimmer et al., 1971). Further details on the interview, the scores and the alcohol use patterns of the population are available in previous publications (3, 7, 26).

2.2 Assessment of Alcohol and Other Predictors

2.2.1 Alcohol Use

Alcohol ingestion was measured by self-report using the QFV interview of Mulford & Miller (1960). This record was quantified in several ways: the AA score, average ounces of absolute alcohol consumed per day (Jessor, Graves, Hanson & Jessor, 1968); the VV score, volume-variability (Cahalan, Cissin & Crossley, 1969); the

QFV index, quantity-frequency-variability (Cahalan et al., 1969); and the AUP, alcohol use pattern, which categorized the number of times per month that a mother reported five or more drinks on an occasion (Little et al., 1977). These were scored individually for wine, liquor and beer, but later we summed them to encode total ingestion from all sources. An additional score, "Number of intoxications during pregnancy," was used for cohort selection but was not used for data analysis because a sampling of notes on the intoxication events revealed reports of intoxications from half a glass of champagne at a wedding reception to three cases of beer (72 cans) over a 1-1/2 day period at New Year's. A set of "supplemental questions" was added after the interviewing had begun in order to compensate for the low ceiling on the standard QFV interview (which stops after asking the frequency of drinking five or more drinks). Any subject who reported ingesting five or more drinks at a time was given the "supplemental questions" which asked the number of times during or prior to pregnancy or pregnancy recognition that 12-or-more, 8–11 or 5–7 drinks had been ingested (see Appendix II-C) (Room, 1970). This score not only raised the ceiling to permit more accurate categorization of the amount drunk per occasion, but also permitted the interviewee to summarize different types of alcohol consumed on one drinking occasion. It is important to note that large individual variation in patterns and rhythmicity of drinking results in different women being classified as "heavy" drinkers depending on the scale used (7). Although no one verbal report can measure the *real* alcohol exposure to the infant, from these many scales covering the breadth of drinking dimensions we were eventually able to estimate the effects of exposure rather effectively (see Chapters 5-8). Tables 2.1 and 2.2 present the alcohol scores used for cohort selection (to be described in the next section). Table 2.3 presents sample statistics for the 13 alcohol scores used in the analyses.

As there was no indication when this study began regarding which alcohol variables might be critical in producing different types of effects in offspring, a variety of alcohol scores were calculated to express differences in timing, level, and pattern of exposure. The questions on alcohol use referred to two time periods: During (D) mid-pregnancy, and for the month or so Prior (P) to pregnancy or to pregnancy recognition. We were particularly interested in the P scores, in that the period of organogenesis is extremely important for teratology research. The period of neurogenesis (reflected in our P scores) is particularly important for research on neurobehavioral teratology (Vorhees, 1986). In this period women have generally not yet altered their normal habits because they are usually not aware of being pregnant. All our alcohol scores except ORDEXC were obtained for both the D and P time periods.

The AA score reflects the overall level of exposure (ounces of absolute alcohol per day). An AA score of 1.0 represents average consumption of about two drinks per day, but the pattern of consumption might be a regular daily drinking pattern or an occasional heavy binge. To clarify the effects of these various drinking patterns several "binge" scores were calculated after the study was underway (65-67) (BINGE,

Table 2.1 Interview Sample and Follow-up Cohort Categorized by ORDEXC (Ordered Exposure Code)

		Interview Sample		Follow-up Cohort [b]	
ORDEXC Definition [a]		Number	Percent	Number	Percent
4	High-Priority	216	14.1%	202	34.7%
3	Low-Priority	118	7.7%	62	10.7%
2	Light-Moderate	780	51.0%	93	16.0%
1	Infrequent	198	13.0%	102	17.5%
0	Abstainer	217	14.2%	123	21.1%
		1529	100.0%	582	100.0%

Notes: [a] Definitions (for greater detail, see Table 2.2):

High Priority: AA≥1.0 pre or during; VV=8 or 11 pre or during.

Low Priority: VV=9 or 10 pre or during; AUP=4 pre or during; QFV=1 pre or during; any intoxication during.

Light-Moderate: any subject not meeting criteria for any other category.

Infrequent: AA ≤0.10 during and pre-recognition of pregnancy and subjects *not* categorized by any of the 19 drinking categories on Table 2.2.

Abstainer: no alcohol use during pregnancy or in the month or so prior to pregnancy or pregnancy recognition.

[b] The follow-up cohort represents all singleton-born subjects with a valid neonatal Brazelton exam together with all subjects seen at any postnatal follow-up.

Table 2.2 Alcohol Scores by Interview Sample and Follow-up Cohort

ORDEXC	Alcohol Score [a]	Subjects Identified By --			
		Each Scale [b]		Priority System [c]	
		Int. sample N = 1529	**FU** cohort N = 582	**Int.** sample N = 1529	**FU** cohort N = 582
High-Priority	1. AA≥1.0 during	36	36	36	36
(1–6)	2. VV=11 during	26	26	5	5
	3. VV=8 during	49	43	49	43
	4. AA≥1.0 prior	110	106	66	64
	5. VV=11 prior	88	80	18	14
	6. VV=8 prior	71	66	42	40
Low-Priority	7. VV=10 during	16	15	2	1
(7–19)	8. VV=9 during	12	10	4	2
	9. VV=10 prior	46	39	11	6
	10. VV=9 prior	32	22	14	5
	11. AUP=4 during	33	33	0	0
	12. AUP=4 prior	109	100	0	0
	13. QFV=1 during	44	41	1	0
	14. QFV=1 prior	110	100	5	3
	15. Intox. ≥5 times	15	13	2	2
	16. Intox. 4 times	7	4	3	0
	17. Intox. 3 times	12	10	2	2
	18. Intox. 2 times	38	29	16	10
	19. Intox. 1 time	95	67	58	31
Light-moderate		780	93	780	93
Infrequent		198	102	198	102
Abstainer		217	123	217	123

Notes: In 1974, ORDEXC and the alcohol scores were prioritized prior to the study according to their presumed effect on fetal welfare.

AA≥1.0: average of at least 2 drinks per day of wine, liquor, or beer in any combination.

VV=11: 45 or more drinks/month and 5 drinks or more on at least one occasion.

VV=8: 17.6-44.9 drinks/month and 5 drinks or more on at least one occasion.

VV=10: 45 or more drinks/month and a maximum of 3-4 drinks on at least one occas.

VV=9: 45 or more drinks/month and never more than 2 drinks on any occasion.

AUP=4: 5 or more drinks at least 4 times a month.

QFV=1: "heavy" drinker defined by Cahalan's criteria which include average daily drinking & binge drinking.

Intox. ≥ 5 times = intoxicated 5 or more times during pregnancy.

[a] "during" = during pregnancy; "prior" = prior to pregnancy or pregn. recognition.

[b] Entries of these columns are not mutually exclusive.
    Int = Inverview; FU = Follow-up.

[c] Entries of these columns are mutually exclusive. Subjects selected by higher priority codes were not eligible for selection at lower priorities.

Table 2.3 Alcohol Block Definition and Descriptive Statistics (N=582)

Alcohol Scores	Abbrev [a]	Mean	SD	Min	Med	Max
Average ounces of absolute alcohol per day						
Prior to pregnancy recognition	AAP	0.58	1.46	0	0.13	25.76[†]
During mid-pregnancy	AAD	0.26	0.56	0	0.05	8.55
Binge ≥5: 5 drinks or more on any occasion						
Prior to pregnancy recognition	BINGE P	0.28	0.45	0	0.20	1
During mid-pregnancy	BINGE D	0.19	0.39	0	0.12	1
Average drinks per occasion						
Prior to pregnancy recognition	ADOCCP	1.82	1.69	0	1.50	13
During mid-pregnancy	ADOCCD	1.68	1.36	0	1.50	13
Max. drinks reported on any occasion						
Prior to pregnancy recognition	MAXP	2.97	2.95	0	2.01	13
During mid-pregnancy	MAXD	2.77	2.73	0	1.92	13
Monthly occasions of drinking						
Prior to pregnancy recognition	MOCCP	12.18	20.14	0	3.45	240
During mid-pregnancy	MOCCD	6.49	11.69	0	1.49	120
Quantity-Frequency-Variability Index						
Prior to pregnancy recognition	QFVP	2.84	1.45	1	2.88	5
During mid-pregnancy	QFVD	2.56	1.20	1	2.53	5
Ordered Exposure Code						
combines timing, dose, pattern	ORDEXC	2.20	1.57	0	2.21	4

Notes: See text for a fuller description of these scores and pertinent references

[a] AA (average oz. of absolute alcohol per day) is a continuous variable; AA=1.00 means an average of 2 drinks per day of wine, beer, liquor, or any combination.

P refers to the month or so prior to pregnancy or pregnancy recognition, D refers to drinking during mid-pregnancy, assessed at the fifth month of pregnancy.

BINGE is a dichotomous variable representing whether or not 5 or more drinks were reported on at least one occasion. This score combines the VV=5, VV=8 and VV=11 of Cahalan et al., 1969.

ADOCC represents the average number of drinks reported per drinking occasion.

MAX is the maximum number of drinks reported for any drinking occasion.

MOCC is the number of occasions per month in which drinking is reported.

QFV is a categorical score (Quantity, Frequency, Variability) summarizing three dimensions of drinking from Cahalan et al, 1969. The order has been reversed for consistency with the other drinking scales, so that 5 corresponds to the heaviest drinking.

ORDEXC is an *a priori* code (Ordered Exposure Code) developed at the outset of this study to describe the presumed risk to the fetus of different drinking patterns, in order to enroll women in the follow -up study: 4 is highest presumed risk.

[†] The next highest AAP score was 9.14 oz.

MAX, and ADOCC). We note that the binge scores as defined in this study reflect a massed versus a spaced drinking pattern, and are not synonymous with, for example, a weekend of drinking. The BINGE score identifies those subjects who reported drinking five or more drinks on some occasion during the relevant time period. (BINGE combines the three binge scores of Cahalan et al. [1969]: VV=5, 8, and 11.) MAX (maximum drinks on any occasion) and ADOCC (average drinks per occasion) are simple counts of the maximum and average drinks per occasion, respectively (Parker & Noble, 1977), reported for the two time periods, D and P. The five-point QFV score derives from a three-dimensional scheme for averaging both daily and binge drinking (Cahalan et al., 1969), while MOCC is a simple count of the monthly occasions of drinking. Finally, we derived an *a priori* five-category drinking score (ORDEXC: Ordered Exposure Code, see Tables 2.1 and 2.2) which was calculated to facilitate selecting the follow-up cohort. ORDEXC is an ordering of the various alcohol scores we calculated in 1974 according to our subjective judgement of their risk to the fetus, from 0 (no risk) to 4 (highest risk) (26).

We initially computed log transformations of the AA, MAX, ADOCC and MOCC scores because of their highly skewed distributions with relatively few extreme cases. The correlations among these 13 alcohol scores are presented in Table 2.4. Note that these correlations range from .39 to .96. Our correlational analyses exclude one subject due to an extreme outlying value for AAP.

2.2.2 Reliability and Validity

We computed test-retest reliabilities for the main alcohol scales utilized in this study (3) and for the caffeine assessments (29). For a sample of 78 subjects systematically weighted for heavier drinkers, the interview was repeated (by the same interviewer) after one week had elapsed. The two sets (D and P) of continuous AA scores correlated .90 and .89 (3) and compared favorably with the continuous D and P scores for caffeine .86 and .94 (29). Reliability for D and P scores, calculated with Kendall's τ, were .85 and .88 respectively for categorized AA scores; .90 and .85 for QFV (wine); .90 and .86 for

QFV (beer); .84 and .85 for QFV (liquor); .68 and .63 for VV scores respectively.

We cannot estimate the validity of self-reports of alcohol use. Note, however, that we made every effort to avoid the obvious biases. The interviews were in the women's own homes, for the most part. Husbands and children were absent, and the whole procedure was designed to be non-threatening.   Furthermore, at the time these maternal interviews were conducted, there was no information available regarding effects of social drinking during pregnancy. This ignorance may have contributed to self-reports more valid than would be likely once the risks were well-known.

2.2.3 Caffeine

We also assessed quantity, frequency, and variability of coffee, tea, and cola consumption, and quantity and frequency of cocoa products. Average mg of caffeine consumed per day summed estimates of the amount of caffeine in coffee, tea, cola beverages, hot chocolate, cocoa, and chocolate candy. This scoring system is described in (29). Some caffeine use during pregnancy was reported by almost every woman, but caffeine use was not associated with child outcomes studied through age 7 years (81). Caffeine, therefore, was not a confounding factor in the alcohol study of these child outcomes.

2.2.4 Tobacco

From the maternal interview, we calculated average mg of nicotine per day by multiplying the number of cigarettes lit per day by the amount of nicotine in the brand smoked. (Analyses of number of cigarettes smoked per day showed, in general, weaker associations with outcomes.) Table 2.5 shows the correlations of nicotine with the 13 different alcohol scores. While most mothers did not smoke, smoking was distributed well across drinking categories, and likewise drinking across categories of smoking in the follow-up cohort. This was a result of the stratification system used in selecting the follow-up cohort from the screening sample.

Table 2.4 Correlations Among 13 Alcohol Scores

	LAAP	LAAD	BINGE P	BINGE D	LADOCCP	LADOCCD	LMAXP	LMAXD	LMOCCP	LMOCCD	QFVP	QFVD	ORDEXC
LAAP	1.00	0.68	0.55	0.39	0.64	0.49	0.65	0.51	0.88	0.70	0.73	0.67	0.73
LAAD	0.68	1.00	0.39	0.48	0.48	0.48	0.49	0.52	0.68	0.87	0.56	0.73	0.63
BINGE P	0.55	0.39	1.00	0.60	0.67	0.50	0.74	0.57	0.53	0.43	0.74	0.58	0.66
BINGE D	0.39	0.48	0.60	1.00	0.49	0.53	0.52	0.64	0.39	0.44	0.51	0.69	0.51
LADOCCP	0.64	0.48	0.67	0.49	1.00	0.78	0.96	0.77	0.75	0.63	0.91	0.77	0.84
LADOCCD	0.49	0.48	0.50	0.53	0.78	1.00	0.76	0.95	0.61	0.61	0.72	0.83	0.77
LMAXP	0.65	0.49	0.74	0.52	0.96	0.76	1.00	0.78	0.77	0.65	0.93	0.77	0.87
LMAXD	0.51	0.52	0.57	0.64	0.77	0.95	0.78	1.00	0.63	0.65	0.74	0.85	0.79
LMOCCP	0.88	0.68	0.53	0.39	0.75	0.61	0.77	0.63	1.00	0.85	0.86	0.78	0.88
LMOCCD	0.70	0.87	0.43	0.44	0.63	0.61	0.65	0.65	0.85	1.00	0.72	0.84	0.79
QFVP	0.73	0.56	0.74	0.51	0.91	0.72	0.93	0.74	0.86	0.72	1.00	0.81	0.91
QFVD	0.67	0.73	0.58	0.69	0.77	0.83	0.77	0.85	0.78	0.84	0.81	1.00	0.84
ORDEXC	0.73	0.63	0.66	0.51	0.84	0.77	0.87	0.79	0.88	0.79	0.91	0.84	1.00

Notes: N=582. Variable names beginning with "L" refer to scores transformed as $\log(x+1)$. These log transformations were computed to lessen the effects of skewness and extreme values in the alcohol scores for use in this chapter and chapter 3 only. Definitions in text and on Table 2.3.

2.2.5 Other Drugs and Medications

Because the use of one drug (alcohol) may be associated with the use of others, we asked about the timing and frequency of use of all drugs and medications taken during pregnancy. This included a list of other drugs and medications. Overall use of illicit drugs in the interview sample of 1529 was low, with only 188 subjects reporting any marijuana use, and only 19 subjects reporting any other illicit drugs; 15 of these 19 subjects were part of the follow-up cohort. Aspirin and acetaminophen were the two medications most frequently taken during pregnancy (by 45% and 42% of the cohort mothers, respectively). Use of these two medications was not significantly related to maternal alcohol use in this sample (see Table 2.5), but aspirin use was associated with IQ deficits and attentional decrements (54). For subjects in the follow-up cohort, we also obtained data on all medications used at delivery. The type of obstetrical medication was not associated with maternal alcohol use (35), and therefore was not a confounder in the neonatal studies.

2.2.6 Diet

As a large nutrition component to this study was not funded, only a few such questions were included in our maternal interview: intake by primary food group in the 24 hours preceding the interview, and number and type of sit-down meals per day. An "OK Nutrition" score summarized the reported intake of basic food groups relative to the standards of adequate intake for pregnant women published by the California State Department of Health, 1975. Heavier drinkers were not significantly different in these dietary characteristics from other women in the follow-up cohort (20). Therefore, diet, to the extent that it could be measured in this study, did not appear to be a confounding factor in this alcohol study, probably due to the primarily well-educated, middle-class women studied (also see Table 2.5).

2.3 Selection Criteria for the Follow-up Cohort

From the interview sample of 1529, we selected about 500 women whose infants constituted the follow-up cohort. As the majority of

Table 2.5 Simple Product–Moment Correlations Between Selected Predictor Variables and Alcohol

	LAAP	LAAD	BINGEP	BINGED	LDOCCP	LDOCCD	LMAXP	LMAXD	LMOCCP	LMOCCD	QFVP	QFVD	ORDEXC
Nicotine, prenatal	0.18	0.15	0.27	0.24	0.29	0.28	0.29	0.30	0.19	0.16	0.28	0.26	0.25
Caffeine, prenatal	0.31	0.25	0.22	0.17	0.34	0.31	0.35	0.29	0.39	0.36	0.35	0.34	0.38
Aspirin, prenatal	0.03	0.00	0.07	0.02	0.04	0.06	0.06	0.06	0.05	0.03	0.05	0.03	0.08
Acetaminophen, prenatal	0.05	0.03	0.05	0.08	0.12	0.13	0.10	0.12	0.07	0.05	0.10	0.11	0.11
Marijuana, prenatal	0.20	0.14	0.26	0.26	0.27	0.22	0.28	0.25	0.20	0.16	0.27	0.26	0.25
Antibiotics, prenatal	0.06	0.09	0.00	0.02	0.06	0.04	0.05	0.04	0.05	0.08	-0.04	0.06	0.04
Nutrition, prenatal	-0.03	0.06	-0.10	-0.06	-0.06	0.00	0.06	-0.01	0.03	0.08	-0.02	0.02	-0.02
Maternal education (yrs)	0.02	0.11	-0.17	-0.10	-0.06	-0.04	-0.07	-0.05	0.10	0.19	-0.03	0.04	-0.01
Paternal education (yrs)	-0.05	0.10	-0.17	-0.08	-0.11	-0.09	-0.10	-0.08	0.03	0.14	-0.07	-0.01	-0.03
Maternal age (yrs)	0.06	0.16	-0.12	-0.07	-0.01	0.01	-0.04	-0.01	0.12	0.18	-0.00	0.06	0.03
Race (Black/other)	0.09	0.03	0.05	0.01	-0.01	-0.06	-0.02	-0.06	-0.01	0.04	-0.00	-0.03	-0.02
Birth order (first/other)	0.10	-0.05	0.15	-0.01	0.12	0.02	0.13	0.02	0.10	0.01	0.14	0.02	0.10
Child's sex	-0.02	0.03	-0.01	-0.04	0.02	-0.00	0.02	-0.00	-0.02	0.00	0.01	-0.02	-0.00
Mother–child interaction	0.00	-0.03	0.00	-0.06	0.00	-0.04	-0.01	-0.02	-0.04	-0.07	0.00	-0.07	-0.03
Preschool	0.16	0.16	-0.01	0.01	0.08	0.08	0.07	0.09	0.20	0.21	0.09	0.11	0.13

Notes: N=582. Nicotine and Caffeine are in log(mg +1); Marijuana is in log(freq.+1); Aspirin and acetaminophen use are binary indicators of use several times per week or more (N=65 and 61 respectively); Antibiotic use is binary for any use during pregnancy (N=66); Nutrition is a count from 0 to 4 of the number of food groups with "adequate" intake (see text); Mother-child interaction is a scale from 0-13 (higher scores indicate deviant interaction); Preschool appears as log(months +1). Correlations for Mother–child interaction and Preschool are based on N=425 and 450. LDOCC = LADOCC.

women in the interview sample were light drinkers, the follow-up cohort oversampled for heavier drinkers. Multiple births were excluded from the analyses. No infant characteristics influenced entry into the follow-up cohort (i.e., no exclusionary criteria such as very low birthweight, cesarean section, congenital malformations and so forth were utilized because we wished to examine the full spectrum of alcohol effects on offspring within the population of 1529 interviewed mothers.) See (26) for details.

Infants for the follow-up cohort were selected daily, at delivery, as follows. ORDEXC scores (Table 2.1) designating categories of risk level drinking were used to assure an even flow of heavily-exposed and lightly-exposed infants into the study (see Table 2.1). The two top ORDEXC categories were differentiated into 19 types of "heavier" drinking. These were rank-ordered, as in Table 2.2, according to our original subjective judgment of their risk for adverse fetal effects. From among the several study infants born at each hospital in each 24-hour period, we could only enroll one per day per hospital in the follow-up cohort to examine as a neonate. Infants of "high priority" (ORDEXC=4) mothers entered the follow-up cohort regardless of other infants delivered that day. If more than two "high-priority" infants were delivered on a given day, enrollment was determined by the rank of their alcohol scores as ordered in Table 2.2. Thus, women with an AAD score of 1.0 or higher were given top priority. The proportion of abstainers and infrequent drinkers was kept comparable in cohort selection. Infrequent drinkers were defined as AA $\leq$ 0.10 and no positive scores on the 19 drinking categories on Table 2.2. Infants of heavy smokers (16 or more mg. nicotine/day) were admitted to the follow-up cohort unless their birthdates coincided with those of the offspring of heavier drinkers. This design enhances the adjustment for possible smoking effects by assuring that the follow-up cohort contained heavy smokers who were not heavy drinkers. If cigarette use did not indicate a clear choice for enrollment, we selected at random.

The composition of the follow-up cohort with respect to alcohol use and smoking is an extremely important aspect of the study design. An additional attempt at balancing the follow-up cohort for important confounding covariates was made in terms of maternal education. Prior to the 7-year exam, an additional 28 families from the screening sample of 1529 were enlisted into the follow-up cohort, both to keep the follow-up sample at around 500 and to help stratify the educational distribution across alcohol categories. Figure 2.2 depicts the effects of stratifying for both smoking and maternal college degree across alcohol categories.

Table 2.1 summarizes how effective the cohort selection process was in raising the proportion of high-priority subjects from 14% (in the interview sample) to 35% in the follow-up cohort, with the fraction of light-moderate drinkers dropping in compensation. 28% of the cohort mothers were binge drinkers (BINGE) prior to pregnancy recog-

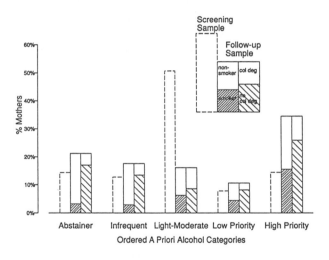

Figure 2.2 Screening and follow-up samples by exposure category. Exposure categories are as in Table 2.1. The Screening Sample totals 1439 singleton born children who were located at delivery and alive at discharge (out of the original Interview Sample of 1529). The Follow-up Sample comprises 582 children seen at at least one of the 5 examinations (day 1, 8 or 18 months, 4 or 7 years). Bars, left to right, within exposure categories: Screening sample proportion; Follow-up sample proportion subdivided by smoking status (smoker/nonsmoker); Follow-up sample proportion subdivided by mother's education (college degree/no college degree).

nition, and 19% during mid-pregnancy. Only 8 women reported alcohol problems. The basic demographic characteristics of the follow-up cohort closely match those of the unselected interview sample (see Table 2.6).

2.4 Demographic Characteristics

We hoped to evaluate alcohol use and pregnancy outcome in a sample that, while demographically broad, nevertheless was more generally middle-class than the samples being studied in the inner cities of Boston (Ouellette et al., 1977) and Cleveland (Sokol, Miller & Reed, 1980). Our two study hospitals together represented a good cross-section of the Seattle population. One hospital (Group Health Cooperative of Puget Sound) was a prepaid health maintenance organization serving primarily a working- and middle-class population. University Hospital, on the other hand, had a somewhat higher proportion of public assistance recipients, as the delivery site for the Maternal and Infant program prenatal clinics and for the Harborview Medical Center prenatal clinic. Yet this hospital also served highly educated families affiliated with the University of Washington. The selection of two large and representative Seattle hospitals for the study, and the inclusion of all available consenting subjects in the interview sample, resulted in sample characteristics that appear to be quite representative of 1975 Seattle generally. Only 8% of the subjects in the interview sample reported public assistance as their primary means of support; 87% were married, and 32% were college graduates. The follow-up sample, despite the larger proportion of heavier drinkers, continues to be basically a white, middle-class group, as was the interview sample. The demographics of our two groups are set out in Table 2.6.

2.5 Sample Maintenance and Follow-up

In the absence of careful sample maintenance, differential loss of certain types of subjects (here, the offspring of heavier drinkers) could seriously interfere with statistical inference in longitudinal studies.

Table 2.6 Maternal Demographic Characteristics of the Interview Sample and Follow-up Cohort

		Interview sample N = 1529	Follow-up cohort N = 582
Race:	White	86%	84%
	Black	9	9
	Other	5	7
Age:	13 - 16	2	2
	17 - 24	33	35
	25 - 32	59	57
	33 - 40	6	6
	41 - 45	< 1	< 1
Parity:	Primiparous	44	43
	Multiparous	56	57
Marital status:	Married	87	84
	Single	9	11
	Other	4	5
Maternal education:	Graduate school	7	7
	College graduate	25	20
	Some college	29	29
	High school graduate	28	29
	Some high school	8	11
	Junior high school	3	4
	Sixth grade or less	< 1	0
Socio-economic status:	Upper	10	9
	Upper middle	21	19
	Middle	27	24
	Lower middle	33	36
	Lower	9	12
Cigarette use:	Non-smoker	75	68
	Smoker	25	32
Pregnancy outcome:[†]			
Prematurity (gestational age < 37 weeks)		4	4
Low Birthweight (BW < 2500 grams)		3	3
Very Low Birthweight (BW < 1500 grams)		< 1	0

Notes: These demographics pertain to the fifth month of pregnancy. SES is determined using education of the mother and occupation of the head of household, according to a modification of Hollingshead's two-factor system (Hollingshead & Redlich, 1958). [†] Prematurity and birthweight statistics are tabulated from 1439 singleton born infants alive at discharge from hospital.

Our follow-up sample was maintained by an outreach worker who located families, scheduled appointments, and provided transportation when necessary. Our sample maintenance techniques are described in two papers (57, 90).

Only 10% of our subjects were lost to the 8-month follow-up; by 18 months, the cumulative loss was only 11%, and, at both 4 and 7 years, 14%. The most common reason for loss was moving out of the area. "Lost" subjects, especially those who had been unable to participate in one segment due to time pressures or illnesses, were often retrieved by the next follow-up. For instance, whereas 5% of those seen at 4 years were not seen at 7 years, the net loss to follow-up from birth was the same. Sample attrition was at the same rate for the drinking mothers as for the others.

As Figure 2.1 describes, the cohort was examined at 1 and 2 days of age, 8 and 18 months, and 4 and 7 years. After the neonatal exams, which were conducted on the neonatal unit of the hospital at birth, all postnatal exams were conducted at the study laboratories at the University of Washington Medical School. All exams were carried out by psychometrists trained to a high degree of reliability in administering tests in a standardized situation. To prevent psychometric bias, the psychometrists had no knowledge of the maternal history or status of any infant either before or after the examination, all scheduling was done by non-examiners, the parental interviews and questionnaires were administered by an outreach worker while the psychometrist examined the child, each examiner saw infants/children from all exposure categories and used all testing rooms, and no data were analyzed until all the data of that wave were gathered.

Test batteries and outcome variables at each age are described in Chapter 3. The 8- and 18-month exams were scheduled within one week of the child's 8- and 18-month birthdays. The 4-year exam was scheduled within one week of the day that the child attained 4 years 3 months of age. The 7-year exam, which took place during the summers of 1982 and 1983, used a different scheduling paradigm. Each child was scheduled for testing during the summer after he/she finished, or should have finished, first grade in school. The age at testing ranged from 6.6 to 8.6 years. This adjustment of the testing schedule was designed to minimize the effects of school attendance on tests of behavior and performance. Each summer, half of the cohort was scheduled for testing in random order. Of the total of 486 examinations given at the 7-year wave, four were considered invalid due to recent testing with the WISC-R, excessive shyness or refusal to speak. The 7-year sample included 28 subjects from the original interview sample brought in to improve the balance of parental education across alcohol groups.

Most of the 7-year exams were scheduled in the mornings, 22% on weekends. The ambient temperature was 80 degrees or less for 89% of the exams; 85% of the children had eaten within three hours of the

Table 2.7 Characteristics of the Children in the 7-Year Cohort (N = 486)

Sex		First born	44%
Boys	54%	First born to mother > 30 years old	5%
Girls	46%		
Age		Preschool experience (N=428 complete)	
< 7 years	10%	None	33%
7 - 7.5	52%	1 - 2 years	63%
7.5 - 8	33%	≥ 3 years	4%
> 8	5%		
		Nursed	
Nutrition at 7 years		Not nursed	30%
Very poor	4%	1 - 8 months	48%
Poor	14%	> 8 months	22%
Moderate	48%		
Fair	25%	Medical concerns	
Good	9%	Vision problems	13%
		Hearing problems	15%
Hand used for name writing		Any fever over 105°	11%
Right	88%	Head injury resulting in	4%
Left	12%	unconsciousness	
Video game playing (monthly)		TV watching (daily)	
None	40%	None	2%
1 - 2 hours	29%	1 - 2 hours	36%
2 - 4 hours	13%	2 - 4 hours	52%
4 - 60 hours	18%	4 - 8 hours	10 %

exam, 96% had had at least 8 hours of sleep the night before, 7% looked tired to the examiner, 3% looked ill to the examiner, 2% had taken a sedative the night before or the morning of the exam (usually allergy medication), and one child had taken a stimulant. (Situational variables such as these were included in the sieve for covariates described in Chapters 6 and 7.) These exceptional children were examined to make sure that their outcomes were close to the sample regressions on exposure.

2.6 Sample Characteristics & Environment: 7 Years

As Table 2.7 notes, 85% of our 7-year subjects were between 7 and 8 years old at the last examination reported here. About half were boys and about half were first-born. Most of the children had had adequate nutrition, as assessed by scoring mother's recall of the child's food intake over the preceding 24 hours. Home and school environment data from the 7-year follow-up appear in Tables 2.8 and 2.9. Eighty-one percent of the children had finished the first grade in school when tested, 9% had just finished kindergarten, and 10% had just finished the second grade.

The children were being raised in demographically low-risk homes (95% remained with their biologic mothers, 19% of the families had experienced a divorce, and fewer than 5% were on welfare) and they attended good schools relative to national norms. IQ at the 7-year exam averaged 107.6, and correlated .77 with the 4-year IQ. At 7 years, 14 children had a WISC-R IQ score of less than 80.

2.7 Covariates

Because human behavior is multiply determined, thoughtful assessment of a multitude of covariates is essential in human behavioral teratology research. Covariates ought to be gathered throughout the child's lifetime, and their effects ought to be assessed whenever outcomes are assessed. Table 2.10 groups some of the approximately 150 covariates we considered.

During the prenatal period, maternal ingestants, diet, and health variables may act directly or interact with other teratogens to produce

Table 2.8 Family Characteristics at the Time of the 7-Year Follow-up (N = 486)

Home environment	%
Household constituency	
Biological mother	95
Biological father	70
Both biological parents	68
No father figure	19
Number of other children	
0	14
1 – 4	84
≥ 5	2
Employment at 7 years	
Mother working	58
Father working	89
Public assistance	4
Major household changes	
Divorce	19
Foster care	3
Death of a parent	2
More than 5 major changes	22
(divorce, foster care, death, etc.)	
Video games in the home	29
Computer in the home	10

perturbations in embryonic/fetal development that produce functional deficits later. We examined the effects of simultaneous exposure to other drugs in the presence of alcohol (using multiplicative interaction terms in the usual linear models). We were particularly interested in interactions between alcohol and prenatal dietary adequacy as they might jointly affect postnatal development.

Follow-up maternal interviews and questionnaires were given at the 8- and 18-month and 4- and 7-year exams to assess other determinants of neurobehavioral outcome scores: childhood illness, accidents, hospitalizations, medications, maternal illness, parental separation or divorce, employment, child care arrangements, schooling, and major changes in the household. These are also presented in Table 2.10.

For the postnatal period, we also assessed such potential predictors as duration of breast feeding, maternal employment, major life changes in the household (using a modification of the Holmes/Rahe Life Stress

Table 2.9 Characteristics of the School Environment at the Time of the
7-Year Follow-up (N = 486)

School environment	%
Private school	16
Percentile of median reading score in district	
< 60th percentile of national norm	36
60 – 70th percentile of national norm	33
> 70th percentile of national norm	31
Percentile of median language score in district	
< 60th percentile of national norm	36
60 – 70th percentile of national norm	40
> 70th percentile of national norm	24
Percentile of median arithmetic score in district	
< 60th percentile of national norm	44
60 – 70th percentile of national norm	36
> 70th percentile of national norm	20
Grade	
Kindergarten	9
First grade	81
Second grade	10

Notes: School environment was assessed by examining the district achievement
scores for the school districts of each child attending a public school.

scale), and mother-child interactions. Mother-child interactions were
assessed at both the 8- and 18-month exam periods using a revised
version (59) of a scale originally developed by Bayley for the
Collaborative Perinatal Project. Other environmental variables
included duration of preschool attendance, type of school attended, and
academic quality of the school, as well as spacing of siblings, number
of adults in the home, and parental attitudes and perceptions of their
children. Home interviews and analysis of HOME scores (Home
Observation for Measurement of the Environment [12]) were carried
out on a subset of women in the study when their children were 12
months old. Compared to Caldwell's norms (Elardo, Bradley &
Caldwell, 1975), mothers in this study typically were providing a
high level of stimulation to their infants. In this substudy, home
stimulation was not associated with self-report of alcohol use during
pregnancy. This study supported the view that these mothers were not

Table 2.10 Primary Covariates by Age of Assessment

Mid-Pregnancy Interview	Medical Records & Neonatal Exam	8 and 18 Month Interviews	4-Year Interviews
Maternal Characteristics	**Infant Characteristics**	**Infant Characteristics**	**Child Characteristics**
Age	Sex	Age at testing	Age at testing
Race	Age at testing	Sensory problems	Sensory problems
Education	Gestational age	Breast feeding duration	Illness, fever, trauma
Marital status	Birth weight	Illness, fever, trauma	Hospitalizations
Parity	Birth length	Hospitalizations	Medications
Gravidity	Head circumference	Vitamins	
Socio-economic status	Apgar scores	Medications	**Maternal Characteristics**
Occupation	Presentation		Illness, hospitalization
Working status	Birth trauma	**Maternal Characteristics**	Separation from child
Lifelong abstinence	Jaundice	Illness, hospitalization	Working status
Years of drinking	Other problems	Separation from child	Caretaking arrangements
Hx alcohol problems		Working status	
Hx pregn. complications	**Environment**	Mother/child interaction	**Family Environment**
Hx deceased children	Delivery medications		Major life changes in household (#)
Prepregnancy weight	Isolette		
Height	Days in hospital		
	To whom discharged		
	Breast feeding		

(table continues)

Table 2.10 Primary Covariates by Age of Assessment (Continued)

Mid-Pregnancy Interview	Medical Records & Neonatal Exam	8 and 18 Month Interviews	4-Year Interviews
Other exposures	**Prenatal Hx**	**Family Environment**	**School**
Cigarette/Nicotine	No. of prenatal visits	Major life changes in	Preschool attendance
Caffeine	Threatened miscarriage	household (#)	Daycare attendance
Aspirin	Mother's weight at delivery	H.O.M.E. scale	
Acetaminophen	Illness & infection during	Caretaking arrangements	**Situational**
Valium	pregnancy		Accompanying person
Other teratogenic drugs	Atypical conditions	**Situational**	Examiner
All other drugs		Accompanying person	Room of testing
	Situational	Examiner	Temperature
Pregnancy	Examiner	Room of testing	Time of day
Nutritional intake	Hospital of testing	Time of day	Day of week
Eating habits	Ambient temperature	Day of week	Month of year
Vitamin supplements	Time of day	Month of year	
Mother vegetarian	Day of week		
Illness/Infection	Month of year		
	Time since feeding		
Family Environment	State at outset		
Source of income			
No. of adults in household			
No. of children ≤ 5 years			
No. children > 5 years			

Home environment	Biological Parents	Family Environment	Situational
Biological mother at home	Mother:	Family Environment Scale (Moos)	Accompanying person
Biological father at home	Race	cohesion	Examiner
Any father at home	Education	expressiveness	Room of testing
No. siblings/children ≤ 5 yrs	Height, weight	conflict	Temperature
No. siblings/children > 5 yrs	Father:	independence	Time of day
No. adults in household	Race	achievement orientation	Day of week
Ratio of children to adults	Education	intellectual cultural orientation	Month of year
Marital status	Height, weight	activity-recreation orientation	
Welfare status	Family Hx:	moral religious emphasis	
Religion & rel. activity	Alcoholism	organization	
Major life changes	Learning disability	control	
death, illness, births	Psychiatric illness	Family Adaptability & Cohesion Scales (FACES II)	
divorces, marriages	Chronic illness	family cohesion	
moves		family adaptability	
job changes, etc.	**Caretaking Parents**		
Computer in home	Education		
Video games in home	Working status		
Smokers in household	Years of surrogate parenting		

(table continues)

Table 2.10 Primary Covariates by Age of Assessment (Continued)

7-Year Interview

School	Child Characteristics
Grade in school	Age at testing
Type of school	Sleep previous night
Type of class	Handedness
Special programs in school	Medications on exam day
Median test scores of school	Caffeine on exam day
	Illness on exam day
	Food intake, day prior
	Sensory problems
	Hx illness, fever, trauma
	Hx hospitalizations
	Medical problems
	Hours TV/day
	Hours video games/month
	Regular medical/dental care
	Immunizations

Notes: These 150 variables are only a representative subsample of those obtained for this study. Other covariates are derived scores calculated from the above (such as weight change during pregnancy). Some of the covariates are also used as outcome variables. This table is reproduced from (50).

providing the type of chaotic home environment often associated with frank maternal alcoholism (12).

Maternal and paternal education were used as surrogates for parental IQ (which could not be measured for 1000 parents within the available budget). We note that the correlations reported in the literature between parent IQ and child IQ (.38 to .46 [Bouchard & McGue, 1981; Smith, Delves, Lansdown, Clayton & Graham, 1983]) are comparable with the correlations we find between child IQ and parent education in the present study (.46 for mothers; .43 for fathers) (63). At least one other researcher involved in human behavioral teratology research has found that maternal education is a better predictor of IQ in young children than maternal IQ (Fried, 1990).

The correlations between the 13 alcohol scores and key covariates are shown in Table 2.5. Six of these covariates involve other prenatal exposures, one is a prenatal nutrition measure, six are basic demographic variables, and two involve key postnatal environmental factors. None are inextricably confounded with prenatal alcohol exposure, and many are uncorrelated with or even totally unrelated to alcohol use in this cohort. For instance, the relation between maternal education and alcohol use is curvilinear: the largest proportion of risk-level drinkers was among the most highly educated mothers, the next highest among the most poorly educated mothers.

This and other consequences of careful cohort selection are important aspects of our study design. Control of potentially confounding variables by explicit experimental design level is far preferable to "analysis of covariance" and other statistical adjustments (see Chapter 6), which may never succeed in disentangling confounded causes and which may thus preclude detection of alcohol effects even when they exist. The large sample size of our cohort was important in view of individual differences in susceptibility to alcohol and to environmental factors of child development. But sample size alone would not have permitted detection of these effects had we not oversampled the highest risk drinkers, stratified smoking across alcohol levels, selected a generally low-risk group of mothers whose primary risk behavior was alcohol use, and excluded women who had not begun prenatal care by the fifth month of pregnancy.

## CHAPTER 3

Test Batteries and Outcome Variables at Each Age

Our study was originally designed to assess three types of outcomes: neurobehavioral functioning, physical growth, and dysmorphology. This monograph deals only with the neurobehavioral outcomes across the first 7 1/2 years of life, as assessed at five standardized test ages: birth, 8 and 18 months, and 4 and 7 years (see Figure 2.1). The primary outcome variables are performance measures, which derive from direct examination or observation of the subjects in a laboratory situation. Additionally, we have obtained reports on the children's behavior from the psychometrists who examined them, their parents, and their teachers.

The test battery at each age was assembled according to contemporary knowledge about outcome variables that might prove sensitive for the detection of the neurobehavioral effects of prenatal exposures and other risk conditions. At the time this study was begun in 1974, there was scarcely any literature on human behavioral teratology. Although some studies had evaluated the long-term effects of maternal smoking during pregnancy, these studies had used an epidemiologic model, as in the traditional studies of low birthweight.

In contrast, the outcomes for the present study, derived primarily from the senior author's clinical experience with Fetal Alcohol Syndrome, cover a much broader range of functions and behaviors. The primary areas of deficit observed in children with FAS are attentional, neuromotor, and mental. We predicted that effects would be observable in these same areas for children of social drinkers, but that the effects would be more subtle than those observed in children of alcoholics (see [37, 46, 65] for a discussion of these issues). According to the dose-response tenet of teratology, one would predict that the milder the dose, the more subtle the effects upon offspring.

Thus, rather than being dichotomous ("normal" vs. "abnormal" on variable "X"), most of our outcomes were continuous, to aid in detecting the subtler effects of social drinking during pregnancy. For example, chronic maternal alcoholism during pregnancy can produce mental retardation in offspring. Therefore, we predicted that social drinking would produce IQ decrements in children of basically normal intelligence, but not frank retardation. In fact, such hypotheses have been confirmed in our earlier cross-sectional analyses (63).

The neonatal exam was particularly important to us because we wanted the opportunity to observe any existing neurobehavioral deficits that might reflect CNS dysfunction even before the infant experienced the home environment and individual caretaking experiences. Functional deficits observed immediately after birth would seem to have a more clearly biologic origin and should be the best markers for adversity of intrauterine environment.

Two of the behaviors most striking in our examination of newborns with FAS were their weak suck and their difficulty in habituating. Rather than "tuning out" redundant stimuli, the babies with FAS that we observed had become increasingly stimulated by sounds in their environment, and thus were seemingly deficient in this important regulatory mechanism so basic to all organisms (Lewis, 1975). Therefore we used the Brazelton Neonatal Behavior Scale on our day 1 examination specifically for its Habituation (Response Decrement) measures. We set up special procedures to assure that the three habituation items were obtained on all subjects. Missing data on the habituation subtest is common in studies using the Brazelton scale because the distressed babies are more likely to be in anything but the state of "light sleep" on which the habituation items depend. The successful use of habituation items as "endpoints" in this alcohol teratology study was contingent on a study design that precluded missing data on these items (16, 35).

Caretakers of babies with FAS often reported that they took an extraordinarily long time to nurse, seemingly because they had a weak sucking reflex. Therefore, rather than relying on the clinical method of judging the adequacy of a baby's sucking reflex by allowing them to suck on the examiner's finger, we developed an automated procedure whereby several parameters of sucking (such as pressure and latency) were assessed with a non-nutritive nipple attached to a pressure transducer (18, 41). A similar procedure had been used by Kron and colleagues (1976) to detect sucking deficits in babies exposed to narcotics *in utero*.

Our goal in planning each wave of data collection was to sample outcomes (such as those described above) that would be most sensitive to the effects of prenatal alcohol exposure on the developing child at the appropriate age of testing. Other considerations also constrained the design, such as the desire to complete three full rounds of assessment during the first 3-year grant period, which was the maximum funding duration possible at that time. The 8- and 18-month exams were simple developmental assessments with their respective behavior observations and global ratings. The 4- and 7-year batteries tapped outcomes from our personal experience with children with FAS, as we have described above for the neonatal exam. The roster of tests by age is summarized in Table 3.1, which also cites earlier publications from this study that describe these procedures in greater detail. In this chapter we describe only those procedures not previously described in published reports.

At the end of this chapter (in Section 3.2) we describe our procedure for aggregating these 474 outcome variables into 15 blocks for ' longitudinal and cross-sectional analyses. Some distribution statistics for each outcome appear in Appendix III-a.

3.1 Procedures for Test Administration, Scoring, and Data Reduction

Certain procedures have been enforced throughout all waves of the study. All data were gathered by highly trained examiners who had no knowledge either before the examination or after of the child's exposures, history, prior test results, or current living conditions. No contact with families, scheduling, or transportation of subjects was carried out by examiners of the children. (All contacts with families were by an outreach worker.) Examiners were trained to a high level of inter-rater reliability and were maintained at this level with monthly reliability sessions. (Reliabilities are presented in the orig-

Table 3.1 Tests Given at Each Exam Age and Primary Citations for
Procedures and Results as Listed in Appendix I

Test	Appendix I Entry
Neonatal	
Day 1: Brazelton (NBAS) 35	
Reflexes and Reflex Thresholds	
Naturalistic Observations [a] 11	
Day 2: Operant Head Turning [a] 4,5	
Operant Sucking [a] 5	
Sucking Baseline [a] 18,41	
Infancy	
8 months Bayley Scales of Infant Mental and Motor	
Development (BSID-8) 20	
Infant Behavior Record (IBR-8)	
Behavior Observations (BO-8)	
Global Ratings (GR-8)	
18 months: Bayley Scales of Infant Mental and	
Motor Development (BSID-18)	
Infant Behavior Record (IBR-18)	
Behavior Observations (BO-18)	
Global Ratings (GR-18)	
Childhood	
4 Years: Wechsler Preschool and Primary Scale	
of Intelligence (WPPSI) 63	
Neurobehavioral Tests 69	
Wisconsin Motor Steadiness Battery (WMSB) 69	
The Tactual Performance Test (TPT) 69	
Finger Tapping (FT) 69	
Grip Strength (GS) 69	
Gross Motor Battery (GMB) 69	
Vigilance Test (Vig-4) 37, 38	
Behavior Ratings (BR-4)	
Behavioral Observations (BO-4)	
Parent Rating Scales (PRS-4; Conners;	
& Werry, Weiss, and Peters)	
Psychiatric Symptom Checklist	
Global Ratings (GR-4) 37	
7 Years: Wechsler Intelligence Scale for Children–Revised	
(WISC-R) 65–67,76	
Wide Range Achievement Test–Revised	
(WRAT-R) 65–67,76	

Table 3.1 (Continued)

Test	Appendix I Entry
Vigilance Test: Continuous Performance Test (CPT-7)	49,65–67
Neuropsychologic Tests	65,67
Children's Memory Test (CMT)	65,67
Tactual Performance Test (TPT)	65,67
Seashore Rhythm Test	65,67
Progressive Figures (PF)	65,67
Memory For Faces (MFF)	65,67
Torque Test	65,67
Verbal Fluency: Blueberries (BB)	65,67
AudioVisual Integration (AVI)	65,67
Name Writing (NW)	65,67
Animal Naming Test (Boston Aphasia Battery)	65,67
Incidental Learning	65,67
Lateral Dominance	65,67
Grip Strength	
Stroop [b]	46, 94
Neurologic Coordination Battery (Neuro)	
Language Tests	
Auditory Attention Span	
Sentence Building Test (SBT)	
Developmental Sentence Scoring (DSS)	
Global Ratings (GR-7)	
Behavior Ratings (BR-7)	49,65,67
Behavioral Observations (BO-7)	
Parent Questionnaire (PQ-7)	
Conners Parent Rating Scale (CPRS-7)	
Eyberg Child Behavior Inventory (ECBI)	
Myklebust Pupil Rating Scale (MPRS)	65, 66, 76

Notes: Appendix III-a lists scores from these tests and additional references. Data from several tasks were not included in the longitudinal analyses due to small sample size available for computation of correlations with other variables in the database:

[a]Naturalistic Observations, Operant Head Turning, Operant Sucking and Sucking Baseline were administered only to subsamples of the cohort.

[b]Stroop was adnimistered to less than one-half of the cohort (only the first summer of the 7-year exam).

inal reports; the citations are collected in Table 3.1.) The neonatal
exams were conducted in special testing rooms within the newborn
area at each of the two study hospitals. Exam rooms and hospitals
were rotated among examiners. In order to standardize the later
assessment conditions, all exams after the neonatal period were conducted at the study's laboratories at the University of Washington.
Time of day and test age were carefully controlled, as already explained. All data were verified three times: once by the examiner
upon completion of the testing, once by the lab coordinator before
keypunching, and once by statistical clerks working with computer-
ized data. Each test and each exam session was given a "validity
score" by the examiner (one reason that our sample sizes often vary
slightly between tests of the same battery). Decisions about the validity of individual tests were made by Ann Streissguth and/or the
project director without knowledge of the subject's exposure history.

3.1.1 Neonatal Assessments

Neonates were examined by two independent teams of examiners, on
both day one and day two of life, in standardized assessment situations prior to discharge from the hospital. Day One involved two
components: The Brazelton Exam and naturalistic observations.
Day Two involved either an Operant Head Turning procedure for the
infants born during the first half of the year or an Operant Sucking
procedure for those born later in the year.

   The Brazelton Neonatal Behavioral Assessment Scale (NBAS;
Brazelton, 1973) was administered to all eligible cohort infants at
7:15am, midway between feedings. Infants were tested on the first
day after delivery that such an examination was deemed medically
advisable. Depending on hour of birth, the testing age was between
9 and 35 hours for 92% of the infants; the median testing age over
all subjects was 23 hours. Scoring and administration of the 27
NBAS items was in accordance with Brazelton's manual, with each
item scored on a 9-point scale. The special procedures we developed
for this study have been described previously (8, 35). Because the
Habituation data were of special interest, infants who could not be

maintained in a state of light sleep long enough to begin the Habituation items were scheduled for another exam midway between the next pair of feedings. Thus we avoided the high frequency of missing data on the NBAS Habituation items that plagues most such studies with this procedure; we obtained Habituation data even on high-risk babies. As Rosett, Snyder, Sander, et al. (1979) have since shown that prenatal alcohol exposure affects the sleep/wake patterns of newborns, these high-risk subjects could easily have been deleted from the sample in the absence of such a protocol.

The special scoring systems we developed for the 21 reflexes that are a routine part of the NBAS are discussed here for the first time. Reflexes were coded on a 4-point scale as follows: 0, stimulus given but reflex not obtained; 1, reflex weak and/or delayed; 2, reflex normal; 3, reflex hypertonic or very strong. Reflexes were originally coded separately on right and left sides; these were combined for the present analyses after screening for asymmetric effects was unproductive. An additional dichotomous reflex code was used (Normal/Abnormal) which compared "normal" (code 2) to everything else (codes 0, 1, and 3). In addition, each reflex was assigned a "threshold" code according to the degree of difficulty (number of trials) needed to elicit it. The threshold codes ranged from 1 to 4, where "1" means easily elicited on the first good trial. While previous analyses of the NBAS data in this study have involved factor scores of the 27 NBAS items as the dependent variables (8, 35), the analyses in this monograph involve the 27 NBAS items themselves, a state change summary rating, and the 21 Reflex items each scored for strength of reflex, abnormality of reflex and threshold to elicit reflex. Procedures for the Operant Head Turning study (4, 5), the Operant Sucking study (5), and the Baseline Sucking study (5, 18, 41) from the Neonatal Day 2 exam have been described previously.

3.1.2 Infancy Assessments

The 8- and 18-month exams included the Bayley Scales of Infant Mental and Motor Development (Bayley, 1969), Behavioral Observations, subjective Global Ratings recorded by the examiners, and structured parent interviews. At each age the Bayley Scales,

scored according to the published manual, included a Mental
Development Index (MDI), a Psychomotor Development Index
(PDI), and Infant/Behavior Ratings (IBR) made by the examiner on
12 behaviors rated on 9-point scales, including some additional IBR-
type scales scales we developed in our laboratory. The Global
Ratings (GR), modified from the Collaborative Perinatal Study, also
used 9-point scales; higher scores were "better." In addition the examiner noted the presence or absence of several aspects of the child's
behavior, such as "unusual hand movements" in the testing situation. These variables are called Behavior Observations (BO). PDI
and MDI data from the 8-month exam have been previously published (20), but this is the first published account of the IBR, GR or
BO data from the 8- and 18-month exams, and of the 18-month
Bayley data.

3.1.3 Childhood Assessments

The 4-year exam included a large neuropsychologic test battery and
parent questionnaires. Previous publications have presented procedures and findings from the 4-year exam, including the Wechsler
Preschool and Primary Scale of Intelligence (63; Wechsler, 1976);
the 4-year Vigilance Test developed in our laboratory (38); and the 4-
year motor data (69) from the Wisconsin Motor Steadiness Battery
(Matthews & Klove, 1978), the Gross Motor Battery developed in
our laboratory (69), and a preschool modification of the tactual performance test (TPT) (Trites & Price, 1979). The additional data presented in this monograph include Behavior Ratings (9-point scales
filled out by the examiner after testing), Behavior Observations (also
filled out by the examiner), and four parental (usually maternal) questionnaires. Selected items or scores from these scales were used in
the longitudinal analyses for the blocks of behavior to which they
were relevant. Items from the Conners Parent Rating Scale
(Goyette, Conners & Ulrich, 1978) and the Eyeberg Child Behavior
Inventory (ECBI) (Eyberg & Ross, 1978; Robinson, Eyberg &
Ross, 1980) and some relevant items from our own parent questionnaire, including a psychiatric checklist developed by Finklestein and
Herman (1978), are also included in the present analyses.

The 7-year exam (see 49 and 65 for procedures) included a large neuropsychologic and attention battery, a language battery, achievement tests, examiner ratings, observations, and parent questionnaires. Questionnaires were also mailed to the children's second grade teachers (65, 66, 76) to obtain data on the Myklebust Pupil Rating Scale (Myklebust, 1981) and other items.

The neuropsychologic tests, described previously (65-67), included the following: the Wechsler Intelligence Scale for Children-Revised (WISC-R) (Wechsler, 1974); the Wide Range Achievement Test-Revised (WRAT-R) (Jastak & Jastak, 1978); the Tactual Performance Test (TPT), the Progressive Figures Test, the Lateral Dominance Test, the Name-Writing Speed task, and our oral-response modification of the Seashore Rhythm Test, all from the Reitan-Indiana Battery (Reitan & Davison, 1974; Seashore, Lewis & Saltveit, 1960; McGivern et al., 1991); the Animal Naming test from the Boston Aphasia Battery (Goodglass & Kaplan, 1972); the Auditory-Visual Integration Tests (Birch & Lefford, 1963; Birch & Belmont, 1964), the modified Torque test (Blau, 1977; Furlong, 1981), the Memory for Faces Test (Milner, 1968); a verbal fluency test "Blueberries," and our modification of the Children's Memory Test of Dodrill and Miller (1982) to which we added a copying designs component and a qualitative scoring system (65, 67). The 7-year Vigilance paradigm (49) was our modification of the Continuous Performance Test (Rosvold et al., 1956).

A language battery was not initially included in the 7-year exam because we had not observed notable language deficits in children with FAS, other than those which might be attributable to intellectual deficits per se. However, in an effort to provide a more comprehensive developmental picture at the 7-year exam, we modified the battery after half the cohort had been examined. We deleted the Stroop and the Aphasia Screening Test words (on which we continued to have difficulty obtaining inter-examiner reliability) and replaced these with a language battery and a neurologic screening battery. Preliminary analysis of the Stroop data (presented earlier [46]) indicated that the 84 children classified ORDEXC=4 (the highest-risk exposure category) took significantly longer on both the color-nam-

ing and the word-naming parts of the Stroop than the 138 children in
the low-risk exposure categories (ORDEXC=0,1,2,3). Even after
statistically adjusting for traditional SES covariates and for Reading
Achievement and IQ, these more heavily alcohol-exposed children
had a slower central processing time for this interesting cognitive
task.

Data from our language battery have not been previously published. Earlier cross-sectional analyses did not reveal significant relationships between prenatal alcohol exposure and language development as measured on these tests, at 7 years of age. The primary language tests included our modification of Johnson's Sentence Building
Task (Johnson & Blalock, 1987), which requires the subject to construct both oral and written sentences based on a set of key words
(dog, jump, pretty, etc.). The task is scored for a variety of syntacti-
cal, grammatical and autographic errors. Additionally, we scored the
written productions according to Lee's developmental scoring system
(Lee, 1987). We also administered a sentence repetition test, the
Auditory Attention Test from the Detroit Tests of Learning Aptitude
(Baker & Leland, 1967).

The neurologic screening test (Szatmari & Taylor, 1984) involved
a set of 11 Right-Left Differentiation items, scored correct/incorrect
(I/O), and five coordination items (thumb and index finger opposition; successive finger movements; alternating supination/pronation
of arm; repetitive toe taps and alternating heel/toe taps). The score
was the number of seconds to complete the required number of
movements. We developed a qualitative rating of apparent difficulty
which was scored by the examiner for each task (high score = more
difficulty). These data have not been previously published.

Previous publications have reported on the procedures and findings
from the 7-year exam as follows. The findings with respect to IQ
scores from the WISC-R, achievement test scores from the WRAT-
R, learning problems, the Myklebust Pupil Rating Scale (filled out
by classroom teachers), and the Vigilance CPT have already been
published (49, 65-67, 76). The three-article series (65-67) also covered findings from the extensive neurobehavioral battery administered
at age 7 and from the examiner behavior ratings.

3.2 Categorization of the Outcomes into Blocks for Analysis

In preparation for the longitudinal analysis, a subset of 474 outcome variables from across all test ages and representing all types of data was selected (it is itemized in Appendix III-a). Software limitations in existence at the time the longitudinal analyses began precluded a set of variables exceeding 500. As this number had to include the 13 alcohol predictor variables, we were unable to analyze more than 487 outcome variables. For this reason, not all of the 7-year neuropsychologic outcomes described in our previous publications (65-67) were included in the present analyses. We retained the 24 most salient outcomes of the 164 reported there.

In order to proceed with the diachronic analyses, the 474 outcome variables were organized into 15 blocks as detailed in Appendix III-a. These groupings are based on face validity; the analyses of Chapter 5 ultimately support the "correctness" of these placements. As Appendix III-a indicates, the blocks often represent fairly broad interpretations of the categorizing constructs. Unlike the case in factor analysis, our methods neither penalize nor misleadingly exploit the assembly of loosely related sets of outcomes in one single block. Before using the outcomes scores for analyses, they were adjusted for age and examiner effects as necessary using multiple regression techniques. Distribution statistics reported in this monograph are raw scores (see Appendix III-a). Appendix III-b presents an alphabetized listing of the acronymns used for the 474 outcomes in the longitudinal analysis.

## CHAPTER 4

Methods of Latent Variable Modeling by Partial Least Squares

In this section we introduce the simplest form of Partial Least Squares (PLS) for the analysis of complex systems indirectly observed. This family of techniques, a hybrid of regression analysis and factor analysis, has recently been applied to diverse scaling problems in the natural and social sciences. For earlier explanations and applications of these methods, refer to Bookstein (1982, 1986), Jöreskog and Wold (1982), or Wold (1975, 1982). The following discussion here and in Section 4.1 is extracted from (66). See also (72).

Partial Least Squares is a method of data reduction designed for exactly the sort of data we face here: An investigator has collected two or more "blocks" of indicators and wishes to summarize the predictive interrelations among the set of all blocks considered together. Each indicator was intended to tap some aspect of a construct underlying its entire block. (For example, the construct for the alcohol items is "exposure," and for the IQ subtests "intelligence.") Yet our interest is not so much in that underlying construct (its factors, their reliability, et cetera) as in its correlations with the other construct or constructs of the full data set, which are also measured indirectly via their own indicators. Regardless of the correlations among IQ subtests, different subtests are sensitive to the effects of alcohol to different extents, and also may be imagined to have been measured with more or less reliability had we had the same child scored by several examiners or by the same examiner over many occasions. We therefore wish to *scale* the items of each block of indicators to best explain the cross-block relationships (correlations). These mutually scaled scores are the *latent variables* (LVs) as they are constructed by PLS for two or more blocks at the same time. Our use of the phrase "latent variable" in this sense derives from the earliest papers on PLS (e.g. Wold, 1975). The reader familiar with the notion of latent variables from latent structural models (e.g., LISREL, Jöreskog and Sörböm, 1984) should not assume that these are "latent" in the same sense—for instance, PLS LVs are modeled without an error term.

Section 1 of this chapter introduces PLS by examining the relationship of the prenatal alcohol block (13 items) with the 11 subtest items of the WISC-R that was given when the children were about 7 years old. We give complete details of a typical PLS analysis, a full explanation of what it does and why. Section 2, which is less detailed, shows a similar PLS technique that can be used in longitudinal analyses. Section 3 discusses the rationale for this method of dose-response analysis, comparing it to other biostatistical approaches to the same question for this type of data. Section 4 presents a detailed plan for the primary statistical analyses in the four chapters that follow.

4.1 Two-block PLS Analysis

To illustrate the PLS technique, we begin with a two-block analysis of the Alcohol Block (consisting of our 13 primary alcohol scores) and the WISC-R Subtest items from the 7-year Mental Block. Table 4.1 displays the ordinary correlation coefficients between each of 13 measures of alcohol exposure and each of the 11 IQ subtests from the WISC-R based on 481 cases for whom IQ tests were available. This array displays a clear pattern of signs: the correlations of most of the alcohol indices with respect to most of the subtests are negative. There appears to be a weak but stable negative correlation between alcohol exposure, as measured in this battery, and IQ as assessed by the components of the WISC-R test battery.

The simple correlations of Table 4.1 are measures of the degree of *linear* association between the alcohol scores and each of the IQ subtests. However, there is in fact no justification for presuming linearity of effects of the (initially) log-transformed AA, MAX, ADOCC, and MOCC scores and the five-point QFV scores along with the binary BINGE variables. Using new methods of data analysis we can

Table 4.1 Correlations Between Measures of Prenatal Alcohol Exposure and IQ Subtest Scores

	INFO7	SIM7	ARITH7	VOC7	COMP7	DIG7	PICC7	PICA7	BLKD7	OBJ7	COD7
LAAP	-0.01	-0.01	-0.07	0.06	0.01	-0.11	0.03	-0.03	-0.08	0.04	-0.08
LAAD	0.00	0.00	-0.03	0.08	0.03	-0.04	0.00	-0.01	-0.05	0.04	-0.05
BINGEP	-0.09	-0.07	-0.19	-0.04	-0.06	-0.13	-0.07	-0.07	-0.14	-0.02	-0.07
BINGED	-0.15	-0.12	-0.15	-0.08	-0.06	-0.12	-0.11	-0.01	-0.13	-0.02	-0.02
LADOCCP	-0.04	-0.05	-0.09	0.00	-0.01	-0.14	-0.05	-0.04	-0.09	0.06	-0.06
LADOCCD	-0.04	-0.05	-0.07	0.01	0.00	-0.11	-0.07	-0.03	-0.03	0.11	-0.01
LMAXP	-0.04	-0.03	-0.10	0.00	0.00	-0.14	-0.05	-0.03	-0.09	0.05	-0.07
LMAXD	-0.06	-0.04	-0.09	-0.01	-0.02	-0.11	-0.08	-0.02	-0.03	0.09	-0.03
LMOCCP	0.03	0.05	-0.01	0.10	0.07	-0.09	0.04	-0.01	-0.03	0.09	-0.07
LMOCCD	0.07	0.08	0.02	0.12	0.09	-0.03	0.03	0.04	0.02	0.11	-0.03
QFVP	-0.03	-0.04	-0.09	0.01	0.00	-0.13	-0.02	-0.05	-0.08	0.04	-0.07
QFVD	-0.01	0.01	-0.06	0.06	0.05	-0.11	-0.04	0.02	-0.04	0.10	-0.02
ORDEXC	-0.01	-0.01	-0.06	0.04	0.03	-0.13	-0.02	-0.03	-0.06	0.09	-0.04

Notes: N=481. The prefix "L" on variable names refers to log–transformed scores.

Table 4.2 Correlations Among 13 Transformed Alcohol Scores

	AAP	AAD	BINGEP	BINGED	ADOCCP	ADOCCD	MAXP	MAXD	MOCCP	MOCCD	QFVP	QFVD	ORDEXC
AAP	1.00	0.61	0.47	0.34	0.57	0.37	0.54	0.37	0.84	0.54	0.61	0.50	0.61
AAD	0.61	1.00	0.38	0.46	0.35	0.42	0.36	0.49	0.67	0.80	0.46	0.64	0.62
BINGEP	0.47	0.38	1.00	0.60	0.78	0.57	0.87	0.63	0.47	0.46	0.79	0.54	0.73
BINGED	0.34	0.46	0.60	1.00	0.55	0.71	0.57	0.82	0.35	0.46	0.51	0.78	0.55
ADOCCP	0.57	0.35	0.78	0.55	1.00	0.68	0.87	0.59	0.44	0.37	0.78	0.58	0.60
ADOCCD	0.37	0.42	0.57	0.71	0.68	1.00	0.63	0.88	0.34	0.40	0.55	0.72	0.52
MAXP	0.54	0.36	0.87	0.57	0.87	0.63	1.00	0.64	0.49	0.44	0.76	0.54	0.69
MAXD	0.37	0.49	0.63	0.82	0.59	0.88	0.64	1.00	0.41	0.54	0.56	0.71	0.61
MOCCP	0.84	0.67	0.47	0.35	0.44	0.34	0.49	0.41	1.00	0.75	0.59	0.45	0.74
MOCCD	0.54	0.80	0.46	0.46	0.37	0.40	0.44	0.54	0.75	1.00	0.51	0.52	0.70
QFVP	0.61	0.46	0.79	0.51	0.78	0.55	0.76	0.56	0.59	0.51	1.00	0.58	0.76
QFVD	0.50	0.64	0.54	0.78	0.58	0.72	0.54	0.71	0.45	0.52	0.58	1.00	0.58
ORDEXC	0.61	0.62	0.73	0.55	0.60	0.52	0.69	0.61	0.74	0.70	0.76	0.58	1.00

Notes: N = 581. In this and all subsequent analyses we have dropped one case for which the reported AAP was most extreme, at over 26 ounces per day.

Table 4.3 Correlations Between Transformed Measures of Prenatal Alcohol Exposure and IQ Subtest Scores

	INFO7	SIM7	ARITH7	VOC7	COMP7	DIG7	PICC7	PICA7	BLKD7	OBJ7	COD7
AAP	-0.06	-0.05	-0.10	0.01	-0.05	-0.11	0.01	-0.05	-0.09	0.01	-0.07
AAD	0.0	-0.01	-0.03	0.07	0.03	-0.04	0.0	-0.01	-0.05	0.04	-0.05
BINGEP	-0.09	-0.07	-0.18	-0.04	-0.06	-0.13	-0.07	-0.07	-0.14	-0.02	-0.07
BINGED	-0.15	-0.12	-0.15	-0.07	-0.06	-0.12	-0.10	0.0	-0.13	-0.02	-0.02
ADOCCP	-0.12	-0.16	-0.20	-0.10	-0.11	-0.16	-0.10	-0.10	-0.17	-0.05	-0.07
ADOCCD	-0.13	-0.16	-0.13	-0.10	-0.08	-0.15	-0.11	-0.07	-0.12	-0.02	0.00
MAXP	-0.11	-0.10	-0.19	-0.09	-0.07	-0.15	-0.10	-0.08	-0.13	-0.03	-0.06
MAXD	-0.12	-0.10	-0.13	-0.09	-0.07	-0.13	-0.10	-0.03	-0.09	0.01	-0.01
MOCCP	0.01	-0.01	-0.05	0.07	0.03	-0.10	0.06	-0.05	-0.04	0.08	-0.06
MOCCD	0.07	0.08	0.02	0.11	0.10	-0.04	0.03	0.04	0.02	0.12	-0.03
QFVP	-0.11	-0.13	-0.18	-0.08	-0.09	-0.14	-0.08	-0.09	-0.15	-0.06	-0.07
QFVD	-0.11	-0.10	-0.14	-0.02	-0.03	-0.14	-0.10	-0.02	-0.12	-0.01	-0.01
ORDEXC	-0.05	-0.05	-0.10	0.02	0.0	-0.14	-0.03	-0.06	-0.11	0.01	-0.06

Notes: N=481. Monotone nonlinear transformation of the alcohol scores were computed using methods described in Sampson et al., 1987 (see #56). They are illustrated in Figure 2. Because of these transformations, the "L" prefix for the log-transformed alcohol scores used in Table 4 has been dropped from the variable names here.

determine "optimal" monotone nonlinear transformations of the alcohol scores for prediction of outcome latent variables. This methodology, explained in (56), is based on nonlinear scaling methods now becoming increasingly common in data analysis (Breiman & Friedman, 1985; Hastie & Tibshirani, 1990). The transforms are the result of a scatterplot smoother ("supersmoother," Friedman, 1984) applied with each alcohol variable, in turn, as the independent variable. In our analyses, the optimal nonlinear regressions appropriate for prediction of each of the outcome blocks happen to be nearly identical among themselves. We therefore use common nonlinear scalings for the alcohol scores in all our analyses. These are taken to be the optimal transformations for the relationship of the alcohol scores with the pool of 158 outcome scores from the eight outcome blocks examined in (67). These scalings are illustrated in Figure 4.1. The correlations of these transformed alcohol scores with each other are shown in Table 4.2 (compare the untransformed matrix of correlations in Table 2.4) and the revised correlations with the WISC-R subtests are given in Table 4.3. The pattern of correlation is now clearer and apparently stronger. All further analysis and discussion of the alcohol effects in this chapter and in the next two is in terms of these transformed alcohol scores.

In Section 2.2.1 we noted our original uncertainty about the appropriate mode of measuring alcohol exposure in utero, owing to lack of information at the outset of the study about the mechanism of the teratological effect. We now see that that uncertainty was justified: a variety of different measures of alcohol exposure have nearly commensurate effects on this particular block of outcome variables. Indeed, the pattern suggests that we seek an underlying construct of "net alcohol exposure," constructed as a weighted average of 13 alcohol scores, and another construct of "net intelligence deficit," constructed likewise as a weighted average of the 11 IQ scores, so as to interpret this pattern of correlations meaningfully. We need, therefore, a procedure for determining the weighted averages and for interpreting the extent to which their single correlation summarizes the entire pattern in Table 4.3.

In combining different estimates of the same quantity that vary in precision, it is standard practice to weight the contribution of each in proportion to its precision, so that the more precise estimates are given more weight in forming the average. Likewise, in attempting to construct a net score (latent variable) for alcohol exposure that is to correlate with intelligence, we should weight the alcohol measures in proportion to their correlation with a sum of the IQ subtests. This is what a Partial Least Squares procedure does.

Such a two-block analysis is typically diagrammed as shown in Figure 4.2. Observed variables are indicated by squares and latent variables by circles. The single line between the two latent variables indicates our intention to explain the pattern of correlations R_{AB} between observables of different blocks in terms of a single pair of latent variables. We are *not* attempting to explain the correlations among indicators of the same block; instead we are determining the linear combinations of the (transformed) indicators in each block which are predictive of items in the opposite block. The coefficients of the LVs represent the *saliences* of each indicator in terms of prediction from or to the other latent variable.

A useful interpretation of the two-block PLS procedure is as a least-squares analysis analogous to ordinary regression. The usual explanation of regression characterizes it as providing a least-squares fit of the "outcome variable" from among linear combinations of the "predictors." In PLS, what we are approximating in such a least-squares logic are not the values of the "outcome score" case by case but instead the *elements of the correlation matrix itself.* We are approximating all the correlations like r_{ij} between the ith alcohol variable and the jth behavioral outcome variable by products $\alpha_i\beta_j$ of *saliences*, the α_i being the saliences for the rows (variables of the first block) of the correlation matrix R_{AB}, and the β_j being the saliences for the columns. We want α's and β's that minimize the sum of squared "errors" $(r_{ij} - \alpha_i\beta_j)^2$ over all the correlations between the blocks.

This minimization is not actually carried out by any single regression (but instead by the singular-value decomposition, as explained in Section 4.1.2, or by an indefinitely long sequence of re-

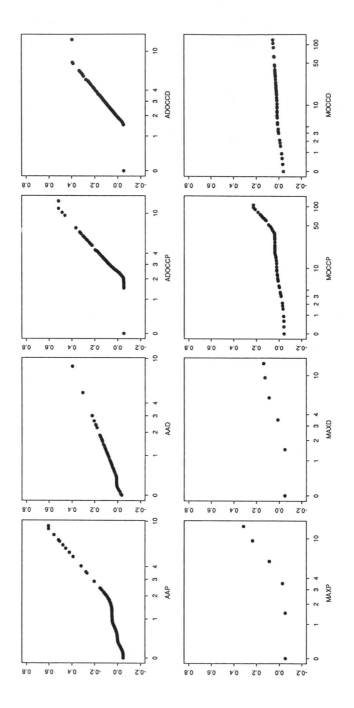

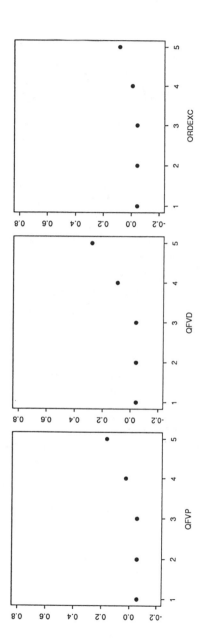

Figure 4.1. Monotone nonlinear transformations of eleven of the 13 original alcohol scores (excluding the two binary BINGE measures) as presented in (67). These were determined to optimize the correlations of the individual scores with the outcome latent variable in the two-block analysis of 158 neuropsychological tests presented in (67). Details of the method are discussed in (56). The large gap between zero and the next positive score on log(ADOCCP+1) and log(ADOCCD+1) was an artifact of the quantity–frequency–variability interview format, in which the smallest possible positive code is 1.5 drinks (the code for response of 1–2 drinks per occasion). This gap is repaired by the nonlinear transformation.

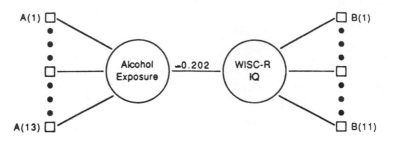

Figure 4.2. Diagram for a two-block latent variable model relating 13 indicators of alcohol exposure to 11 IQ subtests from the WISC-R as presented in (66). The correlation between the estimated latent variables is –0.202.

gressions, as explained below).   Nevertheless there is a close tie between it and the notion of regressions on case values which allows us to interpret these coefficients α_i and β_j. Suppose we already knew one set of these coefficients—say, the α's, the saliences for the rows (alcohol variables) of the correlation matrix R_{AB}—and wished to compute the column saliences, β's (one per outcome), from them. Any particular β—say, β_1, for the first variable of the outcome block—is computed to minimize the sum of the "errors" $(r_{i1} - \alpha_i\beta_1)^2$ over the alcohol indicators indexed by i. But this minimization is an ordinary regression problem: predicting the "dependent variable" r_{i1} by a best multiple β_1 of the "independent variable" α_i. The regression has no constant term, and so (by the usual formula) the value of β_1 is the sum of the products of "dependent" by "independent" variables divided by the sum of squares of the "independent." That is,

$$\beta_1 = \Sigma_i r_{i1}\alpha_i \Big/ \Sigma_i \alpha_i^2$$

In fact, for each j,

$$\beta_j = \Sigma_i r_{ij}\alpha_i \Big/ \Sigma_i \alpha_i^2 \qquad (1)$$

and similarly, for each i,

$$\alpha_i = \Sigma_j r_{ij}\beta_j \,\Big/\, \Sigma_j \beta_j^2$$

(2)

Equations (1) and (2) define the usual iterative algorithm for computation of PLS estimates. For given initial estimates of the α's, one estimates the β's from (1), then substitutes these into (2) in order to compute new estimates of the α's, then returns to (1), and so on. The scales of the sets of the α_i and the β_j are arbitrary. We choose to set $\Sigma_i \alpha_i^2 = \Sigma_j \beta_j^2 = 1$; see expression (3) below.

The numerator of the formula for each α or β can be interpreted as a covariance involving case values over the subjects of the study. The numerator for β, $\Sigma r_{ij}\alpha_i$, for instance, is the covariance of the jth outcome with the "latent variable" $\Sigma\alpha_i A_i$ built using the α's (where the A_i are assumed standardized to mean zero and variance 1). Similarly, the numerator for the α's, $\Sigma r_{ij}\beta_j$, is the covariance of the ith Alcohol variable with the "latent variable" $\Sigma\beta_j B_j$ built using the β's. Thus, the approximation of the correlation matrix expressed in terms of regressions corresponds to our original suggestion: that a net score (latent variable) for, say, Alcohol exposure, should be constructed by weighting the alcohol measures in proportion to their correlation with a corresponding weighted combination of outcome measures. The solution of a least-squares problem about *correlations* is interpreted using the language of latent variables and the saliences of individual variables for the *cross*-correlation matrix.

We can draw an analogy between PLS and principal components (PC) analysis. The first principal component of any set of data is the "score" (combination of variables) which predicts back to the original variables with the least summed squared error. PLS may be thought of as a principal-components analysis *of the cross-correlation matrix all by itself.* Consider each row of the correlation matrix R_{AB} as a separate "variable"—each a profile of correlations with a single alcohol measure. The alcohol latent variable is identical with the uncentered first principal component of these "variables" r_{ij}, $i=1,2,...,13$ (with "cases" indexed by j). That is, the Alcohol saliences are the relative weights of these individual alcohol correlation profiles in the "combination" that best predicts back to them separately. The Outcome saliences are proportional to the "case scores" on this first PC. Equivalently, the Outcome saliences are the principal component loadings for the "variables" $r_{ij}, j=1,2,...,11$ (with "cases" indexed by i), and the Alcohol saliences are the "case scores" for *this* first PC. This duality of component loadings and scores is familiar as the Eckart-Young Theorem underlying much of multivariate statistics, including the singular-value decomposition we recommend for PLS computations in Section 4.1.2. When we report a "second dimension" of Alcohol effect in Section 5.3, it may be thought of as a meaningful second principal component of the cross-correlation matrix, just as the first pair of latent variables represents a meaningful first principal component of the same matrix.

There is a further analogy of PLS with the method of principal components analysis. Principal component analyses are evaluated using the "proportion of (total) variance explained" by successively extracted components. In the case of our PLS latent variable analysis, successive pairs of solutions to equations (1) and (2) above determine scores that represent mutually orthogonal aspects of interblock prediction. Successive pairs of scores (linear combinations of scaled indicators) have successively smaller covariances. We interpret the total of the squared correlations in R_{AB} as the *total predictability* of either block for the other, and each successive pair of latent variables may be said to account for an appropriate fraction of this total, as expressed in equation (3) below. Note, however, that one need not compute actual scores on these linear combinations in order to compute their covariances. Simple algebra, or the singular-value analysis discussed in Section 4.1.2, yields these covariances directly.

There are, in fact, eleven mutually uncorrelated sets of coefficients α_i and β_j which satisfy the pair of equations (1) and (2). (That is, there are 11 principal components of the 13×11 correlation matrix R_{AB}.) These solutions are most conveniently expressed using the matrix notation shown in Section 4.1.2. The particular linear combinations LV_A and LV_B we want are those which have the greatest covariance. When the coefficients are scaled so that

$$\Sigma_i \alpha_i^2 = \Sigma_j \beta_j^2 = 1$$

one can show that the sum of the squared covariances for the eleven pairs of solutions is equal to the sum of the squared correlations in the matrix R_{AB}. We thus refer to the ratio

$$\left(\text{cov}(\Sigma_{i=1}^{13} \alpha_i A_i, \Sigma_{j=1}^{11} \beta_j B_j)\right)^2 / \Sigma_{i=1}^{13} \Sigma_{j=1}^{11} r_{ij}^2 \qquad (3)$$

as the "proportion of the sum of squared cross-block correlations explained by the latent variables LV_A and LV_B." For the Alcohol-IQ analysis, this figure is 87.6%. See Table 4.4 for a summary of this analysis.

The quantity in equation (3) is our measure of "goodness-of-fit" for the two-block analysis. (Others, notably Wold [1982], refer instead to a quantity "Q" much more closely aligned with the LV correlation.) For the more complex longitudinal models, causal models

Table 4.4 Two-Block Partial Least Squares Analysis of Alcohol Exposure Scores and IQ Subtest Scores

Alcohol LV Saliences		LV Saliences for IQ	
AAP	−0.19	Subtests	(WISC–R)
AAD	−0.04	Information	0.34
BINGEP	−0.30	Similarities	0.35
BINGED	−0.32	Arithmetic	0.48
ADOCCP	−0.42	Vocabulary	0.20
ADOCCD	−0.35	Comprehension	0.21
MAXP	−0.35	Digit Span	0.42
MAXD	−0.29	Picture completion	0.25
MOCCP	−0.06	Picture assembly	0.19
MOCCD	0.12	Block design	0.39
QFVP	−0.37	Object assembly	0.08
QFVD	−0.27	Coding	0.13
ORDEXC	−0.20		

Summary	
LV Covariance	1.02
Fraction of Summed Squared Correlation Explained	0.88
LV Correlation	0.20

and multiple regression models, we propose no index of quality of fit at all; we treat these as explanatory decompositions of patterns in sets of correlations already fitted to pairs of blocks by this method.

The PLS dimensions computed do not necessarily bear any relation to principal components of the blocks considered separately. For instance, the first principal component of the IQ block weights the subscales of Verbal and Performance IQ nearly equally, but the PLS analysis selects primarily Digit Span and Arithmetic as expressing the dependence on alcohol. Table 4.5 presents the results of this principal component analysis, which differs considerably from the PLS analysis of Table 4.4. PLS latent variables "explain" the cross-correlation matrix R_{AB} in the sense just described; they are not computed to explain the within-block correlation matrices R_{AA} and R_{BB} as principal components do. This focus on cross-block correlation or prediction, together with the lack of assumptions regarding the structure of within-block correlations, distinguishes PLS analysis from the relatively better known "linear structural relations" modeling approach provided by the LISREL computer package (Jöreskog & Sörböm, 1984); this comparison is dealt with at length in Bookstein

Table 4.5 Principal Component Analysis of Standardized IQ Subtest Scores

IQ Subtest (WISC–R)	Component 1	Component 2	Component 3
Information	0.37	0.21	−0.08
Similarities	0.36	0.27	0.10
Arithmetic	0.33	0.00	−0.11
Vocabulary	0.35	0.32	0.09
Comprehension	0.34	0.29	0.20
Digit Span	0.24	0.16	−0.59
Picture completion	0.28	−0.18	0.09
Picture assembly	0.28	−0.26	−0.10
Block design	0.29	−0.35	0.30
Object assembly	0.26	−0.50	0.34
Coding	0.17	−0.44	−0.59
Eigenvalue	4.54	1.28	0.90
Fraction of variance explained	0.41	0.12	0.08

(1986). Thus PLS does not specifically attend to the reliability of the LV scores it extracts, and different LVs from the same block may have different reliabilities.

Finally, we note that a correlation between latent variables (for this example –0.202, see Figure 4.2) should *not* be corrected for "attenuation" at any stage, in spite of the custom of correcting so in the course of estimating two-block models by maximum-likelihood methods as provided in LISREL. Correction for attenuation is based on an assumption that the indicators of each block are modeled by the underlying factor only, together with error. We have imposed no such model, nor any other assumptions about the within-block factor structure; hence there is no way to compute an appropriate amount of attenuation.

For the IQ data, as shown in Table 4.4, the Alcohol LV is weighted most heavily on the binge-oriented measures ADOCC, QFV, MAX, and BINGE, with greater emphasis on the pre-pregnancy recognition period. The AA and MOCC variables, measures of average consumption level, are clearly not consistent with the general pattern of negative correlations for the items reflecting the dimension of alcohol exposure of interest. The IQ items also vary in the extent to which they are predicted by alcohol. The net IQ LV most appropriate for adumbrating the effects of alcohol is a combination principally weighting Arithmetic and Digit Span, with substantial saliences also for Block Design, Similarities, and Information. These items reflect problems with short-term memory, quantitative functioning, and sustained attention that are apparent in other blocks of outcome measures as well (see below).

In this example the second latent variable pair explains only about one variable's worth of correlations ($9\% \approx 1/11$), and we do not interpret it further. In the examples of the next section, the second latent variable explains an amount of correlation corresponding to 53 variables ($11.2\% \approx 53/474$); we will interpret it further there.

4.1.1 Summary of How to Read PLS Tables

By now we have introduced enough new quantities that a review of the crucial tables 4.3 and 4.4 might be helpful. Table 4.3 is the

complete data for a PLS analysis: a matrix of correlations between
the items of one "block" and the items of another. Table 4.4 is a
model that fits Table 4.3 by one pair of latent variables (LVs).
There are two columns of "saliences," one for each of the blocks of
variables. The entries of each column, when squared, add to exactly
1; hence these numbers are *not* comparable between columns whenever the blocks are of different length. Within each column, the values are coefficients for the latent variable of that block, *and also* the
values are proportional to correlations of the item with the LV of the
other block: these are the two separate functions of "saliences" as
PLS defines them. At the bottom of that table are three numbers
that are useful for thinking about how well the analysis has done:
the correlation between the pair of LVs specified by the coefficients
in these two columns, the covariance of this same pair of scores, and
the extent to which the covariance of these two LVs exhausts the
available covariance between all items of one block and all items of
the other. This fraction is the ratio of the covariance of the first LV
pair, 1.02, to the sum of squares of all the correlations in Table 4.3.
(That sum of squares is $1.02 / 0.88 = 1.16$.)

The first-time reader may wish at this point to skip to Section
4.3.

4.1.2 Two-Block PLS in Matrix Notation

Readers who wish to implement PLS in their favorite statistical
packages will perhaps find convenient the following re-expression in
conventional matrix notation. Let α denote the column vector
$(\alpha_1,...,\alpha_{13})^T$, and β denote the column vector $(\beta_1,...,\beta_{11})^T$, where
superscript T indicates a matrix transpose. Then, equation (2) be-
comes

$$\alpha \propto R_{AB}\beta \qquad (4)$$

(where "$\propto$" means "is proportional to") and (1) becomes

$$\beta \propto R_{BA}\alpha \qquad (5)$$

Substituting (5) into (4) we obtain

$$\alpha \propto R_{AB}R_{BA}\alpha \qquad (6)$$

and substituting (4) into (5),

$$\beta \propto R_{BA} R_{AB} \beta \qquad (7)$$

These equations define α and β as eigenvectors of $R_{AB}R_{BA}$ and $R_{BA}R_{AB}$, respectively. They may be computed more conveniently as left and right "singular vectors" of R_{AB}:

$$R_{AB} = UDV^T \qquad (8)$$

where U is a 13×11 matrix of (orthonormal) left singular vectors, V is an 11×11 matrix of right singular vectors, and D=diag(d_1, ... , d_{11}) is an 11×11 diagonal matrix of (ordered) "singular values." (See, for instance, Mardia, Kent, & Bibby, 1979.) The singular values provide the covariances between the linear combinations $A^T u_i$ and $B^T v_i$ where A and B are the vectors of alcohol and IQ subtest scores, and u_i and v_i denote columns of U and V, respectively. The coefficient vectors we seek for the PLS analysis are then $\alpha = u_1$ and $\beta = v_1$, the linear combinations with maximum covariance. Further linear combinations or latent variables, computed from subsequent singular vectors, may be considered if the first linear combinations do not adequately explain the correlation matrix R_{AB} (or, equivalently, if the first singular value d_1 does not greatly dominate the entire vector of singular values).

Equation (8) can be re-expressed as

$$R_{AB} = \sum_{i=1}^{11} d_i u_i v_i^T \qquad (9)$$

R_{AB} is thus the sum of 11 rank-1 matrices. The first term in this sum, the (scaled) product of the first singular vectors u_1 and v_1, represents the best (least squares) rank-1 fit to the whole matrix R_{AB}.

Our discussion of the analogy of PLS analysis with principal components indicates that we can also compute the singular value decomposition one set of singular vectors at a time—the set of saliences for Alcohol only, or the set of saliences for the Outcomes only—via ordinary principal components analysis. (We will use this interpretation in Chapter 5.) Either set of singular vectors can be thought of as the principal components of the cross-correlation matrix whose columns are the block in question and whose rows represent "cases" corresponding to the variables of the facing block. The principal components must be computed without first subtracting the means of the columns. That is, the columns of U are the eigenvectors of the matrix $R_{AB}R_{BA}$ and the columns of V are the eigenvectors of $R_{BA}R_{AB}$, as shown in equations (6) and (7).

The computations described here can be programmed easily with the aid of numerical analysis subroutines for computing eigenvectors or singular value decompositions. (These are available in a number of widely available mathematical subroutine libraries, such as EISPACK, IMSL, and NAG.) A commercial program (Lohmöller, 1984) can also be used for these simple two-block analyses (and for much more complicated PLS models). The reader should be forewarned, however, that this program does not present the covariances or the fraction of summed squared correlations with which we are concerned. Researchers with access to a computer running the UNIX operating system and the "S" or "S-Plus" package for data analysis and graphics (Becker, Chambers & Wilks, 1988; Statistical Sciences, Inc., 1991) may contact one of the authors (PDS) for special-purpose programs for the analyses described here.

4.2 Explicitly Longitudinal Analyses

This section presents details of some other applications of PLS in this study. The first time reader may choose to skip to Section 4.3.

The two-block PLS model described above does not distinguish among the different waves of the study as ordered in time. We have, of course, kept separate the measurements of similar conceptual content—Attention, Neuromotor, and Mental—at the separate waves of analysis. But when we have combined them in larger analyses of multiple outcome blocks, their temporal ordering has played no role in the computations. For example, in the first set of analyses that we are going to report (Section 5.3), nothing in the treatment of the 4-year Attention block reminds one that it was intermediate in time between the earlier Attention blocks and the 7-year. The same method (standard two-block PLS) that we applied to the 7-year standardized test scores only (66) could be applied to the entire 7-year span of outcomes without any modification. Clearly, one class of information is being underutilized.

4.2.1 Longitudinal Path Models

We can restore the ordering of our blocks most simply by invoking versions of *longitudinal path analysis* to interpret the results of certain PLS analyses and to modify the results of others. The ideas of longitudinal path analysis themselves are not new. Developed originally by the biometrician Sewall Wright in the 1920s, they were introduced to the social sciences in the 1960s (cf. Blau & Duncan, 1967) and can now be computed routinely, for observed (not latent) variables, by computer programs such as LISREL (Jöreskog & Sörböm, 1984). Our version of latent-variable modeling does not accord with the ideas of "structural equations modeling" in many important respects that we have reviewed elsewhere (cf. 68; Bookstein, 1986), and so we do not use LISREL. Our application of these models will be instead within the general context of PLS analysis. There is at present no single exposition to which we can refer the reader for an explanation. The themes we need are two: the idea of a *causal chain* (Wold, 1959) and the idea of a *distributed effect*.

Path analyses are systems of interrelated regressions, such that the variables which are "dependent" in some of the regressions are "independent" (predictors) in others. A good source for the rudiments of this sort of modeling is Chapter 13 of Wright (1968). In a causal chain, variables are measured in time-order, and each variable is "caused" (i.e. predicted by) some or all of the variables that existed earlier; in a *simple* causal chain, each variable is affected only by its immediate predecessor and affects only its immediate successor. Diagrammatically this is the scheme:

$$V_1 \ldots \Rightarrow V_i \Rightarrow V_{i+1} \Rightarrow \ldots V_N$$

where V_i is the ith assessment of variable V (in time order), V_{i+1} the $(i+1)^{st}$, and the arrow means simple regression: that is,

$$E(V_{i+1}) = \alpha V_i + \epsilon_{i+1}$$

where E is the "statistical expectation operator" (E(x) means "the expected value of x"), α is a regression coefficient, and ε_{i+1} is the error of the $(i+1)^{st}$ regression, presumed uncorrelated with the value of V_i and with all the earlier regression errors up through ε_i.

The aspect of a simple causal chain which gives it its importance in practice and which lets us identify it in data is the multiplicative property of correlations down the chain. If $r_{i,i+1}$ is the correlation relating each variable V_i to its successor, then for the statements about uncorrelated error and simple causation to be true the correlation between variables two waves apart must be the product of their separate correlations with the variable between them —

$$r_{i,i+2} = r_{i,i+1} r_{i+1,i+2}$$

— and so on over longer and longer subchains. Another way to say the same thing is to assert that all partial correlations between distant terms of the chain, partialled or conditioned on variables intermediate in the chain, equal zero—

$$r_{i,i+j \bullet i+k} = 0 \text{ for } 0 < k < j.$$

(Of course, by "equal" we mean an approximation appropriately statistically insignificant.) This notation for a partial correlation coefficient is read as 'the correlation between v_i and v_{i+j} partialling on v_{i+k}. If these partial correlations are not zero, then the "proper" causal model is as indicated in Figure 4.3(b), rather than Figure 4.3(a). The curved line in 4.3(b) represents the "lagged" effect implied

(a)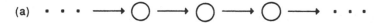

(b)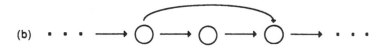

Figure 4.3.   Path diagrams for (a) a simple causal chain and (b) a causal chain with a lagged effect.

implied by a nonvanishing partial correlation.   Such effects immediately raise questions of epistemology: for instance, if the effect of the age-18-months measurement on the age-7 measurement does not "pass through" the age-4 measurement, how, exactly, is it effected? For our longitudinal analyses, we will be able to interpret alcohol's effect on a diachronic construct, like Mental Ability, only if the longitudinal structure of that ability is a simple causal chain.

Lest the reader believe we are demanding too much of our data, here is an example of a real causal chain: one series of Mental Ability scores at ages 8 months, 18 months, and 4 and 7 years. These are the scores MDI8M, MDI18M, FULLIQ4, and FULLIQ7 introduced, along with their subscales and hundreds of cousins, in Chapter 3. The correlation matrix among these four scores using all the available data (ranging from n=392 cases for the MDI18M-FULLIQ4 correlation to n=438 cases for the MDI8M-MDI18M correlation) is shown in Table 4.6.

Table 4.6 Correlations Among MDI and IQ Scores at 4 Ages

	MDI8M	MDI18M	FULLIQ4	FULLIQ7
MDI8M	1.000	0.374	0.198	0.139
MDI18M	0.374	1.000	0.541	0.407
FULLIQ4	0.198	0.541	1.000	0.770
FULLIQ7	0.139	0.407	0.770	1.000

If this were a causal chain, the true regression coefficients would be the correlations just off the diagonals—

$$
\begin{array}{ccccccc}
& 0.374 & & 0.541 & & 0.770 & \\
\text{MDI8M} & \Rightarrow & \text{MDI18M} & \Rightarrow & \text{FULLIQ4} & \Rightarrow & \text{FULLIQ7}
\end{array}
$$

—and all other path coefficients, such as FULLIQ7 on MDI18M, would be zero.

We check cross-correlations as follows:

• between 8 mos. & 4 yrs., $0.374 \times 0.541 =$ 0.202
                                                        (observed, 0.198);

• between 8 mos. & 7 yrs., $0.374 \times 0.541 \times 0.770 = 0.156$
                                                        (observed, 0.139);

• between 18 mos. & 7 yrs., $0.541 \times 0.770 =$ 0.417
                                                        (observed, 0.402).

The largest discrepancy is only 0.017 (vs. a conventional 5% significance threshold of about $2/\sqrt{N} \approx .09$). We may consider it estab-
lished that (within the stringent confines of path modeling of these
four scores) early Mental Ability affects later Mental Ability only
through intermediate Mental Ability.

Given a series of variables in a causal chain, we can proceed to
distribute the effect of alcohol over the chain. By this we mean the
following. The observed correlation of a cause (in this case, Alcohol) with any one variable in a causal chain may be conceptually
divided into two parts: the part attributable to its effects on all
previous variables in the chain, and the part not so attributable, but
instead representing a new effect on only the variable in question
(i.e., its effect on cumulative behavior in the interval after the preceding wave of measurement). In the case of a causal chain, it can be
shown, all the effect of all preceding variables may be expressed as a
correlation with the immediately preceding variable only.

Consider, for instance, the pair of arithmetic IQ subscale scores at
ages 4 and 7 (selected because at the older age this score is a particularly salient indicator of alcohol teratogenesis, as will be shown in
Chapter 5), and represent alcohol, for now, by one of its best single
indicators, the BINGEP score. (All these single variables will be replaced by LVs in the next part of this discussion.) The correlations
among these three variables are:

	ARITH4	ARITH7	BINGEP
ARITH4	1.000	0.487	−0.133
ARITH7	0.487	1.000	−0.189
BINGEP	−0.133	−0.189	1.000

Suppose the arithmetic scores belonged to a causal chain (as will
their LV equivalents in the data of Chapter 5). Then we can *distribute* the alcohol effect over the causal chain as follows:

- net effect at age 4:   –0.133
- effects at age 7:
    - indirect, via age 4
        $-0.133 \times 0.487 =$ –0.065
    - direct, attributable to age 7 only
        $-0.189 - (-0.065) =$ –0.124

This last expression is the numerator of the formula for the partial correlation $r_{Alc,A7 \cdot A4}$. The path analysis would thus be drawn as shown in Figure 4.4, where the parentheses around –0.133 express our intention to partition it in terms of even earlier measures. Note that this is not a "multiple regression" of A7 on A4 and Alc. The effect of A4 on A7 is taken as a simple correlation, not a partial regression coefficient.

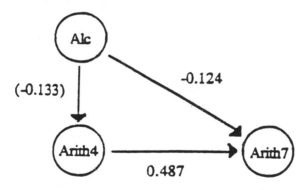

Figure 4.4. Path diagram for the relationship between Alcohol exposure (the BINGEP score) and the arithmetic subscales of IQ at ages four and seven. The correlation of Alcohol with the arithmetic score at age seven (–0.189) is partitioned into an indirect effect (–0.133 × 0.487) and a direct effect (–0.124).

4.2.2 Longitudinal PLS

The technique of Partial Least Squares we have reviewed in Section 4.1 produces single variables as scores on LV formulas that summarize the saliences of blocks of variables for one another. We have explained the method hitherto as if it applied only to blocks in pairs. In that special case, we can express the desired optimum-covariance solution in "closed form" as a single matrix formula, the singular-value decomposition, equation (8).

The two-block case is only the simplest instance of Partial Least Squares analysis. It extends generally to describing any number of blocks of variables connected according to any path diagram (cf. Wold 1982, Bookstein 1982). Think back for a moment to Section 4.1, and recall that the pair of latent variables in the causal assertion *Alc LV* —> *Outcome LV* (see Figure 4.1) was estimated by a least-squares fit of products of saliences (latent variable coefficients) to the correlation matrix R_{AB}.

We can extend this logic to any other path model on latent variables. For instance, the latent variables in a causal chain on three outcome blocks

$$\begin{array}{ccccc} \text{Outcome} & \Rightarrow & \text{Outcome} & \Rightarrow & \text{Outcome} \\ \text{8-mo} & & \text{4-yr} & & \text{7-yr} \end{array}$$

are computed via a least-squares fit of products of saliences (coefficients) to the cells marked "R" of the full correlation matrix of all indicators

	8-mo block	4-yr block	7-yr block
8-mo block	0	R_{84}	0
4-yr block	R_{48}	0	R_{47}
7-yr block	0	R_{74}	0

where the 0's represent "zeros"—large chunks of the matrix that we are simply ignoring: the within-block correlations, and also the correlations between the first and last outcome blocks, which are not directly connected in the path model.

We can compute saliences for all three blocks in models like these by a variant of Wold's interative method as described above. We might begin (step 0 in Figure 4.5) by choosing any tentative pattern of saliences for one block, say, the middle one. For now, assign all these indicators the same relative salience, 1. We add up the indicators of this block using these weights (i.e., take their sum) to arrive at a tentative latent variable score for the middle block (step 1 in Figure 4.5). We then compute (still tentative) saliences for the outer two blocks that are simply the correlations of each item with the LV score just added up for the middle block (steps 2 and 3 in Figure 4.5). In the language of Bookstein (1986), this results in the *net partial predictor* of the middle LV from each of the outer blocks in turn. We combine the indicators of these blocks using these saliences (steps 4 and 5) to get *their* tentative LV scores. Finally (step 6 in Figure 4.5) the saliences of the middle block are updated to be proportional to the correlations of its items with the sum of these two new tentative LV scores for the two outer blocks (each having been computed as the [tentative] salience-weighted sum of its indicators). The LV score of the middle block is recomputed (step 1) using these new saliences, and the whole cycle begins again.

It can be shown that this algorithm must converge to provide the least-squares rank-1 fit to the non-zeroed parts of the correlation matrix using products of the latent variable saliences/coefficients. That is, letting estimates of the latent variable coefficients for the 8-month, 4-year, and 7-year blocks be denoted by α_i, β_j, and δ_k, respectively, we have the elements of the correlation matrices R_{84} and R_{47} approximated as

$$r_{8i,4j} \propto \alpha_i \beta_j$$
$$r_{4j,7k} \propto \beta_j \delta_k.$$

After the LV saliences are computed in this way, we must inspect the correlation matrix of their scores to verify the assumptions of the causal chain — here, whether $r_{LV1,LV3}$ equals the product of $r_{LV1,LV2}$ and $r_{LV2,LV3}$. These assumptions have not been built into the computation (we ignored the whole matrix of cross-correlations between the first and third blocks) and so can serve as an independent check.

Another sort of PLS model that we shall fit corresponds to the path diagram in Figure 4.6 for a "distributed Alcohol effect." In this

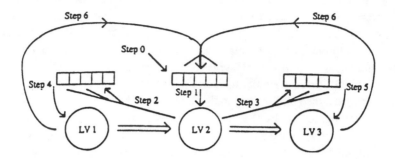

Figure 4.5. Diagram illustrating the sequence of steps in the iterative PLS algorithm for a three-block causal chain model.

scheme the Alcohol dose, computed as a latent variable, affects each of the four Mental outcome blocks in turn, with a strength that we compute as the path coefficient for the direct effect (computed as demonstrated in our simple example with just BINGEP, ARITH4, and ARITH7). Notice that there is some real biological content to this model: we are assuming that the *same* Alcohol LV is responsible for all the outcome blocks—that is, that the pattern of saliences, correlations with the Alcohol indicators, is the same for each of the Outcome LVs. We have marked the longitudinal connections among the outcome blocks with dotted lines because we will compute the saliences for the items of these blocks only with respect to Alcohol. (That is, all the off-diagonal blocks of correlations connecting the outcome blocks are ignored, not just those outcome blocks two waves apart as in the simple causal chain example just described.) The extent to which the computed outcome LVs satisfy a causal chain model can be checked in terms of their correlations as described above for the longitudinal analysis without the Alcohol block.

The reader may already have guessed how we fit models such as these. The logic is the same as for the causal chain "submodel" algorithm already described. We begin by assigning an arbitrary pattern of saliences—all 1's—to all of the blocks. Then, block by block, the saliences of each block are "updated" to be proportional to the correlations of its indicators with the salience-weighted sum of all the in-

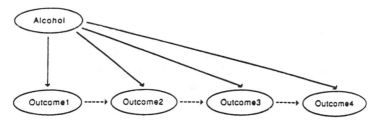

Figure 4.6. Path diagram for a "distributed alcohol effect" in a five-block longitudinal model involving prenatal alcohol exposure and the four Mental outcome blocks at ages 8 months, 18 months, 4 years, and 7 years.

dicators of all the blocks to which that block is connected. For instance, the saliences of the Alcohol variables are proportional to the correlations of the Alcohol indicators with the *sum* of all the Outcome LVs — it is as if, with respect to prediction by Alcohol, there is only one Outcome block, the concatenation of all four blocks' worth of indicators—whereas the saliences of each Outcome block are proportional to the correlations of its items with the Alcohol LV. (Since, typically, the longitudinal correlations among the Mental outcome blocks are stronger than their correlations with Alcohol, if we were to include linkages among the outcome blocks, the resulting Mental LVs would tend to resemble those computed without regard for Alcohol.) The Alcohol LV has been computed optimally to explain correlations with the list of all the outcomes; its effect can be "distributed" across the separate blocks of the causal chain as before. As mentioned earlier, we use these techniques mainly to decompose patterns of correlations arrived at by earlier PLS summaries. Although we speak of "fitting" these models, we do not test their "goodness-of-fit" in any formal way.

4.3 PLS as Dose-Response Analysis

It may be helpful to elaborate on these matters from a somewhat less algebraic point of view. In this section we will talk briefly about PLS as it interacts with four typical aspects of any study: scientific context, design of measurements, interpretation of statistical computations, and comparison to other multivariate techniques.

4.3.1 Scientific Context

PLS is designed for studies of cause and effect in systems under indirect observation. In our study, FAS is known to exist and to be caused by prenatal exposure to alcohol in sufficient quantity. The subject of our dose-response studies is the calibration of effect against cause—of response against dose—in the mildly abnormal case ("social drinking").

In general, PLS is of greatest help neither in studies of entirely normal populations nor for the syndromology of clearly defined groups of "cases." Rather, it is aimed at the combination of these two kinds of study. In this teratological context, PLS is most useful for investigations trying to pursue "downward," into the "normal" range, a cause-and-effect relationship that is known to lead to a syndrome in situations of demonstrably high dose.

4.3.2 Measurements

PLS applies to studies in which cause and effect are each measured variously and redundantly. Our alcohol study includes multiple "soft" measures of the integrated intake of alcohol, peak dose, effect on the mother, and the like, all at two times during pregnancy. The measures of "effect," likewise, include an assortment of nearly five hundred measures of neurobehavioral functions typically found to be altered in the full expression of Fetal Alcohol Syndrome. These outcomes are gathered in "blocks" by child's age (from 1 day to 7 years) and behavioral channel, and the analysis proceeds both separately by blocks and with the outcomes all pooled.

4.3.3 Interpretation

In a good analysis, such as we find for the effect of alcohol measures upon neurobehavioral outcomes, the LV scores may be used to detect high-dose and high-deficit children and to search for covariates that may exacerbate or attenuate the effect of dose. Furthermore, the saliences can be sorted, block by block, to suggest rosters that are particularly sensitive (by virtue of causal relevance and careful measurement) or particularly insensitive (by virtue of causal irrelevance or irreducible measurement imprecision) to the dose-response relation under study. In our study, measures of binge drinking very early in pregnancy will be found the most salient aspects of dose; the salient outcomes include measures of arithmetic skills, attention, and many others. The saliences are reviewed exhaustively in Chapter 5.

4.3.4 Comparison of PLS with Other Statistical Methods for Indirect Studies of Neurobehavioral Phenomena in Humans

PLS may be contrasted with other approaches to the same sort of data. By maximizing covariance between the LV scores, PLS optimizes the usefulness of the analysis for subsequent studies of intervention. Unlike the coefficients of a canonical correlations analysis, the saliences PLS computes have meaning individually even when (indeed, especially when) the predictor block or the outcome block is intentionally multicollinear (66). Along with the scores, the saliences can be computed in any statistical package that has a principal component feature, so that PLS can be applied to vastly larger problems than can more sophisticated optimizations. PLS differs from structural equations models in its lack of most distributional assumptions and in that it invariably ignores the within-block factor structure of the dose measures and the response measures separately. In our experience, this structure is quite irrelevant to the assigned task of cross-block explanation. (For instance [Sec. 7.3], alcohol doesn't affect the general factor of IQ as much as it affects a particular profile of arithmetic deficiency.) As a fit to the cross-correlation matrix rather than the raw data, PLS avoids the difficulty of all likelihood-based structural equation modeling (including multiple regression) that to be interpretable a fitted model must first be "true." While PLS is not designed for the "testing" of "hypotheses," bootstrapping and other resampling data analyses can be applied to substantive aspects of the interpretations that result, such as covariates of LV scores or the reliable identification of types of dose or response measures as particularly salient for each other (Efron & Tibshirani, 1986). For further discussion of these matters, see (72).

4.4 Overview of Data Analysis

Chapters 1 through 3 of this monograph have reviewed all the major themes involved in the design of this study and the collection of its data, and the current chapter has introduced our principal multivariate statistical approaches, which are all varieties of Partial Least Squares. These analyses result in two forms of output, *saliences* and *scores*. Saliences serve as latent variable coefficients and pertain to individual *variables* (here, Alcohol or Outcome). Scores, on the other hand, pertain to the status of a subject on a variable.

These two aspects of the multivariate analysis are separated in the chapters to come. All analyses related to the saliences of the variables are presented in Chapter 5. These discussions might be considered entirely "correlational" except that the scores on each of the 13 Alcohol measures have been transformed by a preliminary nonlinear regression (see Section 4.1). Using the full roster of 474 variables collected into 15 blocks, we explore the pattern of correlations with the Alcohol block as a whole in a very large single two-block analysis of 13×474 correlations. These analyses are based on all but one case (the AAP outlier) of the 582-child pooled follow-up cohort. We will extract a (two-dimensional) circle of profiles of correlation with the Alcohol measures (Sec. 5.2) and represent all 474 variables by their individual correlations (saliences) around this circle of profiles (Sec. 5.3). Small adjustments of the principal profile of alcohol correlations may be considered as combinations "more ADOCC-like" or "more MOCC-like" than the typical profile of correlations with Alcohol, which is slightly binge-weighted. Section 5.4 extends all these findings to a causal chain analysis of the Mental outcomes over time. All these may be characterized as discussions of the *saliences of variables*: reflections of the patterns of correlation between alcohol scores and outcomes.

Chapters 6 through 8, by contrast, deal primarily with properties of the scores as they vary over the subjects of our sample. We begin with the latent variable scores for the two principal patterns of Alcohol Effect presented in Section 5.2. We examine the role of potential covariates and confounding variables, including measures of postnatal environment which could compensate for (or exacerbate) the effects of the prenatal insult by alcohol. We next express the dominant LV pattern from the present chapter both as a profile of 15 partial scores and as a longitudinal sequence of five different partial scores (at ages 0, 8 months, 18 months, 4 years, and 7 years). Consideration of the profile of 15 partial LV (PLV) scores proves to be useful for the detection of "true Fetal Alcohol Effects." Chapter 7 pursues outcomes from our 7-year LD block in greater detail, and Chapter 8 explores the possibility of identifying individual cases of true alcohol damage. All these forms of profile-by-profile analyses are built upon the foundation of one critical PLS analysis of the 13 Alcohol indicators versus the entire group of outcomes.

4.5 Summary

In this chapter we have introduced the principal statistical methods that will be relied on throughout the rest of the volume:

- The methods are all extensions of dose-response analysis to the context of multiple measures for both dose and outcome.
- Our analysis of the effects of Alcohol or any single outcome block or pool of blocks is by consideration of saliences of outcomes as effects of a single Alcohol LV using least-squares fitting of a cross-correlation matrix, a particularly simple version of Wold's Partial Least Squares.
- Our longitudinal analyses are all latent-variable versions of two models familiar from the literature of path analysis: the *simple causal chain* and the *simple causal chain with a distributed alcohol effect*. For the causal chain, all effects are simple correlation coefficients and all "distant" partial correlations vanish; but the coefficients of distributed effects are all path coefficients computed as demonstrated above.
- The extension to latent variable analysis is not in the spirit of structural equation modeling of all the data but in the spirit of Partial Least Squares modeling of (parts of) the cross-correlation matrix.

- The computation of LV saliences and scores proceeds by standard PLS iterative algorithms, as reviewed here. The saliences of each block are computed as if all the blocks "connected to" that block (which are either "causes" or "effects" of the block in question) have been pooled into one single superblock for a temporary two-block analysis.

Alcohol Dose and Alcohol Effects: Partial Least Squares Analyses

5.1 Introduction

Chapter 5 exploits the PLS methods introduced in Chapter 4 to examine the effect of prenatal alcohol exposure on the full spectrum of outcomes obtained across five waves of data collection. Chapter 4 presented a simple two-block example, the prediction of 11 subtests of the seven-year IQ score by the 13 Alcohol scores. This chapter sets out the principal findings of the study in a single very large two-block PLS analysis of the 13 Alcohol predictors against 474 outcomes. As before, we first describe the saliences of Alcohol items for these outcomes and then sort the outcomes by their saliences for the composite Alcohol latent variable scores (two composite measures of dose) that result. Because the findings are two-dimensional, we have an entire "map" of the relation between doses and outcomes to survey; this map, the core of our report of the findings, is discussed in Section 5.3. As in Chapter 4, we also report a longitudinal PLS analysis examining the prediction by prenatal alcohol of the separate waves of data, from day 1 to seven years of age, block after block in the order in which they were collected.

Before proceeding, let us take a moment to re-acquaint ourselves with the meaning of some of the primary alcohol scores as they were introduced in Chapter 2. Three of the scores (actually six, with their P and D components) are "binge-oriented." They differ from each other as follows. ADOCC (Average Drinks per Occasion) is the answer to the question: When you do drink, how many drinks do you usually have at a time? MAX is the answer to: What is the maximum number of drinks that you have had on any occasion (for this time period)? BINGE is a yes-or-no response to the question: Have you ever had five or more drinks on any occasion (during this time period)? These binge-oriented scores contrast with the frequency-oriented MOCC (Monthly Occasions) score, which answers the question: How often did you drink (beer, wine, liquor, etc.) during this time period? In-between are three "volume-type" scores deriving from combinations of frequency and binge measures: the AA scores (average ounces of absolute alcohol per day), the QFV (Quantity-Frequency-Variability Index), and ORDEXC (an *a priori* Ordered Exposure Code developed for this study).

Our PLS analyses, as mentioned in Section 4.1, involve transforming (recoding) each of the 13 Alcohol indicators to "straighten out" the manner in which it predicts the net Outcome LV we are about to report on. The alcohol saliences here and in subsequent chapters reflect these transformations; they talk about *how* each measure becomes salient as a mother's score on it increases. Figure 4.1 shows the transformations to which we were led. On this plot, the height of each little curve roughly matches the salience of the dose measure as it will be reported in Table 5.1 and Figure 5.1. (The match would be closer if each dot were printed with an area corresponding to the number of sample children whose exposure was at that level.)

For instance, the effect of an additional unit of AAD, *according to the PLS model*, is nearly linear on this logarithmic scale. The effect of a unit of AAP is greater at all dosages above 2, and, again, is nearly linear there. The effect of a "peak drink" (ADOCC) is linear above the minimum dose codable on our forms (see Section 9.3 and Appendix II). The effects of the MOCC variables are low at all exposure levels, but, again, high levels of MOCCP have a greater effect than the same high levels of MOCCD.

Actual effects of the categorical variables like ORDEXC, as reflected in their saliences, weight the apparent heights in Figure 4.1 according to the sample size per category, so that ORDEXC=4 (which characterizes some 200 of our follow-up cohort) explains tremendously more outcome deficits than, say, QFVP=5 (which gathers in only a few subjects highly exposed in one particular pattern).

We will have more to say about the differential recruitment of different high-dose profiles in Section 9.1.2. Issues of "threshold"—a level of drinking below which there is "no effect"—are discussed in Section 9.3, after an exhaustive review of the design of our study and the interplay of that design with all the findings of this and the next three chapters.

5.2 Two Patterns of Correlation between Alcohol Dose and Outcomes

As our PLS analyses elucidate the dependence of outcomes on Alcohol dose, the dose measures have considerably more meaning collectively than individually. In Chapter 4, the collective pattern of alcohol scores for the 11 IQ subtests was best described as a single "binge-weighted" profile. Because this first LV accounted for 88% of the squared correlation, no further profiles of relationship were pursued. However, in the very large two-block analysis presented in this chapter, in which alcohol is examined in relation to 474 neurobehavioral outcomes, two distinct alcohol profiles emerge. These reflect the greater richness and diversity of the full roster of outcomes as they are affected by the same 13 alcohol predictors.

This very large two-block PLS Analysis of 13 Alcohol scores by 474 outcomes is presented in Table 5.1 and Figures 5.1–5.3. Figure 5.2 (Sec. 5.3) indicates that our 474 outcomes span a two-dimensional space of profiles of correlation with Alcohol. (We refer to the set of 13 correlations of any outcome measure with the Alcohol scores as a *profile*.) These two dimensions of "Alcohol prediction space" can be described in several ways, as we will see in the discussion of "hikes" (Sec. 5.3). Whatever directions we use to characterize this space of profiles, variables of different blocks can correlate with Alcohol in the same profile, while variables of the same block might differ greatly in their saliences for a given profile of alcohol effects. This is the language of principal components factor analysis (Reyment & Jöreskog, 1993). Specifically, we are talking about the way outcomes cluster on the basis of a scatter of their saliences independent of *a priori* groupings. In this instance there are 474 "cases" (outcome variables), and 13 "variables" the "values" of which are *correlations with alcohol*, outcome variable by outcome variable,

after the alcohol variables have been nonlinearly transformed as in
Figure 4.1. One interpretation of PLS (Sec. 4.1) is that it submits
this set of 13 "variables" on 474 "cases" to a principal components
analysis, so as to extract the underlying dimensions of these profiles
of correlations with the alcohol variables.

From the analysis by PLS we extract the first two meaningful
"principal components" for the correlations of the 474 outcomes by
Alcohol. These components are presented in the first two columns
of Table 5.1; they are to be interpreted as two latent variables for the
Alcohol block. These two columns of saliences are represented as a
scatterplot in Figure 5.1. The decision to stop with two components
traces to the interpretability of the second dimension in plots such as
Figure 5.1, without any corresponding interpretability for the next
one. (In Figure 5.2 the corresponding outcome saliences are set out
as a scatterplot; the outermost 99 points in this Figure are identified
in Appendix IV. These represent the 99 outcomes assessed across all
ages and domains that are the most salient for some pattern of alcohol exposure as identified in Figure 5.3.) The first Alcohol latent
variable explains $4.67^2 = 75.2\%$ of the total sum of squared correlations (29.0) with all 474 outcomes (Section 4.1, equation 3). Its
saliences are nearly homogeneous across our diverse assessments of
dose, except for AAD and the MOCC measures, but somewhat emphasize the earlier (P) measures and, among those, the measures of
bingeing. (Note that these saliences are very similar to those reported in Table 4.3 for the analysis of Alcohol with just the 11 IQ
subscales.) The single alcohol score most salient for the outcome
LV (a pool of all 474 effects, each weighted by its predictability by
the Alcohol LV) is ADOCCP. However, the score on this first
Alcohol LV is a considerably more sensitive measure of dose than
any one indicator, even ADOCCP.

The second Alcohol LV, which explains $1.81^2 = 11.2\%$ of the
summed-squared correlations, has the appearance of a contrast of the
AAs, MOCCs, and ORDEXC against most of the bingeing measures. This form is an artifact of PLS's requirement that successive
LVs for the same block be geometrically orthogonal. We can obtain
a clearer understanding of the structure of prediction by Alcohol from

the plot of the first pair of columns in Table 5.1, each scaled by its LV covariance ("singular value"), the ordinary scatter in Figure 5.1.

Table 5.1 Two-Block PLS Analysis of Alcohol Scores and 474 Outcomes Across 5 Ages

Alcohol	LV Saliences			LV Saliences for 24		
	LV1	LV2		Outcomes Identified in Fig.		
AAP	0.23	−0.26		5.2		
AAD	0.10	−0.52			LV1	LV2
BINGEP	0.32	0.07		HABLIT	−0.112	0.124
BINGED	0.28	0.05		MORO	−0.084	0.104
ADOCCP	0.40	0.25		INCURVTH	−0.064	0.125
ADOCCD	0.33	0.11		ACADADJ4	0.004	0.126
MAXP	0.36	0.17		CSHORB7	0.009	0.124
MAXD	0.28	0.02		CSHORA7	0.041	0.110
MOCCP	0.15	−0.43		ACADADJ7	0.119	0.007
MOCCD	0.02	−0.55		LFMMAZTD	0.106	−0.029
QFVP	0.35	0.08		LAXFA50	0.106	−0.036
QFVD	0.27	−0.09		D1INTMEM	0.095	−0.091
ORDEXC	0.23	−0.23		D1REVCOP	0.104	−0.099
				D3QULCOP	0.091	−0.111
				UNCLVERB	0.006	−0.112
				NEOSTATE	0.002	−0.119
Summary:		LV1	LV2	VOC7	−0.037	−0.111
LV Covariance		4.67	1.81	FOLINSTR	−0.056	−0.112
Fraction of Total Squared				READING	−0.065	−0.100
Correlation Explained		0.75	0.11	VERBIQ7	−0.087	−0.076
LV Correlation		0.33	0.35	FULLIQ7	−0.086	−0.072
				TOTALPRS	−0.092	−0.059
				ARITH7	−0.104	−0.026
				WRATASS	−0.107	−0.019
				COOPRTQ	−0.104	−0.002
				SPADND	−0.110	0.046

Notes: Definitions of the Alcohol variables can be found in Table 2.3. Definitions of the Outcome variables can be found in Appendix IV–b. Distribution statistics and derivation of each outcome can be found in Appendix III. The 24 outcomes are ordered according to their positions in Figure 5.2, beginning in the northwest corner and proceeding clockwise. This table is based on an analysis of a 13 x 474 missing data correlation matrix using all pairwise complete cases in the follow–up cohort of N=581 (excluding the one extreme AAP case).

(See Reyment & Jöreskog [1993] for other examples of this style of factor/latent variable interpretation.) This demonstrates the surprising fact that the set of 13 Alcohol items can be ranked along an almost perfectly linear range (with respect to this set of 474 outcomes). The end-members of this range are ADOCCP and MOCCD;

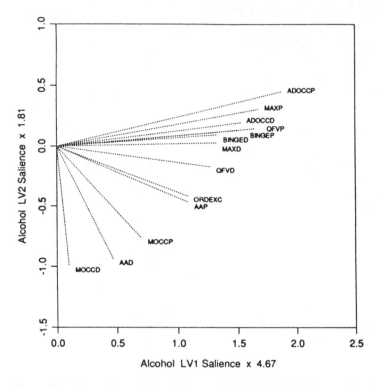

Figure 5.1. Scatterplots of the saliences of the 13 alcohol indicators for the first and second latent variables of the two-block analysis with 474 outcomes. These saliences are printed in the first two columns of Table 5.1. Vectors of saliences from Table 5.1 are scaled by the respective LV covariances (or singular values; see Sec. 4.1.1): 4.67 for LV1 and 1.81 for LV2. Lengths of the dotted lines represent the net salience of the alcohol indicators for the approximation of the elements of the 13 × 474 correlation matrix by the first two latent variable pairs as discussed in Section 5.2. The angle of the line indicates how characteristic each Alcohol score is of the Alc LV. The horizontal line is "most characteristic," but not most salient.

the bingeing measures are all at one end, the non-bingeing measures at the other.

Except for BINGE, the P and D members of each pair are separated by what appears to be a constant displacement, about 20% of the length of the "scale" from ADOCCP to MOCCD. The sorting of the Alcohol items is thus by a combination of bingeing and timing, with the one measure constructed a priori to average both these facets, ORDEXC (see Section 2.2), squarely in the middle, along with QFVD and AAP, which each "compromise" between binge-sensitivity and timing. The net salience of these 13 alcohol measures for the pair of LVs found here may be read as distance from the origin in Figure 5.1 (the length of the ray connecting the origin to the name of the measure). The salience of the MOCCs, AAs, and ORDEXC is considerably less than that of all the binge indicators.

ADOCC-like and MOCC-like Alcohol profiles are correlated in the sample partly because one cannot have drinking occasions (MOCCs) without drinks (ADOCCs), and vice versa. Likewise, the higher AA Alcohol scores result mainly from binge-related drinking patterns: it is hard to imagine how it could be otherwise.

The interpretation of the Alcohol items as spread along a range from ADOCCP to MOCCD is superior to the alternative, a factor rotation. The rotation would place oblique factors through the ADOCCs and the MOCCs and tempt us to express the patterns of Alcohol correlation with outcomes as combinations of these two. We argue that the patterns of correlation with alcohol are better interpreted as weighted combinations of the extreme MOCCD and ADOCCP profiles. Of course, the net magnitude of the MOCC-like correlations with outcomes is lower than that of the ADOCC-like, corresponding to the fact that the first two LV covariances, 1.81 and 4.67, differ in a ratio of 2.6 to 1. Note that the single alcohol indicator having the correlation profile (with the 474 outcomes) most similar to that of the first Alcohol LV is MAXD. That is, it lies closest to the horizontal axis in Figure 5.1. But we can more reliably estimate individual scores on that profile (see Chap. 6) if we incorporate the more salient indicators like ADOCCP.

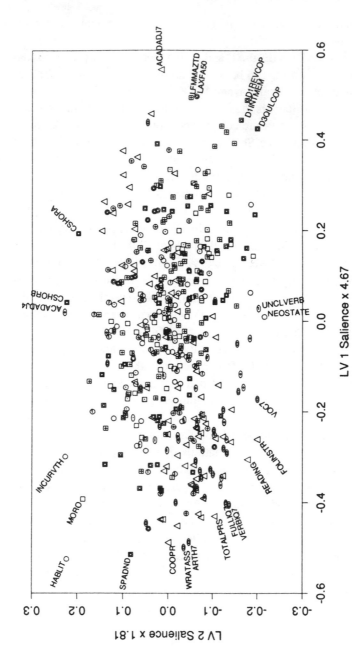

Figure 5.2.

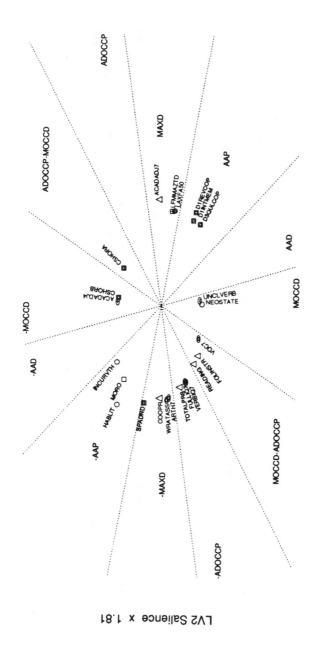

LV1 Salience x 4.67

LV2 Salience x 1.81

Figure 5.3.

Figure 5.2. (See overleaf.) Scatter plot of the saliences of the 474 outcomes for the first and second latent variables of two-block analysis with 13 alcohol scores. Appendix II presents the complete list of outcomes in this scatterplot. Outcomes furthest from the origin in each direction are the most salient for some alcohol score. The full names of the 24 labeled outcomes are included in Appendix III-b. Saliences for these labeled indicators are printed in the last two columns of Table 5.1. Plotting symbols identify the outcomes according to the 15 blocks indicated in Appendix II. Variables from *Attention* blocks are represented by circles, from *Neuromotor* blocks by squares, and from *Mental* blocks by horizontal ellipses. Symbols for neonatal measures are empty while those for 8 month, 18 month, 4 year, and 7 year outcomes are marked by a single dot (•), a pair of dots (••), an enclosed cross (+), and concentric symbols of the same shape, respectively. Triangles mark the indicators for the *Learning Disability (LD)* block, which was measured only at 7 years. The triangles and the empty squares have been pulled out into their own pictures in Figure 7.2 and 7.3 where the LD-7 and NMot-7 LVs are examined in relation to alcohol.

Figure 5.3. (See second page overleaf.) Plot of a superimposition of the 24 Outcome variables labelled in Figure 5.2 along with Alcohol variables from Figure 5.1 that best describe the map directions of the plot. Outcomes located to the right correlate positively with the dominant alcohol LV, which is slightly overweighted for the binge and pre-pregnancy recognition alcohol measures. Outcomes at the top of the vertical axis have generally moderate positive correlations with the binge measures and negative correlations with average volume and pure occasions (AAs and MOCCs), while outcomes at the bottom correlate in the opposite pattern. Outcomes at the SW extreme of the NE-SW diagonal correlate negatively with a "heightened-binge" alcohol score, which represents a more extreme contrast between the binge indicators and the AAD and MOCC scores. Outcomes at the SE extreme of the NW-SE diagonal correlate positively with a "mostly volume" alcohol score, which is a general average of all the alcohol indicators overweighted for the AADs and MOCCs.

5.3 Going on a Hike: Response Saliences for 474 Outcomes

A PLS analysis generates two sets of LVs: in this case, one for Alcohol, one for the outcomes. Figure 5.2 scatters the saliences for the
474 outcomes just as Figure 5.1 scatters those for the 13 Alcohol
variables. While this figure might at first seem like just another elliptical statistical distribution, it has in fact a very rich structure, and
contains more information about Alcohol effects than any other
figure in this book. The most informative zone is the outer hull of
this scatter. To understand this figure, it is convenient to select a
few of the outermost outcomes, and plot them along with Alcohol
variables from Figure 5.1 that best characterize the directions on the
plot. The combination of these is Figure 5.3, to which we will refer
repeatedly in this section. The reader familiar with advanced
multivariate data analysis may recognize this scheme as a variant of
conventional "correspondence analysis" or a "biplot" between the two
sets of variables. (See, for example, Greenacre, 1984.)   Different
outcomes correlate best with different mixtures of the ADOCC-like
and the MOCC-like Alcohol profiles.   A biplot graphically
associates each outcome variable with an Alcohol score with which
it correlates most highly.   Similarly, each Alcohol score is
associated with outcomes. As this topic is perhaps not so common
in the modern curriculum of applied psychology, we pause briefly to
introduce a helpful analogy from a familiar extracurricular activity:
hiking in the woods.

To understand Figure 5.3, it is helpful to think of a homely analogy: a hiker's map. Imagine that the investigator finds herself located at a particular spot labelled "the center" of a great woods.
Statistically, this will represent the origin, the point (0,0), of all
three of the figures 5.1 through 5.3. Outcomes near this point have
the "flat profile" of no correlations with Alcohol at all.

The PLS analysis, and the set of figures that diagrams it, can be
considered to be a map of the "woods" (the set of all 474 outcomes)
as seen from this original spot (the location of "no correlation").
You know that to explain to a hiker how to get from where she is to
another location (a particular outcome), you must specify two instructions: how far to travel, and in what compass direction. In our

analogy, the "length" of the path to a particular outcome is the net explanatory power of the first two Alcohol LVs for that outcome: the amount of the net summed squared correlations of the outcome with the parts of all 13 Alcohol measures accounted for by these two Alcohol LVs. (This length can also be expressed as the sum of squared covariances of the outcome with these two Alcohol LVs.) The "compass direction" in which that path lies is specified not by the usual geographical coordinates ("north" and the like) but by the names of our original Alcohol variables.

Before we begin to describe particular hikes from the origin—the saliences and directions at which particular outcomes can be found—we need to point out some interesting aspects of the map considered as a whole.

1. Directional coverage is complete. In Figure 5.2, the periphery (or, if you will, the "horizon") of outcomes at relatively great distance from the center seems to cover nearly the entire compass rose of all possible directions. In this system, in which every possible direction has a name in terms of Alcohol (see [3] below), every direction is used by some outcome: there is some interesting landmark at a substantial distance along every path. Furthermore, each direction in this two-dimensional space of "profiles" has its own set of outcomes with which the Alcohol score corresponding to that profile has the greatest covariance. Outcomes in some of these directions are "farther away" than outcomes in others: hikes toward the east or west (in the direction associated with MAXD) find outcomes at a greater distance (greater net salience) than hikes toward the north or south. This means that some profiles of alcohol correlation sustain much greater covariance with outcomes (or, salience for outcomes) than others. Outcomes appear with both positive and negative saliences because some are defined as measures of poor performance (e.g., errors on a vigilance task, LAXFA50) and correlate positively with prenatal alcohol exposure, while others are defined as measures of good performance (e.g., an achievement score such as WRATASS) and correlate negatively with prenatal alcohol.

2. The PLS analysis tabulates a crucial fact not shown in the plot: this map, and the two-dimensional scene it diagrams, incorporate 86% of all the power of Alcohol in accounting for the 474 outcomes measured (75% east-west and 11% north-south). In other words, this landscape is (relatively) flat, with less vertical relief than north-south variation. There is no need to use a map any more complicated (say, a contour map) to guide one in one's hiking.

3. Most of the outcomes that are at a relatively great distance from the center lie in the direction through the middle of the range of Alcohol variables. Recall from Section 4.1 that the first PLS Alcohol latent variable lies exactly along the long axis of this scatter: it is the scatter's first principal component. While this single composite Alcohol score adequately accounts for most of the correlations with outcomes (for 75% of all their squared correlations, to be precise), individual outcomes are better accounted for by variations, usually small, in the pattern of relative weighting of Alcohol variables around this main composite. In the main composite, PLS assigned the greatest weight to ADOCCP, the least to MOCCD: these weights are proportional to the easterly coordinates of the Alcohol variables in Figure 5.1. Outcomes toward the ADOCCP sector in Figure 5.3 are salient for a profile of Alcohol correlations weighting ADOCCP relatively more heavily than that; outcomes toward the AAP sector instead correlate with ADOCC and AA about equally. Outcomes toward the northeast or southwest require negative weights—see Hike E below. In terms of our map analogy, we do not miss visiting the interesting outcomes by so very great a distance if we hike only east and west; nevertheless, the other directions bring us closer to a few of the most interesting points on the horizon.

4. The range of map directions that can be described by selective weighting of one or another single Alcohol variable with respect to the central easterly tendency is about 110°, from ADOCCP around through MOCCD. These include all the out-

comes that typically rise when any measure of Alcohol rises. The range of the *opposites* of these directions (variables coded in the "good" direction, which rise as Alcohol falls) is another 110° halfway around the circle of directions from the center. There is a final set of outcomes which correspond to neither of these general tendencies. Such variables have *no* general pattern of rise or fall with increasing dose (regardless of Alcohol measure), but, rather, rise in proportion to one measure of dose (ADOCCP or MOCCD) and fall with respect to another (MOCCD or ADOCCP, respectively). Such correlation patterns contrasting these polar types of dose measure may typify outcomes that are positively sensitive to SES effects, with which MOCC is most correlated, but that are negatively sensitive to binge effects nevertheless. In terms of our map analogy, it is as if nearly one-third of the directions out of the origin can be described by sentences like "walk straight toward Mountain X," where X is a mountain in the Alcohol range, and most of the rest of the possible hikes can be described by the instruction, "hike directly away from Mountain X." However, a few interesting hikes have to be described by the instruction, "walk away from the origin in the direction parallel to the mountain range itself," the direction from one end (ADOCCP) to the other (MOCCD) or the opposite.

Now that we have explained all the hikes we might take with Figure 5.3 as our map, let us actually write the guidebook for this forest. We will refer to 24 different interesting outcomes, those at greatest or nearly greatest distance in each of five pairs of directions. These 24 are listed in Table 5.1. A longer list of 99 such salient outcomes appears in Appendix IV-b. Of these 24 measures, 20 may be characterized as "in the direction of Mountain X" or "directly away from Mountain X." These have a profile of Alcohol correlations characterized by relatively high weight in the vicinity of one or another specific Alcohol variable. The remaining four variables are reached by hikes "parallel to the mountain range," having Alcohol correlations that contrast MOCCD against ADOCCP.

A. For our first hike, we proceed from the origin in the direction of
    the measure ADOCCP. The outcomes we encounter on this
    hike are those for which the correlations with Alcohol weight
    the binge measures a great deal more heavily than does the typi-
    cal outcome, and continue to weight P measures higher than
    D's. We refer to this as the "heightened binge" trail and the
    outcomes we encounter as the "ADOCC-type" outcomes. Three
    of these outcomes showing relatively large Alcohol salience
    (that is, having a relatively large and negative covariance with
    their best summary Alcohol predictor) are Full Scale IQ at 7
    years (FULLIQ7), the verbal subscale of the same test
    (VERBIQ7), and the summary learning disability score
    (TOTALPRS) from the Myklebust Pupil Rating Scale. These
    variables all have correlations with ADOCCP exceeding –0.18
    and nearly zero (or slightly positive) correlations with AAD and
    MOCCD.

B. An adjacent sector of hikes, along the east-west direction of
    maximum net Alcohol explanatory power, leads us to outcomes
    which are not so heavily binge-sensitive or preawareness-loaded
    as the preceding. These outcomes show a profile of correlations
    with Alcohol relatively oriented toward measures like MAXD.
    Here we find outcomes that correlate substantially with most of
    the Alcohol variables, weighting the P's and the binge-type
    scores only a bit more heavily than the others, in more or less
    the pattern of the first column of Table 5.1. A list of seven
    outcomes for which Alcohol is particularly salient on this hike
    might begin with ACADADJ7 (mother's rating of classroom
    adjustment problems), the second most distant (salient) outcome
    in this study. Four of its correlations—with the BINGEs,
    MAXP, and ADOCCP—are above 0.20; those with the AAs
    and MOCCs are below 0.06. Also easterly on this path are
    LFMMAZTD (fine motor score for log time spent tracing the
    maze with the dominant hand at age 4) and LAXFA50 ("false
    alarms," or impulsive errors, on the AX-component of the 7-
    year Vigilance task), both having peak correlations greater than

0.20 with ADOCCP and correlations less than 0.10 with AAD and the MOCC variables. Heading west, we find COOPR7 (teacher's rating of impulsivity vis-a-vis cooperation from the Myklebust PRS), the two standardized arithmetic scores (ARITH7, from the WISC, and WRATASS, from the WRAT), and SPADND, *less* difficulty with supination/pronation of the dominant hand at age 7. All these variables show a profile of correlations with the Alcohol measures that is the opposite of that for ACADADJ7 or LAXFA50: all generally negative, and peaking at or over –0.20 for one of the MAXs or ADOCCs. The result for the subjective SPADND rating is unexpected and may be related to the subject's haste or carelessness in performance of the task; see Chapter 9. (Alcohol-exposed children were generally not among those rated as having difficulty with this task.)

C. Hikes in another direction are generally slightly shorter than those just preceding (representing slightly less net explained co-variance of the Alcohol profile with the outcomes). These hikes are to outcomes whose correlations with Alcohol are not really binge-weighted at all. Rather, their profiles emphasize measures that, like ORDEXC or AAP, attempt to represent "net dose" averaged over all of our alternate measures. These "AAP-type" outcomes include three neonatal scores: HABLIT (poor habituation to light, from the Brazelton scale), MORO (weak Moro reflex), and INCURVTH (high threshold for a good incurvation response); all improve in the absence of dose. HABLIT, the most distant (most salient) outcome in this direction, has correlations with alcohol ranging from -0.108 (MAXD) to -0.189 (MOCCP), a consistency unusual for the salient outcomes among these data. Three other outcomes are error scores from the CMT task at the 7-year exam: D1REVCOP, D1INTMEM, and D3QULCOP. These tap all the kinds of errors (reversals, poor integration, and poor quality) on an assortment of tasks described in Chapter 3. The actual correlations encountered show some divergences from the profile— D3QULCOP correlates 0.223 with AAP, D1REVCOP 0.262—

perhaps owing to the strongly J-shaped distributions of these CMT scores (see [67]), which render the correlations less stable than sample size would otherwise indicate.

D. There are no interesting hikes toward or away from AAD or MOCCP. The last hike toward or away from a "mountain" brings us to the "MOCCD-type" outcomes at due north or due south in Figure 5.2 or 5.3. These show nearly zero correlation with most of the binge measures. The effect of Alcohol here is somewhat difficult to interpret because high-MOCCD is the drinking pattern typically associated with high-SES parents. In these unadjusted analyses, then, this pair of causes—high education but also high drinking occasions—leads to competing effects on most of our behavioral and socioeconomically stereotyped outcomes. One "outcome" on this hike—high maternal expectations at age 4 for the child's academic adjustment (low scores on ACADADJ4)—is likely an SES effect of this sort. (When real data on academic adjustment become available at 7 years, the structure of correlations with exposure changes greatly; see ACADADJ7 on hike B above.) Three others (NEOSTATE, "baby's ability to sustain state" from the Brazelton scale; UNCLVERB, "unclassifiable verbalizations at the 18-month exam"; and CSHORB, "fewer errors on the second [easier] of the three Seashore tests") show Alcohol-related deficits in the expected direction. It is fortunate that the hikes in this direction are relatively short, as very strong Alcohol effects not correlated with binge scores would be very difficult to interpret convincingly. The correlations with the "occasions" Alcohol scores (AAs and MOCCs) are modest, no more than 0.14, as fits the generally lower explanatory power of the second LV profile of correlations with Alcohol.

E. There remain the hikes to the northeast or southwest in Figure 5.3, hikes "parallel to the mountain range," arriving at outcomes characterized by a profile of positive correlations with the ADOCCP-like variables and negative with the MOCCD-like, or the opposite. These outcomes can often be imagined to be en-

hanced by SES but damaged by bingeing, and so are most sensitive to the low-SES high-binge profile. (This is not to say that
many mothers' drinking behavior falls into that classification.
We are describing patterns of correlation with drinking on this
map, not patterns of drinking *per se*.) In fact, SES measures
such as parental education and occupational status are modestly
positively correlated with MOCCD and negatively correlated
with ADOCCP. The four landmarks at farthest distance along
this hike are errors on the first Seashore task (CSHORA), poor
vocabulary scores on the 7-year WISC (VOC7), a teacher rating
of poor instruction-following on the Myklebust PRS
(FOLINSTR), and a teacher rating of poor reading skills
(READING).

5.4 Remarks on Teratological Method

Of the many implications this overview of our findings bears for be-
havioral-teratological method, we would like to emphasize one in
particular here. Potentially severe cost is incurred whenever studies
are limited to fewer measurements of alcohol, fewer measurements of
outcome, or the analysis of alcohol by outcome measures one at a
time. Studies of the variables AA only, for instance, would not tap
the binge-related aspects of alcohol salience. The outcomes salient
for AA *exclude* a strip through the center of the salience scatter in the
direction of the "heightened binge" variable (northeast-southwest
axis). Such a study, for instance, would not uncover the outcome
variable TOTALPRS—although located on the circumference of our
set of outcomes, it is hardly correlated with AA at all. Conversely, a
study limited to measures of binge drinking would miss a strip of
outcomes around the "mainly volume" axis through the center in the
direction of MOCCP—outcomes like NEOSTATE, which correlate
mainly with the AA and MOCC variables, but correlate strongly
nevertheless. Studies of Attention at a specific age, or of LD alone,
or any other particular combination of functional modality and age,
would conceal the two-dimensional nature of the saliences of outcome measures for alcohol. In other words, different blocks corre-

spond to different understandings of the nature of alcohol teratogenesis.

In our view, additional sensitivity to the effects of alcohol will not be achieved by the design of more and more sensitive tests. (By analogy, designers of IQ tests do not achieve precision by the construction of more and more delicate single questions.) Instead, additional sensitivity in behavioral teratology results from the additive combination of a very widely spread battery of measures covering as many aspects of neuropsychological functioning as possible at as many ages as possible. That is, *behavioral teratology is best studied in breadth, not in depth.* There appears to be a great variety of "moderately good" measurements, but a complete dearth of "very good" measurements. *There is no gold standard for measuring alcohol-induced brain damage* across the first 7 years of human life; rather, the presence of alcohol damage is a truly latent variable, one developed more and more clearly by longer and longer series of outcomes, studied more and more patiently.

We can best present this argument for breadth of coverage graphically, via the display of Figure 5.4. The horizontal axis represents the 474 outcomes of the study, in numerical order (as listed in Appendix III). The vertical dotted lines separate the 15 blocks of out-

Table 5.2 28 Outcomes of Greatest Net Salience for Alcohol Categorized by Block

No. of Outcomes (out of best 28)	Block Number	Block Name	Abbreviation
1	1	Attention—neonatal	Att–0
1	2	Motor—neonatal	Mot–0
1	9	Attention—4 years	Att–4
4	10	Motor—4 years	Mot–4
2	12	Attention—7 years	Att–7
4	13	Neuromotor—7 years	NMot–7
6	14	Mental—7 years	Ment–7
9	15	LD—7 years	LD–7

Notes: Net salience is $4.67 \times (\text{LV1 salience})^2 + 1.81 \times (\text{LV2 salience})^2$. These 28 outcomes are all those falling outside of a circle of radius 0.4 drawn on Figure 5.2. They are identified (by magnitude) in Figure 5.4.

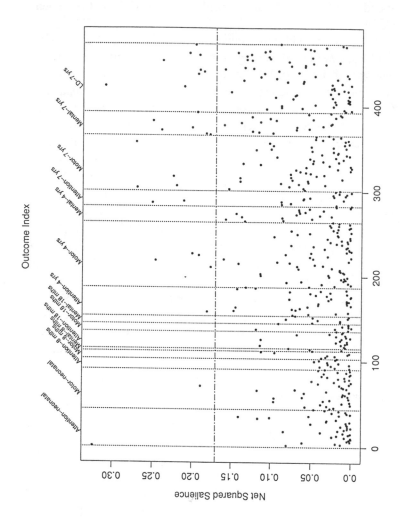

Figure 5.4. Plot of the net squared salience of the 474 outcomes for the first two alcohol latent variables in chronological order as they are listed in Appendix II. The dotted vertical lines separate the outcomes by block. The dashed horizontal line allows identification of the 28 outcomes of greatest net salience for prediction by the first two Alcohol LVs. The higher the dot, the more salient that outcome is for the two alcohol latent variables.

comes; the spaces between the lines are proportional to the number of variables block by block. The vertical axis represents the net squared salience of the outcome in question to the appropriate combination of our two patterns of alcohol dose. (It represents the contribution of the two patterns of alcohol dose to the total sum of squared correlations involving the given outcome.) The blocks of the 28 best outcomes, by this criterion, are distributed as in Table 5.2.

These 28 variables overlap with those labelled in Figure 5.2 and listed in Table 5.1, but they are not the same because this tabulation takes into account the differential weighting of the LV1 and LV2 axes. In fact, these 28 variables are all those plotted outside a circle of radius 0.40 on Figure 5.2.

We see that all channels are represented, and three different ages. At the same time, it is becoming clear that the mild effects on behavior that represent the effects of Alcohol at low doses cannot easily be observed in the infant or toddler as a passive responder to "stimuli," but go best with the active cooperation of the subject in the cognitive component of tests at pre-school age and beyond.

We believe these implications are not in any way specific to the study of alcohol teratogenesis, but apply throughout behavioral teratology. Teratogenic insults are multidimensional; so are consequences. They cannot be studied one of each at a time. In any channel of behavioral decrement, and in any study of near-normals, there will be an upper limit on the "amount" of damage attributable to the teratogen. Further increases in the "variance explained" (that misleading conventional criterion of "meaning" in most studies) can be achieved not by designing more and more delicate indicators but by multivariate statistical procedures for combining different indicators, of both exposure and effect, in light of an explicit model for the redundancy with which the causal process under study has been measured. PLS, at root, is a model for just this redundancy; we recommend the technique wherever developmental investigations take the form, as ours does, of a quasi-experimental study of response to dose.

5.5 Longitudinal Analysis

The analyses just preceding have not made any use of the temporal ordering of our waves of measurement. If we are interested in the explicitly longitudinal structure of the alcohol effect—the manner in which it appears to "infuse" into the outcome LVs age after age—we must turn to the longitudinal path models as described in Section 4.2. We have three general constructs that might be followed longitudinally in the appropriate way: Mental ability, Attention, and Neuromotor function. Analyses of the latter two blocks show no causal chain, with or without respect to any consistent Alcohol effect. For Mental ability, however, the models described in Section 4.2 appear to fit our data reasonably well. The relevant quantities of the PLS analysis are collected in Table 5.3.

The longitudinal structure of Mental abilities is, in simplest overview, exactly the causal chain that we already sketched for our demonstration of longitudinal PLS in Section 4.3. Our blocks and their variables are as follows (see Appendix III, blocks 5, 8, 11, and 14). At 8 months we used the age-standardized MDI and two seven-point ratings (General Mental Development and Overall Impression). At 18 months, there are nine indicators: the age-standardized MDI,

Table 5.3 Longitudinal Structure in "Mental" Blocks

(a) Correlations Computed from a Causal Chain Analysis without the Alcohol Block

	8-mo LV	18-mo LV	4-yr LV
LV 18-mo	0.402		
LV 4-yr	0.248	0.540	
LV 7-yr	0.196	0.402	0.765

(b) Correlations Computed by Linking Each Outcome Block with the Alcohol Block

	Alcohol LV	8-mo LV	18-mo LV	4-yr LV
LV 8-mo	.09			
LV 18-mo	.10	.38		
LV 4-yr	.15	.25	.51	
LV 7-yr	.22	.18	.38	.76

again; three sub-tabulations of verbalizations among Bayley items 80-163 (Receptive, Expressive, and Other—recall this latter was salient for the second, "occasions" Alcohol LV); ratings of general mental development and language production quantity, quality, and spontaneity; and an overall rating. At 4 years, we used full-scale IQ, verbal and performance subscales, all nine separate scale scores, ratings of general mental development and language development, a psychometrist's overall impression, and four mothers' ratings (expectation for academic adjustment, school concerns, learning difficulty, and odd speech). Finally, the 7-year Mental battery included IQ and its subscales; the three WRAT-R scales; three ratings (general mental development, language development, overall impression); and seven mean counts (length of oral and written utterances, and DSS, misspellings, phonetic errors, and oral and written syntax errors per sentence).

The causal structure of this sequence of blocks, considered without reference to alcohol, is straightforward. A system of four latent variables, one per block, shows correlations as in Table 5.3(a). Reconstructions of distant items lie within $\pm.03$ of products of immediately off-diagonal correlations (for example, $0.402 \times 0.540 \times 0.765 = 0.166$, vs. the correlation of 0.196 actually observed between the LVs at the two ends of the chain). The latent variables are all general averages over most of their blocks. At 8 months, the saliences of the three items (a Bayley score and two ratings) are equal. At 18 months, the net MDI is the best score, but all scores except language spontaneity have a substantial salience. At 4 years, IQ and all its subscales, and also all the psychometrist's ratings, show satisfactory saliences (but none of the mothers' ratings). At 7 years, again, the LV involves IQ and seven of its subscales (all except OBJ7 and COD7), the WRAT-R and Stroop scores, and the psychometrists' ratings, but none of the 7-year word and error counts.

We next consider LV correlations computed from a five-block PLS analysis linking each of the four outcome blocks to the Alcohol block as described in Section 4.2.2 and Figure 4.6. The correlations among the LVs of the chain are essentially unchanged (Table 5.3b) even though the formulas for the outcome LVs — i.e., the saliences

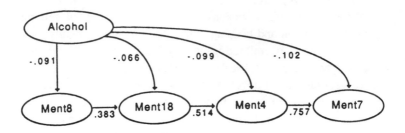

Figure 5.5. Alcohol effect on a Mental causal chain.

of the individual variables—are substantially different. The Alcohol LV responsible for the longitudinal prediction of IQ is weighted mainly on the binge indicators, especially ADOCCP; it is a slightly binge-heightened modification of the first pooled Alcohol LV, aligned approximately with the variable QFVP in the alcohol profile space plot in Section 5.2. The correlations of this alcohol LV with the outcome LVs are, wave by wave, −0.091, −0.101, −0.152, and −0.217, corresponding to distributed effects (see Section 4.3) of −0.091, −0.066, −0.099, and −0.102: a pattern of apparently *even infusion* of alcohol damage at successive waves of analysis (Figure 5.5). The coefficient of −0.102 might be interpreted equally well as the effect of the Alcohol LV on a residual of the Ment-7 LV after regression on the Ment-4 LV, etc.

The variables of the outcome LVs at each age have saliences that are nearly proportional to their saliences in the first LV of the comprehensive two-block analysis (with all other outcomes) of Section 5.2. The outcome LV at the 8-month wave does not show much salience for the Bayley scale, only for the ratings. At 18 months the Bayley scale score *is* salient for alcohol, and also the ratings for general mental development and overall language quality and the overall impression. At 4 years, the LV reflecting Alcohol incorporates all of the longitudinal 4-year LV except for the language development rating; and, at 7 years, the Alcohol-related LV differs from the longitudinal 7-year LV only in a greater salience for overall impression and for one of the error counts, mean syntax errors per written sentence.

Thus not only does there exist a causal chain of Mental abilities, but an Alcohol variable is salient for it with a steadily increasing correlation corresponding to a steady addition of coherent "new causation."

Such a finding is important and suggestive: important, inasmuch as it shows the role of later waves of measurement in refining the understanding of alcohol effects as observed in toddlers; suggestive, in that it might permit an attempt at a *forecast of deficit,* whereby one pattern of mental deficit at an early age attests to the probability of alcohol teratogenesis and then to a future profile of increasingly detectable deficits at later ages, as the alcohol effect continues to appear with such substantial saliences. We return to this issue of forecasting in Section 6.3 after a more detailed discussion of the construction of a block-by-block scoring system that permits regressions of LVs within cases across time.

Table 5.4 Absence of Longitudinal Structure in "Neuromotor" Blocks

(a) Correlations Computed from a Causal Chain Analysis without the Alcohol Block

	Neonatal LV	8-mo LV	18-mo LV	4-yr LV
LV 8-mo	0.33			
LV 18-mo	0.13	0.44		
LV 4-yr	0.09	0.27	0.38	
LV 7-yr	−0.07	0.12	0.34	0.63

(b) Correlations Computed by Linking Each Outcome Block with the Alcohol Block

	Alcohol	Neonatal LV	8-mo LV	18-mo LV	4-yr LV
LV Neonatal	0.34				
LV 8-mo	0.14	0.06			
LV 18-mo	0.14	0.02	0.22		
LV 4-yr	0.25	0.08	0.19	0.30	
LV 7-yr	0.41	0.10	0.20	0.29	0.28

For us to explore the "new" effect of Alcohol on any outcome in this way, it is not necessary that the outcome relate to earlier waves via a causal chain. The most salient single outcome LV for Alcohol effects at age 7, for instance, is the Neuromotor block. As Table 5.4 shows, there is no Neuromotor causal chain. The NMot-7 LV correlates 0.28 with NMot-4, but a full 0.29 with NMot-18, even though those two correlate only 0.30 with each other (leading to a predicted NMot-7 to NMot-18 correlation of $0.28 \times 0.30 = 0.08$ under a causal chain model). Instead, as we shall see in Chapter 6, the strongest predictor of NMot-7 from age 4 is Ment-4, with a correlation of 0.46; the correlation with Att-4, at 0.28, is almost as strong as the "autocorrelation" with NMot-4. (The LVs here are those computed by saliences with respect to the pooled Alc LV1, not by separate analyses against Alcohol.) We adjusted NMot-7 for *all* these precursors—the multiple R is 0.472, barely larger than that due to Ment-4 above—and then computed the correlation of the Alc LV with this adjusted score. That correlation, 0.29, is almost all of the correlation of Alc LV1 with "unadjusted NMot-7," which is 0.33. This value from Table 8.1, is the actual correlation, attenuated for missing data as explained in Chapter 6, between the NMot-7 score and the pooled Alcohol LV of Table 5.1.) That is, almost all the effect of Alcohol on the NMot-7 outcome is "new" with respect to effects on the age-4 latent variables.

5.6 Summary

This chapter has considered the structure of correlations between the 13 Alcohol variables and the 474 outcomes reviewed in Chapter 3. We first reported one crucial two-block PLS analysis of the entire set of these correlations, and then examined more closely the patterns of Alcohol effect over time. While the study design treated these outcomes as a set of many "blocks" of related measures at each of five ages, this first PLS analysis investigates them rather differently, sorting them instead by the typical patterns of their profiles of correlation with the 13 Alcohol items.

We saw that this space of possible profiles of Alcohol effect is two-dimensional. The Alcohol items of the prenatal questionnaire are sorted along a nearly straight line in this space. At one end of the line lies ADOCCP (that is, here are the profiles of correlation most heavily emphasizing ADOCCP). This is the single indicator most highly correlated with the outcomes as a whole set, but it is not the "most typical" Alcohol indicator, the one with the most typical patterns of correlation with the outcomes. Those more typical patterns, derived from the first Alcohol LV, are more characteristic of MAXD or BINGEP (the indicator we break out in Appendix III). At the other end of this range of Alcohol correlation profiles lie the profiles emphasizing no binge items or even emphasizing the AA and MOCC exposure measures; these typically involve lower net amounts of correlation than those profiles emphasizing bingeing.

To review the 474 outcomes in the light of this range of Alcohol correlational profiles, we concentrated our attention upon the two dozen outcomes most strongly correlated with one or another interesting Alcohol profile, and reported these in order of the Alcohol variable or contrast that best typified that profile. The "ADOCC-type" items were VERBIQ7, FULLIQ7, and TOTALPRS. These are the most purely binge-sensitive outcomes. Slightly less binge-sensitive outcomes (the MAXD type, in the direction of greatest Alcohol salience overall) include ACADADJ7, COOPR7, ARITH7, WRATASS, LFMMAZTD4, LAXFA507, and SPADND. The "AAP-type" outcomes (the "mainly quantity" type correlating roughly evenly with all 13 Alcohol measures) include three neonatal measurements, HABLIT, MORO, and INCURVTH, and three items from the CMT7 task: DIREVCOP, D1INTMEM, and D3QULCOP. Some outcomes which are nearly wholly binge-insensitive in their Alcohol dependence (the "MOCC-type" outcomes) are NEOSTATE, UNCLVERB, ACADADJ4, CSHORB. These are somewhat difficult to interpret, as the pattern of high MOCC is associated with high SES, representing a competing influence upon the outcome. The remaining sector of Figure 5.3 represents the variables that are both enhanced by SES effects (high MOCC) and damaged by bingeing (high ADOCC), and hence are most salient for an Alcohol correlational profile of ADOCC versus MOCC or the opposite. These outcomes include CSHORA, VOC7, FOLINSTR, and READING.

We see, therefore, that all the main patterns of possible Alcohol saliences—from ADOCC-type through MOCC-type and back via their contrast—are entailed in the description of the set of all the outcomes. We see, also, that a great variety of types of outcome (from neonatal attention scores through laboratory measurements, psychometric measurements, and ratings at age 7 years) are found to be salient according to one or another of these profiles.

Although the main PLS analysis treated the entire list of 474 outcomes as one roster to be sorted over a two-dimensional map, we also examined the correlations between prenatal Alcohol and the four domains of behavior as they were measured over the five waves of examination. This is the study of "causal chains" as we explained it in Chapter 4. For the Mental domain, there is a causal chain of quite clear definition. A single Alcohol score, of the QFVP-type (slightly binge-overweighted), is salient for each of a series of 4 Mental LVs with path coefficients ranging from $-.07$ to $-.10$. The Mental LVs are correlated nearly as well across time as the single MDI and IQ scores discussed in Section 4.2.1; and the effect of Alcohol upon them is quite consistent. That is, a coherent Alcohol LV accounts for the Mental LVs with a steadily increasing correlation corresponding to a steady addition of "new causation," all the while these Mental LVs account for each other in the usual autocorrelated fashion.

In contrast, the other principal domains of measurement, Neuromotor and Attention, do not support a strong longitudinal model of the effects of Alcohol. Instead, they represent a different pattern of relationship. For both of these, almost all the effect of Alcohol on the wave-7 outcome is "new," at least in terms of the similarly named block at the 4-year wave. Several possibilities are suggested to explain these findings. On the one hand, the "new" Neuromotor and Attentional effects of alcohol measurable when the children are 7 years old may represent some type of "sleeper" effect dependent on the fuller central nervous system development manifested at 7 years of age. On the other hand, some environmental factor occurring at this age could be exacerbating the effects at this age—so that children with unimpaired Neuromotor and/or

Attentional functioning are able, as a result of the academic experience, to make greater strides in these domains by age 7 relative to age 4. A third possibility, which has some support from the data, is that the behaviors measured at 4 and 7 years were not equally reflective of the underlying construct of the domain. We will see in Chapter 8 that the NMot-7 latent variable nevertheless supports a longitudinal analysis of a different form: a retrospective longitudinal detection task. To explain this possibility we must first show how we generate numeric scores, subject by subject, corresponding to these lists of latent-variable saliences; the next chapter begins with this explanation.

The findings for the present chapter deal only with patterns of correlation between the 13 Alcohol measures and the 474 outcome scores. In Appendix V we draw together an alternative summary of our analysis in which findings about correlations are paired with findings about the corresponding scores of individual subjects.

## CHAPTER 6

Longitudinal Analyses of Latent Variable Scores, with Covariate Adjustments

In the last chapter we introduced our fundamental question: What are the long-term effects of prenatal alcohol exposure? This actually entails three subsidiary questions: What dimensions of alcohol exposure best account for child outcomes? Which child outcomes are best accounted for by prenatal alcohol exposure? Is there a longitudinal structure to these outcomes across time? In Chapter 5 we used LV saliences to answer these questions. Now we attend to individual subject scores in order to explore the extent to which correlations with alcohol are attributable to competing predictions by covariates, such as smoking, nutrition, or parental education.

For each of our 581 subjects we derive an LV score for alcohol that is the salience-weighted sum of that subject's scores on each of the 13 alcohol measures. Likewise, each subject has an Outcome LV score computed from all 474 outcome measures. In order to study the longitudinal sequence of covariates together with alcohol effects on outcomes we also compute separate Partial LV scores (PLVs) for the collections of outcomes measured at each wave of examination.

After explaining our approach to computing and analyzing latent variable scores in the face of the inevitable problem of missing data, Section 6.1 displays the fundamental scatters of dose and outcome LV scores that reify the analyses of correlations in Chapter 5. Section 6.2 introduces our modification of the classic procedure of "covariate adjustment" to suit the PLS context. We review the usual terms of analysis of covariance—"explanation," "effect," "significance"—and indicate which have equivalents in the PLS approach; we also clarify the problem of temporal coherence when adjusting an outcome composite of observations at many different ages. The section then presents our best arguments for the stability of the alcohol-outcome effects reported in Chapter 5 against "adjustment" for any of a variety of plausible covariates and confounding variables, including measures of postnatal environment that could exacerbate or compensate for the effects of the prenatal alcohol insult. In section 6.3 we disaggregate the principal outcome latent variable into PLVs according to the five waves of examination. The analysis of these wave-specific parts of the outcome LV allows us to study the explicitly longitudinal structure of Alcohol effects more generally than we could in Chapter 5, and, in particular, better to estimate "new" (previously unobserved or unmeasured) alcohol effects that become apparent at each new age of examination, as the maturation of our subjects permitted us to assess steadily more complex processes as outcomes.

6.1 Computation of Latent Variable Scores with Missing Data

Any large longitudinal study, even one with a loss to follow-up as low as ours, must cope with substantial amounts of missing data. The correlations in the matrices analyzed in Chapter 5 were computed from all available cases on each pair of the outcome variables. (There are no missing data in the block of 13 measures of alcohol exposure.) Thus, each of the 13×474 correlations may be based on a slightly different sample of children. A total of up to 581 children, measured on at least two occasions across the waves of this study, contributed to these calculations. (One child, who had an exceedingly high AAP score and a clinical diagnosis of FAS, was dropped from our analyses as noted in Tables 4.2 and 5.1.) However, no children have complete data on all 474 outcomes. Some variables were measured only during either the first or second summer of the 7-year follow-up period (see Table 3.1 and Appendix III). Thus to compute outcome latent variable scores as linear combinations of the 474 individual outcome scores, we must effectively fill in missing values in some way.

After considering a variety of approaches for dealing with missing data, we decided to base all our analyses on the following calculations. We first filled in missing values on the outcomes with the outcome means (which are zero once the variables are "z-scored") and then rescaled the filled-in variables to have unit variance once again. We could then compute the linear combinations $LV_A = \sum \alpha_i A_i$ and $LV_B = \sum \beta_j B_j$ explained in Chapter 4 using saliences (coefficients) derived from the 13×474 missing data correlation matrix (Table 5.1) applied to the rescaled mean-filled outcomes. Simple correlations involving the outcome latent variable LV_B as defined here are substantially attenuated because of this filling-in of means. More sophisticated estimates of missing values might be employed to lessen the attenuation. However, the simple incorporation in correlation (or regression) analyses of case weights reflecting the amount of (salient) complete data provides an adequate solution.

For each case a "net salience" of the non-missing data was computed as the sum of the absolute values of the saliences for the non-missing outcomes on that case. If m_{ij} is an indicator for missing data, coded 0 when variable j (j=1, 2, ... , 474) is missing on case i and coded 1 otherwise, then the weight for the ith case is $\sum m_{ij} |\beta_j|$. Cases which are missing values on those outcomes alcohol are expected to have LV scores most biased toward zero because of the filling-in of mean values; but these cases will receive little weight in statistical analyses relating the outcome LV to the Alcohol LV and other covariates.

For the comprehensive two-block analysis summarized in Table 5.1, an estimate of the correlation between the two linear combinations $LV_{Alcohol}$ and $LV_{Outcome}$ can be computed algebraically using only the missing data correlation matrix (correlations computed using all pairwise complete data; i.e., a different sample size for each correlation). This is 0.33, as reported in Table 5.1. Now that we have actual scores for the LVs of greatest interest, however, we can go beyond the algebraic manipulations that PLS embodies to actually consider their joint distributions in this sample. The simple Pearsonian correlation actually observed between the two LV scores computed as above after substituting mean values is 0.29. For this example, case weighting has little effect because both the covariance in the numerator of the correlation coefficient and the variance of the

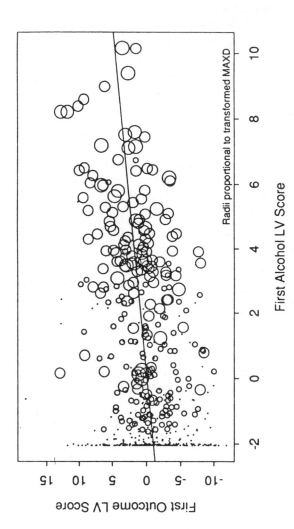

Figure 6.1. Scatterplots of scores on the first and second Alcohol-Outcome LV pairs for the two-block analysis of 13 measures of prenatal alcohol exposure and 474 outcome measures across 5 waves of measurement from birth to seven years. (Least squares lines are drawn to highlight the trend in these scatters.) The algebraically computed LV correlations are 0.33 for the first LV pair and 0.35 for the second LV pair. The correlations computed from these scatterplots are 0.29 and 0.31, respectively, owing to attenuation caused by missing data. For the first LV pair (a) cases are coded by circles having radii proportional to the value of MAXD; for the second LV pair

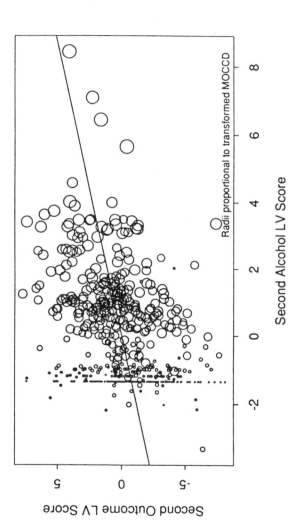

Figure 6.1. (continued) (b) cases are similarly coded by circles having radii proportional to the value of MOCCD. These two were chosen because correlations of outcomes with MAXD most closely match the shape of the correlation profiles with Alc LV1, and correlations of outcomes with MOCCD most closely match the shape of the correlation profiles with Alc LV2. The vertical clusters of points near −2 in both figures represent those cases with zero scores on all the Alcohol measures, i.e., the abstainers. These variables are not z-scored, but are normed so that their covariance is the corresponding singular value of the full 13 × 474 cross-correlation matrix of all the dose measures by all the outcomes, as explained in Chapter 4. Hence the slopes of the lines are not proportional to correlations.

LV score in the denominator are attenuated by the missing values. (Nonetheless, it is important to utilize the case weighting in regression analyses of LV scores.)

Figure 6.1 presents scatter plots of the estimated scores for both the first and second Alcohol and Outcome LV scores, those for which the saliences are summarized in Table 5.1. The vertical streak at the left of the plots incorporates all the women who reported no alcohol consumption on any of the alcohol scores. In Figure 6.1(a) the points are coded with circles having radii proportional to the (transformed) MAXD score, which is most characteristic of the first Alcohol LV as explained in Section 5.2; in Figure 6.1(b) the points are similarly coded with circles having radii proportional to (transformed) MOCCD.

Although the first LV pair explains most of the structure in the cross-correlation matrix (75% of the sum of squared cross-correlations versus 11% for the second LV pair), the scores for the second LV pair are correlated at about the same strength as the scores for the first LV pair. The estimated correlations are 0.33 for the first pair and 0.35 for the second pair; the weighted correlations of the estimated LV scores are 0.29 and 0.31, respectively. The difference is that the first pair of LVs have greater variance, and so explain far more covariance via that correlation; that covariance, in fact, is what PLS is optimizing (recall Section 4.1).

This first LV is also more reliable, in that its coefficients are more homogeneous, so that it more stably taps the underlying structure of positive correlations among most items in the Alcohol block (Sec. 2.2.1). One can think of the first principal component as approximating the "most reliable" scale that could be formed from the block: the first factor of the block (specified by the usual model for factor analysis; see, for example, Bookstein, 1991, Chap. 4) . The first Outcome LV is much more closely aligned with that first factor than is the second.

6.2 Adjusting Alcohol-Outcome Correlations for Covariates

6.2.1 A Note on Defining Terms

Here and in Chapters 7 and 8 we shall frequently alter the language of our data analyses from that of Partial Least Squares to that of conventional multiple regression analysis. Sometimes this is because of an interest in scores, sometimes because of an interest in computing "predictions" of the same age-7 outcome by multiple earlier indicators including Alcohol. The reader should keep in mind that three crucial terms change their meaning from one context to the other.

1. "Explanation." Partial Least Squares "explains" the covariance pattern between blocks; multiple regression "explains" the variance instead, of only one variable at a time.

2. "Effects." In Partial Least Squares, these are the *saliences*, which are proportional to the correlations of the variables of one block with the latent variable representing another block. In multiple regression, the coefficients are not proportional to correlations; each represents the covariance of one predictor with the outcome "holding the others constant." There is no equivalent to the quoted phrase in PLS.

3. "Statistical significance." A PLS model has essentially one "significance level" for an assessment of whether sets of saliences (singular vectors in a two-block analysis) are "well-defined." The null hypothesis is that the vectors of saliences are ill-defined in the sense that they have no central tendency when considered as unit vectors on a (hyper-) sphere. We can assess this significance level using bootstrap methods (see 66). Multiple regression models have multiple "significance levels," one for each predictor as well as an overall level. We do not examine overall measures of significance or of fit for these multiple regression models.

In addition to these three terms, which are shared between discussions of PLS and discussions of regression, we will reserve two terms to strictly distinguish between these contexts. We will say either that alcohol "predicts" or that it "accounts for" an outcome. (Neither of these statements implies, in general, causation.) PLS *accounts for* correlations, and thus in PLS analyses we have found an alcohol LV to *account for* a pattern of correlations with outcomes. Regression *predicts* case values, and so in our regression analyses we will find that alcohol scores *predict* outcome scores. This sense of the word "prediction" is identical to its ordinary use in regression analysis. The phrase "account for" is sometimes found in regression, but in this book we have reserved it for the PLS context alone.

6.2.2 Covariate Lagging

In the teratological literature, it is customary to "adjust out" the effects of covariates upon a teratogenic outcome by a multiple regression in which the insult and the covariate jointly predict the outcome. That is, the effect of the insult is estimated "holding the covariates constant," and vice versa. This familiar procedure must be used carefully as it can be inappropriate for many covariates measured *after* the birth of the child. It is equivalent to first adjusting both outcome and Alcohol for their "joint" linear dependence on the covariates and then observing the correlation of the two residuals. Such procedures are nonsense whenever they result in "adjusting" the alcohol score for one of its own effects.

Only in the context of an explicit longitudinal analysis does it make sense to "adjust" Alcohol for the values of variables measured up to eight years after the dose was incurred. For straightforward assessment of alcohol effects without regard for longitudinal pathways, it seems to us appropriate to "adjust" outcomes only for those covariates for which no dependence on alcohol dose is conceivable, such as race or other preconception demographics, and for examiner effects and other situational effects on exam day. Initial analyses are not adjusted for all other intervening variables, such as video games in the home, which could conceivably be consequences (indirect effects) of Alcohol exposure as much as they are independent "causes" of the outcome.

The adjustment for situational effects is carried out separately prior to any PLS analysis. Test score by test score, age at testing

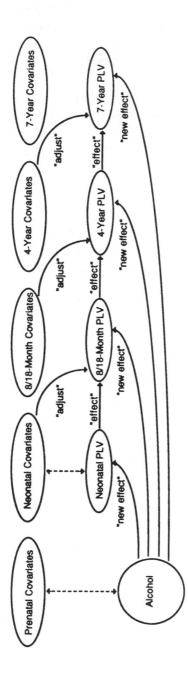

Figure 6.2. Diagram explaining the role of lagged covariates in the analysis of LV scores in a longitudinal study. (See Section 6.2.2 for discussion.)

and dummy variables for examiner were entered into regressions of each outcome measure in a multiple regression jointly with AA, and any age or examiner effects found significant in this computation were corrected as raw scores.

Beyond this conceptually very early step, which should be considered an adjustment of raw data rather than any sort of "modeling," the role of covariates in our explanations is twofold. Our principal interest in them is as they challenge our causal (dose-response) interpretation of the alcohol-outcome LV correlation. The response to the challenge is to remove the effects of the covariates upon alcohol (or of alcohol upon the covariates) and the effects of the covariates upon the outcomes and then test the resulting partial correlation again. We will see that its import for teratology does not change. To challenge a claim of dose-response relationship regarding an LV it is appropriate to consider all covariates regardless of the time at which they were measured.

But of course the information about outcomes represented by correlations with these covariates is valuable and should not be discarded. It is explicitly preserved in the longitudinal analyses of Section 6.3, where we wield it to quantify "new" Alcohol effects wave by wave. "New" alcohol effects are those not predictable by deficits or effects at earlier times. The *effect* of Alcohol upon 7-year outcomes, for instance, will be taken to be the correlation of the appropriate Alcohol LV with the 7-year Outcome PLV after adjusting for the 4-year PLV *and all of the covariates measured up through age 4*. The "new" Alcohol effect cannot run via old covariates; in other words, we adjust the Alcohol effect only for old covariates, not for new ones. The path model for these covariance adjustments is indicated in Figure 6.2. For an extended discussion of the role of covariates in longitudinal research, see Cochran (1983), or Mosteller & Moynihan, eds. (1972).

6.2.3 Adjusting the Large Two-Block PLS Analysis for Covariates: Predicting the Principal LV Scores

Demographic characteristics, prenatal and neonatal covariates including prenatal exposure to other possible teratogens, and measures of postnatal environment may be predictive of the outcome latent variable or may serve to confound, mitigate, or exacerbate the effects of prenatal alcohol exposure expressed in terms of the Alcohol latent variable. In this section (and in Section 6.3) we consider these possibilities.

On the basis of our previous experience and preliminary data analyses, we identified a large number of covariates to consider in model building. Table 2.10 lists over 150 potential covariates which have been examined previously in this study in relation to the child outcomes. Table 6.1 lists the 61 relevant to analyses in the present monograph. We grouped these according to the waves of measurement (not necessarily the waves at which their effects might be expected to be observed). As indicated in Table 6.1, we began with 19 demographic and genetic factors (which, of course, are likely to influence the postnatal environment) measured at or before the birth of the child. Next were nine measures of maternal prenatal use of other drugs: nicotine, caffeine, marijuana, aspirin, acetaminophen, and antibiotics. Eleven measures of the postnatal environment at the 8- and 18-month follow-ups comprised the third group of covariates. We considered four measures of the postnatal environment at four years and 18 measures at seven years.

For covariate adjustment of the large two-block PLS analysis represented in Table 5.1 (13 Alcohol scores × 474 outcomes across five ages for 581 subjects) we use the two Alcohol LVs this analysis produced. Following upon the discussion in Chapter 5 of the two-dimensional pattern of alcohol effects, one might consider model building for outcome latent variables associated with any sector from the scatterplot of Figure 5.3, including the ADOCCP-type profile and the AAP-type profile. We consider it sufficient to analyze just the principal outcome LVs indicated in Table 5.1: the "MAXD-type" profile and the "MOCCD-type" profile. All these regressions are on the full sample of 581 cases. Note that these analyses cannot embody the covariate lagging approach just suggested (Sec. 6.2.2), as these outcome LVs are computed from outcome variables measured across all five examination periods.

Table 6.1 Covariates and Potential Confounding Variables Considered for the Main Outcome LVs

Pre/neonatal demographics and covariates:
- Sex: child
- White: indicator of white mothers
- Black: indicator of black mothers
- Fatheduc: father's education (yrs.)
- Motheduc: mother's education (yrs.)
- Mothdegree: mother's academic degree
- Mother's age
- SES: socioeconomic status (Hollingshead)
- OKnutrition: maternal prenatal (4 pt scale)
- Parity (log)
- Indicator for first born
- Maternal marital status
- Children in the household (#)
- Children younger than 6 yrs (#)
- Children older than 5 yrs (#)
- Adults in the household (#)
- Maximum occupation status
- Maternal thyroid disease
- Maternal metabolic disease

Other exposures
- Nicotine (log mg/day)
- Cigarettes (log count/day)
- Marijuana (log freq/month)
- Caffeine-prior (log mg/day)
- Caffeine-during (log mg/day)
- Aspirin (log #/month)
- Aspirin (indicator for more than 4 occasions/month)
- Acetaminophen (log occasions/month)
- Antibiotics for illness

8/18 month environment
- Nursing (log # weeks)
- Children in household at 8 mths (#)
- Children in household at 18 mths (#)
- Adults in household at 8 mths (#)
- Adults in household at 18 mths (#)
- HhChg8: # Household changes at 8 mths (log)
- HhChg18: # Household changes at 18 mths (log)
- HhChg8Low: Household chgs, 8 mths, low SES (log)
- HhChg18Low: Household chgs, 18 mths, low SES (log)
- MIISss8: Mother-infant interaction scale at 8 mths
- MIISss18: Mother-infant interaction scale at 18 mths

4 year environment
- Children in household at 4 yrs (#)
- Adults in household at 4 yrs (#)
- Household changes at 4 years (log)
- Household chgs, 4 years, low SES (log)

7 year environment
- Maternal marital status
- Maternal employment
- Father figure employment
- Indicator for lives with biologic mother
- Indicator for lives with biologic father
- Indicator for lives with foster parents
- Lives with surrogate mother
- Lives with surrogate father
- Child nutrition (4 pt scale)
- Children in household (#)
- Children younger than 6 yrs (#)
- Children older than 5 yrs (#)
- Adults in household (#)
- Child/adult ratio in household
- Household changes, 7 years (log)
- Household changes, 7 years, low SES (log)
- Indicator of preschool attendance
- Grade of child

Underlined entries are abbreviations/covariate names that are used in subsequent tables.

We followed an informal forward stepwise procedure in building the regression models, requiring nominal significance at the .05 level (corresponding approximately, for this sample size, to a partial correlation greater than 0.095) in order for variables to remain in the multiple regression model from step to step. To accommodate missing data, all regression analyses were weighted using for case weights the "net salience" measures discussed in Section 6.1. We began with the 19 demographic and genetic covariates and selected what appeared to be the best predictors of the outcome LV from this group. We proceeded to examine the measures of maternal use of other drugs for effects that correlated with the outcome after adjustment for the fundamental demographic effects. This was followed by consideration of the 8- and 18-month postnatal family/environmental measures (including mother-child interaction, which could also be considered as a possible outcome influenced by the condition of the child), and then the 4-year environmental measures. At each stage we examined the relative importance of the Alcohol LV as a predictor of the Outcome LV after adjustment for all the other covariates. (Note that some of these predictions appear to be running "backwards in time," whenever, for instance, a 4-year environmental measure "predicts" an outcome LV score incorporating substantial salience for the neonatal observation HABLIT. The problem is not a serious one inasmuch as the outcome LVs are dominated by the 7-year data; see Tables 5.1, 5.2.) We note which 7-year covariates would enter the regression equation next, although they are excluded from our tabled results for the reasons explained in Section 6.2.2.

At this point we considered separate regression models by sex to explore possible interaction effects, and finally we considered multiplicative interaction terms involving the Alcohol LV by each of the predictors in the "final" model. The data were examined for many types of interactions (such as Alcohol or Sex by other main effects in the model). In view of the number of interactions considered, the few marginally significant interaction effects are not reported here.

We are not claiming that these regression models are "true": that is, these models should not be taken to have identified "the significant predictors" of the outcome LVs. We examined the regressions primarily to determine whether the pattern of association between the Alcohol measures and the outcomes could be explained by adjustment for the primary correlates of child outcome and whether there were factors that might exacerbate or mitigate the apparent Alcohol effects expressed in terms of our two main latent variables. We make no formal tests of hypotheses about covariate effects *per se*. In fact, the substantial correlations among groups of pre- and post-natal covariates make the search for a "true" model meaningless. Detailed interpretation of environmental influences on child outcomes should be assessed using the language of latent variables as explained in (56).

The result of the analysis of the primary Outcome LV identified in Chapter 5 is summarized in Table 6.2. The regression model includes those covariates meeting the criteria described above. These are: sex of child, indicators for white and black race, parental education, maternal prenatal nutrition, aspirin use during pregnancy, number of children younger than 6 years of age in the household, nursing, and mother-child interactions at 18 months. The coding of these scores is described in Table 6.1. The directions of these covariate effects in terms of the Outcome LV are as follows (a high score represents poorer performance): males do worse than females; both whites and blacks do worse than other racial groups (mostly Asians and American Indians); lower parental education (both maternal and paternal) is related to poorer performance; poor prenatal nutrition relates to poorer performance; maternal prenatal aspirin use relates to poorer performance; the presence of more young children in the household relates to poorer performance; absence of nursing, and deviant mother-child interaction scores relate to poorer performance.

It is of interest that other facets of prenatal experience (in addition to Alcohol) appear to have an enduring association with child outcomes through age 7, notwithstanding our cautions about interpreting the value of regression coefficients. While sex of child and parental education are well-known covariates in developmental research, others, such as prenatal nutrition and aspirin exposure, are seldom considered, although they have been noted in previous reports on this data set (54, 63) up through 4 years of age. Three postnatal covariates were related to the Outcome LV: nursing, deviant mother-infant interactions, and number of young children in the household. Of interest is a recent report indicating that alcohol use while breast-feeding relates to poorer motor performance at 12 months (Little, Anderson, Ervin, Worthington-Roberts & Clarren, 1989). As post-natal alcohol use by mothers was not recorded in the present study, it is not possible to distinguish the prenatal from the postnatal effects in those mothers who drank. However, the apparently positive effect of nursing in the present study suggests that the prenatal alcohol effects in this study are the most salient of the factors recorded at the time of the 7-year exam. Only grade of child—a possible conse-quence of alcohol exposure—would be added as a "significant" predic-tor of the outcome LV. Adding this covariate does not change the magnitude of the estimated Alcohol effect. We note that nicotine and caffeine, among the strongest covariates in terms of their correlation with alcohol, are not in the final list of covariates adjusted in Table 6.2. This is because they are not significant predictors of these long-term outcomes in this data set. The absence of caffeine effects on child outcomes across the first 7 years of life has been extensively investigated in previous papers from this study (e.g., 69).

The model in Table 6.2 explains about 42% of the variance in the estimated Outcome LV scores. It is remarkable that the Alcohol LV remains not only highly significant for the Outcome LV after ad-justment for these other factors, but is in fact, after sex of the child, the "most significant correlate" of the Outcome LV. Its partial corre-lation exceeds even that of paternal education, which is the best pre-dictor of most measures of child performance. We do not report probabilities on a null hypothesis—"p-values"—as we do not believe this regression analysis represents a "true" model in any sense. For instance, it does not take account of the process of data analysis that led to the definition of the Alcohol and Outcome LVs as maximally salient for each other. In our view, the p-values associated with in-dividual terms in a multiple regression should be viewed with ex-treme caution. In fact, the problems of "significance testing" are far milder for PLS, governed as it is by one single test for the reliability of the vectors of saliences (see Section 6.2.1), than for all other techniques of multiple, competing hypotheses exploited anywhere else in the current literature of developmental teratology. Nonetheless, the regression models strengthen our confidence in the reality of the primary Alcohol-Outcome relationship.

A parallel analysis of the second Outcome LV is summarized in Table 6.3. Again, the Alcohol-Outcome relationship appears quite stable against adjustment for covariates. The second Alcohol LV is the "most significant" predictor in a multiple regression model that explains approximately 39% of the variation in the second Outcome LV. Nursing and sex of the child are the next strongest predictors in this particular regression. Note that the number of children in the household and the number of children under six years of age have opposite effects in this multiple regression equation—effects which are not apparent without adjustment for the other terms in the model. These are likely artifacts of multiple regression.

Table 6.2 Summary of Multiple Regression Analysis for First Outcome LV (Covariate Adjustment)

Variable	simple r	partial r	Coef.	S.E.	t
Sex	−0.20	−0.30	−2.26	0.37	−6.16
White	−0.13	0.10	1.83	0.80	2.30
Black	0.24	0.15	3.60	1.12	3.23
Fatheduc	−0.43	−0.24	−0.40	0.08	−4.95
Motheduc	−0.40	−0.10	−0.19	0.10	−1.95
OKnutrition	−0.24	−0.15	−0.53	0.17	−3.38
# Children < 6 yrs	0.04	0.17	0.86	0.25	3.51
Aspirin (log)	0.18	0.16	0.57	0.17	3.38
Nursing (log)	−0.33	−0.17	−0.46	0.13	−3.62
MIISss18	0.21	0.21	0.43	0.10	4.47
Alcohol LV1	0.29	0.26	0.37	0.07	5.42

Notes: $R^2 = 0.42$; N = 428 (581 cases minus 153 due to missing data on Fatheduc, Nursing, and MIISss18). All correlations and regression statistics incorporate case weights computed as explained in Section 6.1. The "simple" correlations are correlations with the response LV ignoring all other predictors in the model; "partial" correlations are adjusted for the other predictors. See Table 6.1 for definition of terms. Higher scores on the Outcome LV represent poorer performance.

The next section, and then Chapter 7, will pursue a rather different approach to the assessment of covariate effects upon smaller sets of outcomes that have a well-defined factor structure.

6.3 Partial Latent Variable Scores

The partial correlations of alcohol with our principal outcome LVs are very stable against adjustment for covariates measured at any wave of data collection; our confidence that this represents a true dose-response relationship is increased. It is of interest, therefore, to see whether this demonstrated effect of alcohol can be somehow distributed over the different ages at which we measured our subjects. We carry out this analysis by *disaggregating* the single outcome LV score from Table 5.1 into four partial latent variables, or PLVs. (The 8-month and 18-month data blocks are combined because they are separately so small.) We concentrate upon the first of the two pooled outcome LVs, the one salient for the "moderately binge-weighted pattern of alcohol saliences" (the "MAXD profile") that defines the

Table 6.3 Summary of Multiple Regression Analysis for Second Outcome LV (Covariate Adjustment)

Variable	simple r	partial r	Coef.	S.E.	t
Sex	−0.14	−0.22	−1.11	0.24	−4.65
Fatheduc	−0.40	−0.15	−0.20	0.06	−3.21
SES	0.42	0.12	0.39	0.16	2.44
OKnutrition	−0.22	−0.11	−0.26	0.11	−2.35
#Children in house	−0.01	−0.11	−0.39	0.18	−2.22
#Children < 6yrs	0.04	0.15	0.74	0.23	3.17
Nursing(log)	−0.33	−0.25	−0.42	0.08	−5.20
MIISss18	0.22	0.20	0.27	0.06	4.28
Alcohol LV2	0.33	0.30	0.50	0.08	6.37

Notes: $R^2 = 0.39$;   N = 428 (581 cases minus 153 due to missing data on Fatheduc, Nursing[log], and MIISss18). All correlations and regression statistics incorporate case weights computed as explained in Section 6.1. The "simple" correlations are correlations with the response LV ignoring all other predictors in the model; "partial" correlations are adjusted for the other predictors. See Table 6.1 for definition of terms. Higher scores on the Outcome LV represent poorer performance.

first LV in Table 5.1 and the horizontal axis in Figures 5.1 and 5.2. Scores on the first latent variable that we plotted in Figure 6.1(a) can then be thought of as sums of four "partial latent variable scores" (PLVs), each representing the sum over one examination wave of the saliences times the scaled (mean zero, variance one) variable values for that wave. We computed these four PLV scores explicitly, case by case, and normalized each to mean 0 and variance 1. Analyses of these PLVs on all the cases in the data set utilize the "net salience" case weights described above. In Chapter 8, we will disaggregate these scores further, into a collection of 15 PLVs that are subdivided by domain as well as by time.

At the conclusion of all this arithmetic, each of our 581 cases has a profile on four partial LV scores, one for each block, each having mean zero and variance one. The distributions of these PLVs, Figure 6.3, show them to be satisfactorily symmetrical in most cases. Their matrix of intercorrelations, Table 6.4, shows that the PLVs for the last three ages are substantially inter-correlated, but these do not correlate with the neonatal ("Wave-0") PLV even though it, too, correlates highly with Alcohol exposure. The Alcohol LV is most highly correlated with the Outcome PLV from the Neonatal period, next most highly with the 7-year PLV and the 4-year PLV, but very little with the 8–18-month PLV. In retrospect, it is difficult to say to what extent this discrepancy represents the sensitivity of the tests selected at birth, 4 and 7 years, or instead certain characteristics of the developmental sequence that makes the middle infancy period less salient for teratologic outcomes (see Table 6.4). (We reserve until

Table 6.4 Correlations Among Four Age-specific Partial LV Scores and the First Alcohol LV

	Alcohol LV1	PLV-0	PLV-8/18	PLV-4
PLV-0	0.38			
PLV-8/18	0.15	0.07		
PLV-4	0.22	0.08	0.40	
PLV-7	0.25	0.05	0.38	0.63

Notes: Correlations incorporate case weights computed as explained in Section 6.1.

Chapter 8 further discussion of the PLVs broken down by time and domain. There we will see that the outcome block PLVs measured at the same wave are generally correlated.)

Now we examine the impact of alcohol on the child performance outcomes, considered wave by wave. Table 6.5 summarizes the findings of the PLS analysis of Chapter 5 by wave of measurement.

While the saliences of individual outcome scores are those of the large two-block PLS analysis reported in Section 5.3, it is convenient to report them in order of wave of measurement. The profile of outcomes we see as we trace the impact of alcohol across the various ages at which the children were examined is as follows. At Day One, on the Brazelton Examination, prenatal alcohol was associated

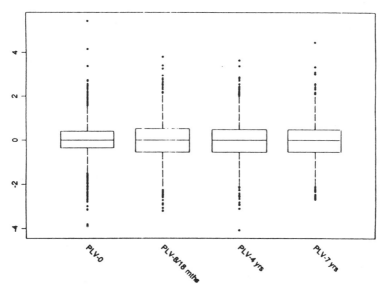

Figure 6.3. Boxplots of the five Partial LV scores, showing reasonably symmetric distributions of scores. The PLV scores, and also those in Chapter 8, have been z-scored. Positive scores are those positively predicted by alcohol dose, i.e., performance deficits. The central box ranges from sample 25th percentile to sample 75th percentile. The dashed lines continue out to 10th percentile and 90th percentile above and below. Other dots are single subjects. These PLVs are further disaggregated by domain of measurement in Figure 8.1.

with poorer habituation, a weaker Moro reflex, difficulty in eliciting several newborn reflexes (walking and placing thresholds), sustained head movement (head lift), resistance to and hypertonic recoil from passive movement of arms, immediate incurvation reflex, fewer smiles, excessive hand-to-mouth activity, and weak crawling attempts. At age 8 and 18 months, the Bayley Scales and Infant Behavior Record did not yield any relationships as strong as those at the other ages. At 4 years prenatal alcohol related to poorer mental development, poorer arithmetic skills, and poorer information-processing as well as a cluster of behaviors including poor attention span, poor goal directedness, frequent verbalizations, and excessive interruptions. At 7 years, by far the largest number of outcomes were related to prenatal alcohol exposure, including poor arithmetic and spelling skills, memory for digits, impulsive errors on a vigilance test, and poor written skills, including verbal syntax, and mean length of utterance. (Other items from the Neuromotor and LD Blocks will be discussed in Chapter 8.)

We now turn our attention to the longitudinal path model for the effect of prenatal alcohol at 4 ages of development, with appropriate covariate adjustment. Figure 6.2 diagrams this process. Table 6.6 summarizes a sequence of four multiple regression models, based on Figure 6.2, that allows us to assess "new Alcohol effects" as they are revealed in the succession of waves of measurement. First, in Table 6.6(a), is an analysis of the Wave-0 PLV. From the collection of prenatal genetic and environmental factors, only race (an indicator for Blacks, who score worse, on average, on this PLV) appears as a nominally significant correlate of the Wave-0 PLV along with the Alcohol LV. The partial correlation of the Alcohol LV with the Wave-0 PLV, adjusting for race, is quite high, approximately 0.37. This is nearly identical to the unadjusted correlation reported in Table 6.4.

Continuing to move forward on Figure 6.2, our analysis of the Wave-8/18 PLV includes adjustment only for the pre/neonatal environmental factors (Table 6.6b). Thus covariates such as nursing, mother-child interaction, and assessments of household changes are reserved for adjustment of the Wave-4 PLV. Sex, education of the

Table 6.5 Child Outcomes at Each Age Most Salient for Alcohol (LV1) from the PLS Analysis Disaggregated by Exam Age

Age 0 (Brazelton Exam and Reflexes)
- Habituation to Light (poorer)
- Habituation to Rattle (poorer)
- Smiles (fewer)
- Walk Threshold (delayed)
- Incurvation Threshold (instant)
- Hand-to-Mouth Activity (more)
- Passive Arms Reflex (hypertonic)
- Moro Reflex (weaker)

Age 8–18 months (Bayley Mental & Motor Scales and Infant Behavior Record)
    (None as salient as those at other ages)

Age 4 years (Neurobehavioral Battery)
- Frequent Verbal Interruptions and Excessive Talking (more)
- Fine Motor: Time in Error (parent rating) (more)
- General Body Tone (examiner rating) (hypertonic)
- Attention Span (examiner rating) (poorer)
- Goal Directedness (examiner rating) (poorer)
- General Mental Development (examiner rating) (poorer)
- WPSSI Full Scale IQ (lower)
- WPSSI Arithmetic Subtest (lower)
- WPSSI Picture Completion Subtest (lower)

Age 7 years (Neurobehavioral Battery)
- Written Syntax Errors (Johnson Sentence Building Test) (more)
- Mean Length of Utterance, Written (Johnson Sentence Building Test) (lower)
- Errors of Commission, AX Task (more)
- WISC-R Digit Span (lower)
- WISC-R Block Design (lower)
- WISC-R Arithmetic (lower)
- WRAT-R Arithmetic (lower)
- WRAT-R Spelling (lower)

father, and (log) parity are all apparently significant correlates of the Wave-8/18 PLV, while the correlation of the Wave-0 PLV with the Wave-8/18 PLV (and, hence, the indirect effect of the Alcohol LV through the outcomes measured at birth) is negligible. The direct or new effect of Alcohol measured over the time from 8 to 18 months is reflected in the partial correlation of 0.13 between the Alcohol LV and the Wave-8 PLV. This value, too, is little changed from the unadjusted correlation in Table 6.4.

The Wave-8/18 PLV is a highly significant predictor of the Wave-4 PLV (partial correlation 0.32) along with sex, indicators for whites and blacks (both scoring worse on average than the pool of all other races, with blacks scoring lowest), and parental education, both father's and mother's (Table 6.6c). From among the 8-to-18-month environmental measures, the 18-month mother-child interaction appears as a highly significant correlate of the Wave-4 PLV. (It is less clearly significant after inclusion of the Alcohol LV.) Inclusion of this mother-child interaction score reduces the sample size for the regression analysis by 57 cases (to 428) because of missing data. The computed partial correlation of alcohol with the Wave-4 PLU is estimated to be 0.18 after all these adjustments. Thus, despite the high autocorrelation of the (Alcohol-related) Wave-8/18 and Wave-4 PLVs, we estimate the direct or new effect of Alcohol measured at 4 years to be about 0.18. That is, most of the unadjusted correlation of 0.22 (Table 6.4) can be interpreted as "new effect."

Finally, our analysis of the Wave-7 PLV considers adjustment for the Wave-4 PLV (and the Wave-0 and Wave-8/18 PLVs) along with genetic and environmental factors measured up through the age-4 examination. The summary in Table 6.6(d) indicates that the pair of PLVs from Waves 8-18 and Wave-4 are important correlates of the Wave-7 PLV along with sex, an indicator for blacks, father's education, and an indicator of household changes for low-SES families. The partial correlation/new effect of Alcohol is estimated to be 0.15; the marginal (unadjusted) correlation was 0.25.

We conclude that each wave of measurement has tapped substantially new effects of prenatal alcohol exposure neither explained by prior environmental factors nor expressed in terms of deficits measured at earlier ages. We have already shown a similar progressive infusion of alcohol effect upon the Mental part of this sequence (Fig. 5.5). The magnitude of this steady infusion of Alcohol effect seems commensurate with an equally steady "drip" of gender effect across the successive waves of the study, with partial correlations for Sex ranging from –0.13 to –0.18, the minus sign meaning that girls score better. Similarly, parental education appears to have new favorable consequences for successive waves of measurement, consequences not explained by outcomes (related to parental education) at earlier ages.

6.4 Summary

In this chapter we have studied individual children in terms of their scores on the Alcohol and Outcome LVs defined in Chapter 5 by analysis of the cross-correlation matrix for the 13 prenatal alcohol measures and all 474 outcomes considered in this monograph.We be-

Table 6.6 Longitudinal Sequence of Regression Models for Age-specific Partial Latent Variables (see Figure 6.2)

(a) Regression model for PLV-0

Variable	simple r	partial r	Coef.	S.E.	t
Black	0.09	0.16	0.61	0.16	3.81
Alcohol LV1	**0.38**	0.37	0.14	0.015	9.49

N=581; $R^2 = 0.16$

(b) Regression model for PLV-8/18

Variable	simple r	partial r	Coef.	S.E.	t
PLV–0	0.07	–0.01	–0.01	0.048	–0.20
Sex	–0.13	–0.13	–0.27	0.095	–2.87
Parity (log)	0.11	0.14	0.31	0.098	3.13
Fatheduc	–0.23	–0.23	–0.08	0.017	–4.96
Alcohol LV1	**0.15**	0.13	0.05	0.019	2.75

N=480; $R^2 = 0.10$

(table continues on next page)

Table 6.6 (Continued) Longitudinal Sequence of Regression Models

(c) Regression model for PLV–4

Variable	simple r	partial r	Coef.	S.E.	t
PLV–0	0.08	–0.06	–0.06	0.044	–1.28
PLV–8/18	0.40	0.32	0.29	0.042	6.93
Sex	–0.16	–0.17	–0.32	0.091	–3.50
White	–0.05	0.12	0.46	0.195	2.37
Black	0.17	0.12	0.67	0.273	2.44
Fatheduc	–0.32	–0.11	–0.05	0.020	–2.23
Mothdegree	–0.35	–0.16	–0.16	0.049	–3.32
MIISss18	0.15	0.10	0.05	0.024	2.05
Alcohol LV1	**0.22**	0.18	0.07	0.018	3.67

N=428; R^2 = 0.31

(d) Regression model for PLV–7

Variable	simple r	partial r	Coef.	S.E.	t
PLV–0	0.05	–0.12	–0.09	0.037	–2.37
PLV–8/18	0.38	0.16	0.12	0.037	3.32
PLV–4	0.63	0.49	0.46	0.040	11.50
Sex	–0.19	–0.18	–0.28	0.076	–3.70
Black	0.24	0.16	0.56	0.165	3.39
Fatheduc	–0.42	–0.30	–0.10	0.015	–6.33
HhChg18Low (log)	0.11	–0.12	–0.19	0.079	–2.44
Alcohol LV1	**0.25**	0.15	0.05	0.015	3.08

N=426; R^2 = 0.52

Notes: All correlations and regression statistics incorporate case weights computed as explained in Section 6.1. Sample sizes vary in tables (a) – (d) depending on how many cases had data available for the selected covariates. See Table 6.1 for definition of terms.

gan with explanations of how we compute latent variable scores in view of missing data and how we approach the analysis of competing effects of covariates measured over the first 7.5 years of this longitudinal study. We then proceeded through a sequence of analyses of outcome latent variable scores computed at two different levels: LV scores aggregated over all 5 waves of measurement of outcomes, and PLV scores specific to only one or two of those waves.

First we considered scores on the two composite principal latent variables from Chapter 5; these were computed from all 474 outcomes. Next we considered "partial LV" (PLV) scores computed by disaggregating the principal outcome LV according to the waves of examination. Our analyses of the principal outcome LVs and of the examination-wave specific PLVs were by multiple regression on the principal Alcohol LV and covariates. The analysis of the examination-wave PLVs was explicitly longitudinal according to a procedure which allowed us to estimate "new effects" of prenatal alcohol exposure—effects manifest at a later age which were not predicted by alcohol-related outcome deficits at earlier ages.

We draw a pair of striking conclusions from these analyses of LV scores.

1. The principal Alcohol-Outcome LV correlations are *not* confounded by any of our measured genetic, demographic, or environmental covariates. Indeed, in the context of a multiple regression equation, the Alcohol LV score for the first Outcome LV—that corresponding to the moderately binge-weighted or "MAXD-type" Alcohol profile—explains nearly as much variance in the Outcome LV scores as the combined effects of paternal and maternal education, or the single "most significant" predictor, child's sex. In view of the fact that parental education has generally proved to be the most significant correlate of a wide variety of child outcomes, that prenatal Alcohol exposure has effects of nearly the same magnitude on this Outcome LV provides strong support for the assertion that these Alcohol effects are "real." Thus our consideration of all 474 outcomes in a PLS analysis has permitted us to identify a dimension of

alcohol effects in children which is only slightly confounded by the usual environmental effects.

2. The longitudinal analysis of PLV scores shows that "new effects" of prenatal alcohol exposure have been identified at each successive wave of examination. That is, PLV scores representing alcohol-related deficits at later ages reflect child characteristics which were previously unobserved or unmeasured in that they were not fully explained by earlier alcohol-related deficits and environmental covariates. Thus, for example, although the 7-year alcohol-related PLV is highly correlated (0.63) with the 4-year PLV, it retains a significant partial correlation of 0.15 with the principal Alcohol LV even after adjustment for the 4-year PLV, earlier PLV scores, and other covariates such as child's sex and parental education. (The last two covariates may also be said to demonstrate new effects on child outcomes at 7 years.) Had we stopped our longitudinal study of prenatal alcohol effects at any age earlier than 7 years, the findings against alcohol would not have been as strong.

## CHAPTER 7

Alcohol Effects on Learning Problems, Achievement Scores and IQ, with Covariate Adjustments

In all previous chapters, we have examined how prenatal alcohol affects the underlying processes of attention, neuromotor and mental development across the first seven years of life. The integrity of these underlying neurobehavioral processes should support the basic task of academic learning that is the main preoccupation of children during the school-age years. In this chapter we study how well the children meet the academic challenge of school, by examining learning problems defined in a variety of ways.

The study children were examined at the end of the first grade in order to evaluate how well they met the behavioral and performance demands of school. In this chapter we examine these data as a learning disabilities block (LD-7).

In Section 7.1 we describe our LD-7 block, which contains 81 items with some face validity for learning problems at 7 years. Then we use a two-block PLS analysis to examine which alcohol scores are most salient for these learning problems and which types of learning and behavior problems are most salient for alcohol. In this section we also assess the relevance of one of the "traditional" methods of evaluating learning disabilities, namely that of "IQ minus achievement." We will discover that this construct is an inappropriate outcome for a behavioral teratology study.

As we expect that some of the learning and behavioral problems are related to important sociodemographic variables, in Section 7.2 we describe a new method for examining covariate effects on some standardized measures of individual performance. This method allows

143

us to statistically adjust for SES effects only on those aspects of a data set that are truly SES-related.

Finally in the last section of this chapter, Section 7.3, we describe how we use this covariate adjustment system to examine prenatal alcohol effects on two standardized tests relevant to learning problems assessed at the 7-year evaluation: the WISC-R, and the Myklebust Pupil Rating Scale. In each of these we apply a covariate adjustment to the summary score and then study the prenatal alcohol effects on the individual items that make up that adjusted summary score.

7.1 Learning Problems and the LD-7 Block

The term "learning disability" was apparently first used and defined by Kirk (1962). The term referred to a discrepancy between a child's apparent capacity to learn and his or her level of achievement. This was a useful construct for the classroom—perhaps children whose poor academic performance was incongruent with their intellectual capabilities might require different pedagogical methods than those whose academic performance was limited by their abilities. A review of the LD classifications for 49 of 50 states revealed that 28 of the states included IQ/Achievement discrepancy criteria in their LD guidelines (Frankenberger & Harper, 1987). This characterization of LD is sketched by the right-hand shaded area, "LD [Kirk]," in Figure 7.1.

For our purposes, which involve the causes rather than the consequences of low achievement, we propose to adapt the "Minimal Brain Dysfunction" (MBD) model popular in the 1960s and 70s (e.g., Strauss & Lehtinen, 1947; Strauss & Kephart, 1955; Clements, 1966; Gross & Wilson, 1974). This definition presumes that learning problems are due to minimal brain dysfunction when they occur in the presence of hyperactivity, perceptual motor deficits, impulsivity, emotional instability, short attention span, coordination deficits, distractibility, diverse neurologic signs, or abnormalities of the EEG (Clements & Peters, 1962). It follows that any *cause* of minimal brain damage, such as parental alcohol exposure, applies

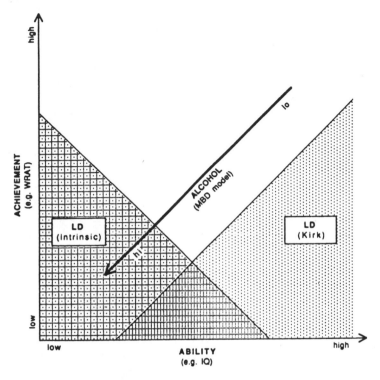

Figure 7.1. Alternate characterizations of "learning disability." Axes are hypothetical ability and achievement scores. "LD Kirk," region of ability-achievement discrepancy; alcohol does not predict to this category. "LD intrinsic," region of lowered ability **and** achievement; alcohol predicts to this category (our "minimal brain damage" model) along the regression vector shown.

jointly to IQ, Achievement, and many other indications. This model of learning disabilities (sketched by the left-hand shaded area, "LD [intrinsic]," in Figure 7.1) is much more in line with that more recently endorsed by the National Joint Committee for Learning Disabilities (NJCLD), 1981:

'Learning disabilities' is a generic term that refers to a heterogeneous group of disorders manifested by significant difficulties in the acquisition and use of listening, speaking, reading, writing, reasoning or mathematical abilities. These disorders are intrinsic to the individual and presumed to be due to central nervous system dysfunction. Even though a learning disability may occur concomitantly with other handicapping conditions (e.g., sensory impairment, mental retardation, social and emotional disturbance) or environmental influences (e.g., cultural differences, insufficient/inappropriate instruction, psychogenic factors), it is not the direct result of those conditions or influences.

This characterization of learning problems as consequences of central nervous system (CNS) dysfunction is sketched with a solid line in Figure 7.1, indicating the role of prenatal alcohol as one cause of learning disabilities. This definition is compatible with the broad array of potential indicators of learning problems assembled in our LD-7 Block (see Appendix III, Block 15). The analyses in this section will help determine which of these potential indicators of learning problems are, in fact, associated with prenatal alcohol exposure in the young school-age child.

It is clearly not possible to "diagnose" LD the way a broken bone can be seen in an x-ray. It is, in fact, a *latent classification*, related to the sort of latent variables we have been discussing throughout this monograph. Furthermore, the developmental nature of LD implies that assessment of a subject's learning disability at 7 years of age is only a first glimpse of a full career of abilities and disabilities. Our block thus represents only a sampling of the earliest information relevant to the concept of LD.

Although it might be argued that earlier deficits predispose a child for learning disabilities, our LD-7 block was assembled entirely from data gathered in conjunction with the 7-year-old examination. The 81 items in this block derive from questionnaires administered to teachers (the Myklebust Pupil Rating Scale [24 items] and other questions derived for this study), to parents (the Conners Parent/Child Rating Scale and other questions derived for this study), and to psychometrists who had administered psychological tests to these subjects in our laboratory. Performance test scores were not included in the LD-7 Block except for those comprising the traditional LD classification "IQ minus achievement." With the exception of these latter three "difference" scores, all data in the LD-7 Block derives from subjective ratings or actual academic classification. A listing of these items and some distribution data is presented in Appendix III.

7.1.1 PLS Analysis of Alcohol Effects on LD-7

PLS analysis of the LD-7 block against the Alcohol block shows it to be the most cleanly structured of all our outcome blocks: 88% of the full 13×81 cross-correlation matrix is explained by a single pair of LVs. That for Alcohol is the profile we have called "heightened binge," along the direction through ADOCCP in Figure 5.3. The correlation between alcohol and the learning disabilities block is 0.24. Table 7.1 shows that the LD-7 LV correlates substantially with all the binge indicators (P more strongly than D) but nearly zero with the frequency scores (AA and MOCC). We diagram this in Figure 7.2 by superimposing the line expressing this two-block PLS analysis over the points of the LD-7 block as they have already been displayed in Figure 5.2.

Figure 7.2 presents all 81 items from the LD-7 block in relation to their saliences for Alcohol. As in Figure 5.2, where these LD items were presented with all other outcomes, those items farthest from the origin are the most salient for Alcohol. The corner of the plot in which the variables fall is an artifact of their coding direction; in reality, all show the expected association with Alcohol. Just as in the PLS analyses of earlier chapters, we see that prenatal alcohol is related to outcomes assessed in our study in a variety of ways. The behavioral composite of alcohol-related learning problems in the second grade is diverse. Some of the most salient consequences of prenatal exposure include parent's ratings ACADADJ7 and SOCADJ7 (academic and social adjustment to school by the second grade), SPECPROG and SPECMATH (participation in special school programs, in particular for arithmetic), and teachers' ratings of Cooperation/impulsivity, Spelling, Retains information, Comprehends words, Grammar, Tactfulness, Word recall, and Arithmetic, as well as the total Myklebust PRS score (see Sec. 7.3.2 below). This is precisely what we hoped to see: a clear structure for the correlation matrix of LD-7 by Alcohol, showing certain outcomes to be coherently salient for a particular alcohol profile.

In a previous paper from this study (79) we reported a relationship between one alcohol score (BINGE) and one specific LD indicator (special programs in school). We found that 24% of the children whose mothers had reported binge drinking during pregnancy were in special remedial programs, compared with 15% of the rest of the group. The present findings are consistent with this earlier analysis, but go far beyond them. In the present PLS analysis, involving the Alcohol block (13 variables) and the LD-7 block (81 variables), we

Table 7.1 PLS Analysis of the LD Block

Alcohol LV Saliences		7–Year LD LV Saliences	
AAP	0.19	SPECMATH	0.16
AAD	−0.04	SOCADJ	0.19
BINGEP	0.33	ACADADJ7	0.22
BINGED	0.29	TOTALPRS	−0.19
ADOCCP	0.43	WORDRECL	−0.16
ADOCCD	0.29	COMPWD	−0.18
MAXP	0.39	ARITHTQ	−0.16
MAXD	0.27	RETAIN	−0.18
MOCCP	0.10	SPELLING	−0.18
MOCCD	−0.09	COOPR7	−0.20
QFVP	0.39	GRAMMAR	−0.18
QFVD	0.22	TACTFUL	−0.18
ORDEXC	0.22	•	
		•	
		•	

Summary:	
LV covariance	2.43
Fraction of squared correlation explained	0.88
LV correlation	0.24

Notes: Only those outcomes labelled on Figure 7.2 are listed here. The saliences here derive from a separate two–block analysis of Alcohol against the LD–7 variables only. They may be thought of as the projections of the points in Figure 7.2 along the long axis of the scatter there.

have the opportunity to see how the whole binge-weighted alcohol profile relates to a broad array of interrelated LD outcomes observed in 7-year-old children.

This behavioral composite, combined with alcohol-related performance deficits on the other Blocks, is supportive of the MBD characterization of LD. The "discrepancy" model of learning disabilities, proposed by Kirk, finds no support in these analyses. Three such discrepancy scores (IQ minus WRAT Reading; IQ minus WRAT Spelling; and IQ minus WRAT Arithmetic) were in the list of 81 variables examined in relation to IQ. All of these "discrepancy" scores correlated around zero with prenatal alcohol.

While the contrast of IQ with Achievement may be useful in a classroom context, it does not appear to be promising for teratology

Table 7.2 PLS Analysis of the NMot-7 Block

Alcohol LV Saliences		7–Year NMot LV Saliences	
AAP	0.27	CSHORC	0.19
AAD	0.25	D1REVCOP	0.27
BINGEP	0.28	D3QULCOP	0.24
BINGED	0.28	ELEMD	−0.19
ADOCCP	0.31	D5MEM	−0.20
ADOCCD	0.31	D1INTMEM	0.25
MAXP	0.31	RL1C	−0.16
MAXD	0.28	RL2E	−0.20
MOCCP	0.22	TIDDOM	−0.17
MOCCD	0.15	FSMDND	−0.17
QFVP	0.31	SPADDOM	−0.17
QFVD	0.32	SPADND	−0.27
ORDEXC	0.26	.	
		.	
		.	

Summary:	
LV covariance	1.91
Fraction of squared correlation explained	0.75
LV correlation	0.41

Notes: Only those outcomes labelled on Figure 7.3 are listed here. The saliences here derive from a separate two–block analysis of Alcohol against the LD–7 variables only. They may be thought of as the projections of the points in Figure 7.3 along the long axis of the scatter there.

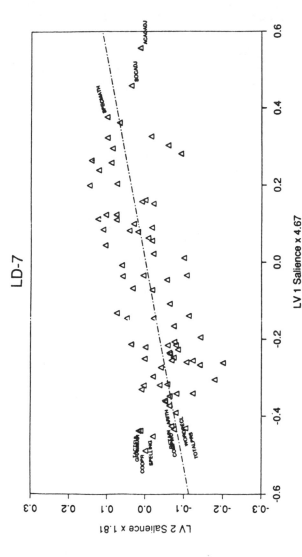

Figure 7.2. This scatter is a detail of the very large PLS analysis (Fig. 5.2) of the 13 Alcohol Scores by the 474 child outcomes. The detail separates out the 81 child outcomes included in the LD Block. Outcomes that are most salient for alcohol (at either end of the distribution) are labelled. The line superimposed across the scatter represents the LD PLV calculated in the separate Alc × LD Block PLS analysis (13 × 81). The direction of the line may be referred to the compass directions shown in Figure 5.3 for the types of alcohol LV most salient for these scores (here the binge-type scores).

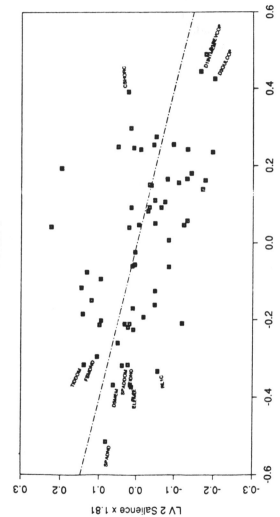

Figure 7.3. This scatter is also a detail from Figure 5.2, now separating out the 65 child outcomes included in the NMot-7 Block. Outcomes most salient for Alcohol are labelled. The superimposed line represents the NMot PLV calculated in a separate Alc ¥ NMot Block PLS analysis (13 ¥ 65). The direction of this line here corresponds to the mainly volume-type alcohol score from Figure 5.3.

research. IQ (or ability) does not cause Achievement to rise the way
weight training causes muscles to grow. In the teratogenic context,
IQ and achievement are more appropriately viewed as joint
consequences of a single underlying general factor that we have
previously called "minimal brain damage" (recall Figure 7.1).
Alcohol, then, can en-gender MBD, of which both ability and
achievement are among the observed consequences. At this earliest
educational period, we expect that Alcohol will account for ability
more strongly than for achievement, and indeed this is what we find.
Furthermore, Alcohol does not account for *all* components of ability
as measured on our IQ test, but rather for a specific pattern or profile
of scores that we will discuss below. Because covariates affect
primarily the general IQ factor, we may obtain a more precise
estimate of the alcohol-related components of IQ by the PLS
analysis that allows us to detect that particular pattern of behavioral
deficits most strongly associated with alcohol (see Section 7.2).

7.1.2 Comparison of the LD-7 Analysis to the NMot-7 Analysis

Figure 7.2 extracts from the overall PLS analysis of all 474 outcomes (Figure 5.2) the symbols corresponding to the outcomes of
the LD-7 block we have been discussing, and Figure 7.3 does the
same for the outcomes of the NMot-7 block, which will provide an
instructive contrast. The oblique lines superimposed over these figures correspond to the first Alcohol LV for PLS analyses of alcohol
against the items of one or the other of the blocks separately, either
LD-7 (Table 7.1) or NMot-7 (Table 7.2).   The obliqueness of the
lines implies that the blocks are salient for the 13 alcohol scores in
somewhat different patterns: LD-7 is somewhat more sensitive to
the binge-type scores (examine the sector in its direction in Figure
5.1), while the outcomes of NMot-7 are somewhat less sensitive to
these scores and somewhat more salient for the volume-type scores.
This is plain as well from the comparison of the relevant columns in
Tables 7.1 and 7.2.

The relation of the LD-7 block to alcohol is strikingly one-dimensional. This is clear in the tightness of the scatter in Figure 7.2
and in the fraction of summed squared correlation for its separate PLS

analysis: 88%, according to Table 7.1. In comparison, the scatter of saliences for the NMot-7 block, Figure 7.3, lies in a broader ellipse, corresponding to the explanation of only 75% of the relation to alcohol by one single block-specific alcohol LV, Table 7.2.

But the more binge-sensitive alcohol LV with which LD-7 is aligned is less reliable than the mostly-volume LV for which NMot-7 is most salient. Partly for this reason, as the tables show, the LD-7 LV is correlated 0.24 with its alcohol LV, whereas the NMot-7 LV is correlated a full 0.41 with its alcohol LV. In spite of the better fit of the rank-one (one-dimensional) PLS model for the alcohol-LD cross-correlations, the predictive power of the resulting pair of latent variables is lower than that for the relation of alcohol to the NMot-7 score, for which the fit of the basic PLS model to the cross-correlations is worse. (This illustrates the point made in Chapter 4 that the two figures of merit of the two-block PLS analysis, covariance of the LV pair and fraction of summed squared correlation explained by the LV pair, are logically independent.) The stronger dose-response relation of alcohol to the NMot-7 LV permits the detection (in the next chapter) of some individual children who appear truly fetal-alcohol-affected, in that they show systematic alcohol-related deficits across all waves of observation. No such detection is possible using the LD-7 LV because it does not correlate as well with alcohol; in fact, it does not correlate at all with alcohol within the subset of the 100 most exposed subjects (see, again, Chapter 8).

We suspect that the beginning of the second grade is simply too early to detect stable individual patterns of LD—not enough learning has taken place by this time even in the non-exposed children. Furthermore, with the exception of the IQ minus achievement "discrepancy" scores, the LD Block contains primarily behavior ratings by teachers and parents, not expected to be as sensitive a measure of MBD at this age as the laboratory neurobehavioral tasks comprising the NMot-7 Block. Finally, the "causes" of the behaviors in the LD block are much more diverse in this age group than just alcohol; they include strong SES effects and many other factors. (In contrast, there is relatively little SES effect upon the particular profile which is the NMot-7 LV.)

7.2   A New Method for Covariate Adjustment for Latent Variables

In this study we measured over 150 potential covariates, expecting from the child development literature that some would be associated with the outcomes reported. To the extent that these are also associated with alcohol, their influence on these outcomes might erroneously be attributed to alcohol unless some type of covariate adjustment was utilized in the analysis. Chapter 6 included multiple regression analyses adjusting ordinary two-block PLS LV scores for covariate effects. In this section, we consider a technique which instead adjusts the formulas of those PLS LVs *before* scores are computed. The adjustment is superior to that in Chapter 6 in that no particular roster of covariates need have been specified. In two interesting cases (IQ and the Myklebust Pupil Rating Scale), it will be possible to adjust out the effects of the covariates before any LV scores are computed at all, by removing the general factor of each block before scoring.

For this purpose, we recall that although PLS ignores within-block factor structures, they do exist and are the subject of a huge literature. As an example, consider the case of SES (which we use here to refer to our strongest SES-type covariates such as parental education, race, etc.). SES strongly affects child IQ and Achievement (more strongly, indeed, than does Alcohol). We could imagine a model in which Alcohol and SES somehow "jointly" affect IQ, but fitting such a model would engage us in the search for the proper scaling of SES, nonlinearities of its effect on IQ, and the like, all of which lead us far from our principal concern with Alcohol. It is more straightforward to argue that any SES effect upon IQ should be reviewed before we adjudicate Alcohol effects. Furthermore, this SES effect is likely to be an effect upon the ordinary IQ "general factor," the Full-Scale score, which is, more or less, the sum of our 11 items. We can perhaps adjust away all these effects (and also those of any other covariates) without even computing them if we instead adjust out the "effects" of Full-Scale IQ.

The simplest way to do this is to subtract a constant from each of the 11 IQ saliences so that the new, adjusted saliences sum to zero. The resulting "adjusted LV" is geometrically orthogonal to the full-scale score and taps the effects we expect from Alcohol after a complete elimination of all effects upon Full-Scale IQ, whether they owe to our covariates or any other determinants. The reader may choose to think of this as an "adjusted" LV in which it is the formula, not the score *per se*, that has been "adjusted." It is customary to refer to variables that vary around a uniform factor prediction as "profiled." Here, we shall refer to *profiled IQ LV* scores, etc., to distinguish these new scores from the unadjusted IQ LV scores, etc., with which we began. Any additional covariate effects upon these profiled LV scores are to be estimated by the usual multiple regression methods; but any such further "adjustments" in the pursuit of the arguments of this monograph (about the effects of alcohol) prove unnecessary. It will turn out that indeed all the covariate effects on these subblocks were borne by their general factors; the effects of covariates upon the profiled scores will be found insignificant in all the examples to follow. Notice that we are *not* adjusting out any of the covariates according to their measured values, of SES or anything else: instead we are suppressing the common factor of the subscale under study, IQ or "behavior problems," through which we have reason to expect that covariate effect ought to be channeled. As a result, it no longer makes any difference what selection rule might have been applied to winnow through the full list of 150 covariates for those that apply; to the extent that a covariate affects the scale's general factor, its effect is cancelled (adjusted away) automatically.

7.3 Determining Profiles of Alcohol Effects from Standardized Tests

We used this new method of covariate adjustment to determine profiles of alcohol effects on three standardized measures from our 7-year exam: the WISC-R IQ test, the WRAT-R Achievement Test, and the Myklebust Pupil Rating Scale filled out by classroom teachers. The method works well for the WISC-R and the Myklebust. For these, a profiled profile shows clear Alcohol effects nearly free of

SES confounding. This approach does not work for the WRAT-R, which was not intended to sum to a single score. In a profiled analysis using the strategy just reviewed, the less salient WRAT scores, Spelling and Reading, did not contribute to any contrast with Arithmetic that concentrated the effects of Alcohol. The WRAT "profile" does not serve to suppress the effect of covariates, but seems, at least in respect of the delineation of alcohol effects in the sample of seven-year-olds, to be pure noise. No further analysis of WRAT-R will be reported here.

7.3.1 Full-Scale IQ

We begin our exposition with an example of a conventional regression model such as has been previously reported from our project. Our example deals with the case of IQ as measured by the 11 subscales of the WISC-R at the 7-year exam. The matrix of correlations between the 13 Alcohol indicators and these subscales was presented in Table 4.1. That table does not give the correlations of these indicators with FULLIQ7; these range from 0.09 to –0.19. The correlation of FULLIQ7 with the Alcohol LV appropriate to that block is 0.17.

It is important to examine the extent to which this coefficient 0.17 is expressing causes of IQ that are different from Alcohol, yet, like SES, correlated with it to some extent. Exploration of potential covariates, without Alcohol in the model (as in Chapter 6), identified 11 variables from Table 6.1 that together explained about 36% of the variance in the full-scale IQ score. (Prior to these adjustments—indeed prior to any of the computations of this monograph—there were some "examiner effects" and a time-of-day effect that were adjusted out subscale by subscale.) This regression model for 7-year IQ, computed on 481 cases, is summarized in Table 7.3. The predictors of 7-year IQ are similar to those reported in our previous analysis of 4-year IQ scores (63).

Correlations of our usual 13 Alcohol measures with FULLIQ7 partialled on these 11 covariates ranged from about 0 to –0.10. The single alcohol measure with the highest partial correlation was BINGED. When included in the model, this binary indicator has a re-

Table 7.3   Regression analysis for Covariates of WISC-R IQ at 7
Years.

Variable	simple r	partial r	Coef.	S.E.	t
Sex	0.02	0.04	0.98	1.07	0.92
Black	−0.31	−0.20	−9.49	2.19	−4.33
Fatheduc	0.42	0.22	1.18	0.24	4.84
Mothdegree	0.44	0.20	2.63	0.60	4.39
OKnutrition	0.24	0.11	1.25	0.50	2.48
# Children < 6yrs	−0.07	−0.16	−2.66	0.75	−3.53
Aspirin (occ/mo > 4)	−0.13	−0.10	−3.53	1.64	−2.15
Sex*Aspirin (occ/mo > 4)	−0.08	−0.14	−9.74	3.27	−2.98
Nursing (log)	0.30	0.17	1.39	0.38	3.65
HhChg18Low (log)	−0.08	0.14	3.68	1.22	3.02
Child's nutrition	0.20	0.11	1.45	0.63	2.31

Notes: N=481. Residual standard error = 11.58. $R^2 = 0.36$.

gression coefficient of −12.65 with a standard error of 6.09 (and, hence, a Student t-ratio of 2.08). Closer examination of transformations of alcohol variables and their interactions with other terms in the model suggested the collapsing of AAD (net alcohol ingestion during midpregnancy) into a step function. The dichotomy cuts AAD at one ounce or more (approximately two drinks per day, on average). We also use its interactions (products) with paternal education and with measures of household size at various ages. These three terms increment the total R^2 by about .021; the F-statistic on 3 and 466 df has a nominal p-value below .01. Findings similar to these were published in an earlier report from this study (79).

The Alcohol LV from PLS, when substituted for this set of three alcohol-derived predictors, contributes little to this regression (partial correlation 0.07, regression coefficient 0.30, t=1.5). That is, the Alc LV really does not improve the prediction of FULLIQ7 at all. But it was not supposed to: FULLIQ7 represents the "general factor" of IQ, the LV for predicting the IQ subscales by a full-scale score, not for their prediction by Alcohol.

As a first step in the clarification of the effect of Alcohol on IQ, therefore, we might substitute the IQ LV computed by PLS in Chapter 4 for that supplied by the publisher (i.e., for Full-Scale IQ).

The effect of the covariates is still large ($R^2 = 0.34$). The Alcohol LV now has a partial correlation of 0.12, conventionally "significant" at about the p=.01 level, and the nominal significance of the three-term alcohol effect involving the dichotomization of AAD increases similarly (p<.001).

This issue of alcohol interactions involving variables having significant main effects already confounded with alcohol has arisen in many of our earlier publications on this sample. Our earlier analyses of the alcohol effects on 7-year outcomes reported that two postnatal environment interactions (Alcohol by lower parental education and by more older children in the household) predicted decrements in "intellectual functioning" (the IQ latent variable) (76); and parental education interacted with Alcohol in predicting a very broad neurobehavioral LV (66). Similar findings were reported on a cross-sectional study of Full-Scale IQ at 7 years (76). None of these "interactions" drained substantial covariance from the Alcohol main effect.

In the presence of unbalanced designs such as ours in respect of Alcohol and SES, for instance, nonlinearities of the SES effect may appear as interactions instead. See also Bookstein (1990). To avoid this confounding of nonlinearity with interaction, we partial out the effects of SES by instead "removing" all the "effects" of the IQ score that SES might be expected to modify, linearly or otherwise.

The situation becomes hugely different when we substitute the *profiled IQ LV* for the previous (unprofiled) IQ LV. Recall from Section 7.2 that the value of this profiled LV is the value of the LV computed *after* adjusting the saliences by subtracting their grand mean, so that they now sum to exactly zero. In effect, we have regressed full-scale IQ out of the individual block scores *after* computing the two-block PLS analysis in respect of alcohol. The profiled saliences, plotted in Figure 7.4, now represent a contrast between scores of subscales like ARITH7, subscales highly salient for alcohol dose, with scores of subscales such as OBJ7 that are much less salient for alcohol dose. When the IQ LV formula is profiled in this way, the effect of the covariates drops from 32% of the variance to about 4% (which is only marginally significant).

Consideration of the 13 alcohol measures reveals QFVD as the best single predictor of profiled IQ, now with a partial correlation coefficient of –0.17, just slightly better than the Alcohol LV with a partial correlation of 0.16. The Alcohol LV thus explains another .026 of the variance (over half as much as the effect of all the "covariates" combined). *This is exactly what the Alcohol LV is supposed to do*: account for the *pattern* of deficit, not "explain" the "variance" of IQ.

The partial correlation coefficient of the Alcohol LV and the IQ profile LV, 0.16, is little changed from the original correlation of 0.17 between the Alcohol and IQ LVs. Thus the combination of PLS and profiling has made the multiple regression unnecessary (ex-

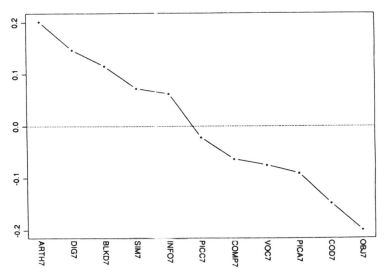

Saliences for Centered IQ LV

Figure 7.4. Saliences of the IQ scales with respect to Alcohol, plotted as a centered profile. The "profiled IQ LV score" that uses these centered values for its saliences will be uncorrelated with any covariate of IQ that affects all the subscales equally—any covariate that, like SES, appears to operate by affecting the General Factor of IQ.

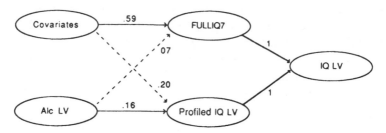

Figure 7.5. Path model explaining the decomposition of the IQ LV into FULLIQ7 (an IQ score computed with equal weights/saliences for all subscales), predicted mainly by covariates, and a profiled IQ LV predicted more substantially by Alcohol LV1. Path coefficients of 1 from FSIQ and the profiled IQ LV into the IQ LV are fixed by construction (see text). Coefficients for paths from the Alc LV are partial correlations; on paths from the covariates, coefficients are the multiple correlation coefficients for regressions without Alcohol. The effect of profiling is to nearly double the partial correlation with the alcohol LV and drop that with parental education by a factor of three.

cept for purposes of verification that covariates affect the general factor, FULLIQ7, not the profiled score). In this case, the explanatory power of the Alcohol LV persisted unchanged across the circumvention of covariate main effects that originally explained eight times as much variance. Of course we have not "created" any new alcohol effect. We have left unchanged the portion of the variation of IQ, subscale by subscale, that is salient for alcohol. Owing to the suppression of the covariate effects on their common factor, however, we have increased the corresponding partial correlation to about 0.17; in addition, we have made any further search for covariates unpromising, since the most significant predictor of raw child's IQ, parental education, has now ceased to be a significant predictor in the profile.

Figure 7.5 summarizes this analysis. The numbers labelling the arrows are regression coefficients. The coefficients of "1" connecting each of FULLIQ7 and the profiled IQ LV to the IQ LV indicate that the sum of FSIQ (with constant saliences across the subscales) and the profiled IQ LV exactly yields the original IQ LV.

7.3.2 The Myklebust Pupil Rating Scale

We analyzed the battery of 24 Myklebust items (each coded on a scale from 1–5 as indicated in Appendix III) in the same manner as the IQ subscales. A regression model for the total score (sum of 24 items), built following the procedure described in Chapter 6, suggests eight covariates measured up through the 4-year measurement period. These explain approximately 28% of the variance in the Myklebust total score (Table 7.4). (Had we considered 7-year covariates, we would have found that the number of children older than 5 in the household significantly improves this prediction, with a partial correlation of –0.15. "Adjusting" for this extra covariate actually slightly increases the partial correlations with the Alcohol measures.)

Correlations of the 13 Alcohol indicators with the Myklebust PRS partialled on these eight covariates range from near 0 to –0.11 for QFVP. This single best Alcohol measure has a coefficient of –18.23, standard error 7.55, and t-value 2.41. The Alcohol LV from the comprehensive two-block PLS analysis has a partial correlation

Table 7.4 Regression analysis for Covariates of Myklebust Total PRS Score

Variable	simple r	partial r	Coef.	S.E.	t
Sex	0.20	0.23	5.86	1.18	4.95
Black	−0.26	−0.17	−9.51	2.56	−3.71
Fatheduc	0.38	0.21	1.25	0.27	4.56
Mothdegree	0.33	0.10	1.46	0.65	2.23
Aspirin (occ/mo > 4)	−0.15	−0.11	−4.49	1.84	−2.44
Nursing (log)	0.26	0.12	1.10	0.43	2.58
HhChg18Low (log)	−0.05	0.11	3.14	1.37	2.30
MIISss18	−0.21	−0.17	−1.15	0.32	−3.60

Notes: N=464. Residual standard error = 12.64. $R^2 = 0.28$.

of –0.09. As in the case of the IQ analysis, measures of prenatal alcohol exposure contribute relatively little to the model for the Myklebust total PRS score as judged by R^2 or partial correlation.

Replacing the total score by the Myklebust LV (from a two-block analysis of the 13 Alcohol measures against 24 Myklebust items [67]), the partial correlations with Alcohol increase slightly (to –0.12 for QFVP and –0.10 for the Alcohol LV). But the profiled Myklebust LV, computed in the same manner as the profiled IQ LV, has only 7% of its variance explained by the joint effect of these eight covariates, and the partial correlations with the Alcohol measures increase substantially. The most significant individual alcohol measure, MAXP, now bears a partial correlation of –0.15, and many others have partial correlations exceeding –0.10, while the Alc LV

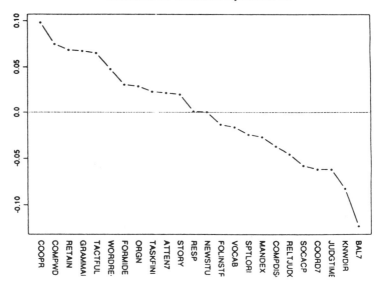

Figure 7.6. Saliences of the Myklebust items with respect to Alcohol, plotted as a centered profile.

has a partial correlation of –0.14. Figure 7.6 plots the profile of profiled saliences. In the multiple regression of the Myklebust profile LV on the Alc LV and covariates, only the indicator for blacks appears to remain clearly significant. The partial correlations of the Alcohol scores are now mostly greater than 0.10, with BINGEP, QFVD, and the Alcohol LV all exceeding 0.15. Thus, as was the case for IQ, the Alcohol LV explains well the pattern of deficit on the Myklebust items. On the other hand, the usual SES-like covariates, which correlate with the total score, do not predict this profiled LV. Their effects are rather on the Total PRS score, which has been subtracted out explicitly.

7.4 Summary

We began this chapter by constructing Learning Disability as a latent variable. Using PLS, we examined which of the 81 assorted manifestations of learning problems assembled in our LD-7 block were most salient for Alcohol. Among the most Alcohol-salient components of the LD-7 LV were academic problems as determined by both the school and the parents and also the total score on the Myklebust Pupil Rating Scale (which signals children at risk for learning disabilities). Within that scale, a series of classroom behaviors were also salient for Alcohol, including memory and language problems (Retains information, Word recall, Comprehends words, Grammar) but also problems with behavioral regulation (such as Cooperation/impulsivity). There were also strong Alcohol saliences for academic and social adjustment problems as rated by a parent, and placement in remedial arithmetic programs. The diversity of this LD-7 LV indicates that already by the end of the first grade in school there are manifest not only learning problems associated with prenatal alcohol exposure but also problems of social adjustment not previously noted in this cohort in assessments from the preschool period.

The Alcohol LV most salient for learning problems in the second grade is the "heightened binge" profile, which incorporates all of our binge measures of alcohol (particularly in the pre-pregnancy period) but not the volume measures (such as the AA scores) or the number of drinking occasions. Compared to the more biologic NMot-7 LV examined in the next chapter, however, the LD-7 LV at grade 2 reflects stronger SES influences.

We have described a new method of covariate adjustment in batteries of strong factor structure. When covariates affect mainly the general factor, their effects can be nearly eliminated by centering the profile so as to eliminate the general factor. While this adjustment is carried out *after* the PLS analysis, and so leaves the algebraic ordering of the outcome saliences unchanged, it may also be thought of as adjusting the outcomes for any covariate influences they have in common *prior to* our PLS study of alcohol effects. For both the Mykelbust Pupil Rating Scale and the WISC-R IQ battery, this adjustment clarifies the effect of the Alcohol LV without any loss in its predictive power.

The analyses in this chapter indicate that for a teratology study such as this, the "IQ minus Achievement" construct of learning disabilities leads to impossible conceptual difficulties. We cannot attribute any part of "achievement adjusted for IQ" to alcohol inasmuch as the effect of Alcohol is stronger upon IQ than upon Achievement itself at this young age. It is SES-adjusted IQ profile, not IQ-adjusted Achievement, that shows the effect of Alcohol most clearly at this first examination within the school-age years.

## CHAPTER 8

Detection of Individual Children with Alcohol-Related Profiles

In this final chapter of data analysis, we begin to consider the following pair of difficult questions: Who are the individual children affected by prenatal alcohol? How do we detect them? We approach these questions by asking whether individual subjects with elevated Alcohol effects at one age or on one domain also show elevated Alcohol effects at other ages or on other domains.

We begin by computing Partial LV scores as explained in Section 6.3, but now disaggregating the scores on the principal Outcome LV score of Section 6.2 into 15 PLV scores, one for each of the blocks defined by measurement wave and domain. That is, for each of the 15 outcome blocks we compute the sum of the saliences times the scaled (mean zero, variance one) variable values for that block. The 15 sets of derived PLV scores are then standardized to mean zero and variance 1 for easy comparison across ages and domains.

The distributions of these PLV scores are shown in Figure 8.1. Their matrix of intercorrelations, Table 8.1, shows some interesting patterns. The variables measured at the same wave are generally correlated—those among the four age-7 measures average about 0.5, for instance, as do those among the three age-4 measures—whereas the "longitudinal" correlations relating LVs of the same name at different waves are generally lower. An exception is the correlation of 0.70 between the age-4 and age-7 Mental LVs. Furthermore, the Ment-4 PLV score actually correlates quite substantially with *all* the age-7 PLV scores. (We will see some consequences of this strength of correlation later.) The other strong cross-wave correlations involve the Learning Disabilities PLV, which correlates 0.4 to 0.5 with all of the age-4 PLVs. But we do not pursue this interesting observation

165

Table 8.1 Correlations Among 15 Partial LV Scores and the First Alcohol LV

	AlcLV	Att-0	NMot-0	Att-8	NMot-8	Ment-8	Att-18	NMot-18	Ment-18
AlcLV		0.33	0.28	0.18	0.12	0.07	0.10	0.12	0.07
Att-0	0.33		0.28	0.08	0.07	0.04	0.01	0.04	-0.00
NMot-0	0.28	0.28		0.08	0.05	0.10	0.00	0.01	0.07
Att-8	0.18	0.08	0.08		0.14	0.11	0.05	0.09	0.04
NMot-8	0.12	0.07	0.05	0.14		0.62	0.21	0.19	0.22
Ment-8	0.07	0.04	0.10	0.11	0.62		0.30	0.27	0.36
Att-18	0.10	0.01	0.00	0.05	0.21	0.30		0.62	0.74
NMot-18	0.12	0.04	0.01	0.09	0.19	0.27	0.62		0.59
Ment-18	0.07	-0.00	0.07	0.04	0.22	0.36	0.74	0.59	
Att-4	0.17	0.02	0.02	0.00	0.06	0.06	0.25	0.21	0.28
NMot-4	0.24	0.15	0.07	0.06	0.17	0.20	0.28	0.29	0.26
Ment-4	0.11	0.04	-0.01	0.03	0.13	0.22	0.38	0.35	0.46
Att-7	0.15	0.10	0.02	0.05	0.04	0.04	0.24	0.26	0.25
NMot-7	0.33	0.10	0.06	0.06	0.16	0.16	0.26	0.30	0.27
Ment-7	0.16	0.05	0.03	0.08	0.09	0.14	0.31	0.32	0.34
LD-7	0.19	0.02	0.01	0.09	0.10	0.14	0.31	0.27	0.34

(table continues on next page)

	Att-4	NMot-4	Ment-4	Att-7	NMot-7	Ment-7	LD-7
AlcLV	0.17	0.24	0.11	0.15	0.33	0.16	0.19
Att-0	0.02	0.15	0.04	0.10	0.10	0.05	0.02
NMot-0	0.02	0.07	-0.01	0.02	0.06	0.03	0.01
Att-8	0.00	0.06	0.03	0.05	0.06	0.08	0.09
NMot-8	0.06	0.17	0.13	0.04	0.16	0.09	0.10
Ment-8	0.06	0.20	0.22	0.04	0.16	0.14	0.14
Att-18	0.25	0.28	0.38	0.24	0.26	0.31	0.31
NMot-18	0.21	0.29	0.35	0.26	0.30	0.32	0.27
Ment-18	0.28	0.26	0.46	0.25	0.27	0.34	0.34
Att-4		0.47	0.54	0.36	0.28	0.36	0.47
NMot-4	0.47		0.51	0.34	0.34	0.37	0.39
Ment-4	0.54	0.51		0.38	0.46	0.70	0.55
Att-7	0.36	0.34	0.38		0.34	0.43	0.49
NMot-7	0.28	0.34	0.46	0.34		0.56	0.45
Ment-7	0.36	0.37	0.70	0.43	0.56		0.65
LD-7	0.47	0.39	0.55	0.49	0.45	0.65	

here, as our task in this chapter is to detect those children who show specific patterns of Alcohol-related disability across ages and domains.

The correlations in this 15×15 matrix are, with only one exception, positive. This is somewhat surprising even though all were computed to correlate positively with one shared Alcohol LV. As correlations averaged 0.18 between the Alcohol LV and the outcome PLVs, Alcohol typically accounts for only about $0.18^2 \approx .03$ of the correlation actually observed (on a simple common factor model). The PLV correlations are much larger than this, expressing instead the apparent dependence of these collections of outcomes on joint causes other than alcohol: for instance, secondary heritable factors that are channel-specific, interactions of attention or information pro-

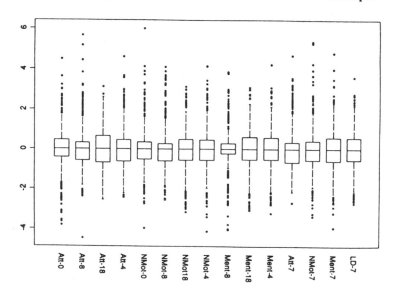

Figure 8.1.   Box plots for 15 PLV scores. The horizontal axis organizes the fifteen age- and channel-specific partial LVs whose correlations are shown in Table 8.1   Vertical is as in Figure 6.3, PLS-standardized scores adjusted for missing data as explained in Chapter 6. The graphics of the "boxes and whiskers" are likewise as in that figure.

cessing with the instructions for other tasks, and the general factor of maturational timing.

Two of these PLVs correlate particularly well with Alcohol dose: one from the neonatal exam (the Att-0 block) and one from the 7-year exam (the NMot-7 block). The correlations (on slightly different subsets of subjects) are both 0.33. Yet surprisingly, the correlation between these two PLV scores is itself only 0.10, which is indistinguishable from the product, (0.33)(0.33), of the separate regres-

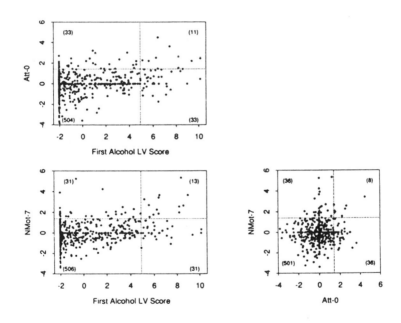

Figure 8.2. Scatterplots of the Neonatal Attention and 7-year Neuromotor PLVs against the first Alcohol LV (from the pooled analysis) and against each other. Dashed horizontal and vertical lines identify the top 7.5% of the scores on the respective LVs. The figures are labelled with counts of the number of cases falling in each of the four quadrants defined by these dashed lines. The horizontal and vertical streaks of black dots at zero for the Att-0 and NMot-7 PLVs mark cases missing data at that measurement wave.

sions upon Alcohol. That is, these two PLVs seem to share no common factors *except* Alcohol. It is of interest to see how these findings can be unfolded into a systematic search for the true value of that common factor, at least for a subset of subjects.

Figure 8.2 presents the scatters of these two PLVs against the Alcohol LV and against each other. It is clear that the correlation of the PLVs with each other is negligible save for a few cases that are high on both. However, the scatters of these two PLVs, in relation to Alcohol, suggest the possibility of screens for detection of alcohol damage by taking strips from the top of the scatters (high-outcome samples). First we will examine the Alcohol LV by the NMot-7 PLV. We begin by intersecting the scatter in Figure 8.2 with lines that demarcate the top 7.5% of each distribution. From among the top 44 cases with the highest doses, we count 13 subjects who are also among the 7.5% worst on the NMot-7 PLV. In terms of their neuromotor functioning at age 7 years, we can call them both exposed and apparently affected by Alcohol. From this figure we can see that 13 of the 44 most highly exposed children (30%) had this specific pattern of neuromotor deficit at age 7 years, compared to only 6% (31 out of 537) of the rest of the sample.

We next ask whether the abnormal score on NMot-7 for these 13 subjects high on both scores could have been detected on any earlier battery. Figure 8.3 shows the profiles of all 15 outcome PLVs for this subset of 13 subjects, both individually, ordered by Alc LV score, (a), and as a pool (b). A glance at Figure 8.3(b) reveals that there was no common pathway between birth and 8 years—no consistent pattern of earlier deficit across domains and ages. The general elevation of the individual profiles, however, indicates that although they lacked a consistent *pattern* of earlier disability, as a group these children *were* deviant at earlier examinations. For instance, we have neonatal data on 11 of the 13 subjects who were most highly exposed and most deviant on neuromotor function at 7 years. Of these eleven (see Figure 8.3a), seven or eight already had deviant scores on Att-0, that is, at day 1. Of the three who were not deviant on Att-0, one was deviant on NMot-0. Thus 9 of the 11 individual subjects with the worst alcohol-related neuromotor deficits at 7 years of age had already had marked attentional or neuromotor deficits as newborn babies. The two children with alcohol-related NMot deficits at 7 years who did *not* appear to be deviant as neonates were both close to the mean on the Ment-7 PLV despite their neuromotor problems. We also note that 6 of these 13 children with Alcohol-related neuromotor problems did not, as yet in the second grade, appear deviant on the LD-7 PLV. As noted previously, the NMot-7 LV was more salient for alcohol than the LD-7 LV. (But only three of these subjects were better than 1 standard deviation below normal on the Ment-7 LV, and none were performing better than our sample mean.) We might anticipate a reversal of these positions on the next assessment of LD.

The finding that the NMot-7 signal is not predicted by any particular earlier pattern of deficits is consistent with a different statistical approach to the same question, by regressing the NMot-7 PLV on the 4-year PLVs for the entire sample. (These regressions are based on the correlations in Table 8.1.) In spite of the correlation of 0.46 between NMot-7 and Ment-4, the Alcohol LV still correlates 0.29 with the residual of NMot-7 after adjustment for all three age-4 scores, and still correlates 0.25 even after adjustment for all 11 earlier PLVs, of whatever wave. In other words, the effect of Alcohol on NMot-7 is primarily on the "new" part of this LV—it seems to appear between the 4-year and 7-year waves of measurement.

In spite of the fact that the Alcohol effect on NMot-7 is not explained by earlier outcomes, a striking pattern is manifest in Figure 8.3. All but 24 of the earlier 121 PLV scores (13×11=143 minus 22 missing observations) are in the direction of alcohol damage. Only two of these 13 children (ID f, who is who is distinctly better than average on eight of the 11 scores prior to age 7, and ID d) were able to substantially exceed average performance levels on any of the earlier PLVs. *This is no artifact of the correlations among these outcomes in the pooled data set.* Only for Ment-4 is the correlation with NMot-7 above 0.4. Because the standard deviations about these regressions are nearly 1.0, using these correlations for "prediction" of the other PLVs from NMot-7 would lead us to expect substantial

High Alc/NMot-7 Cases

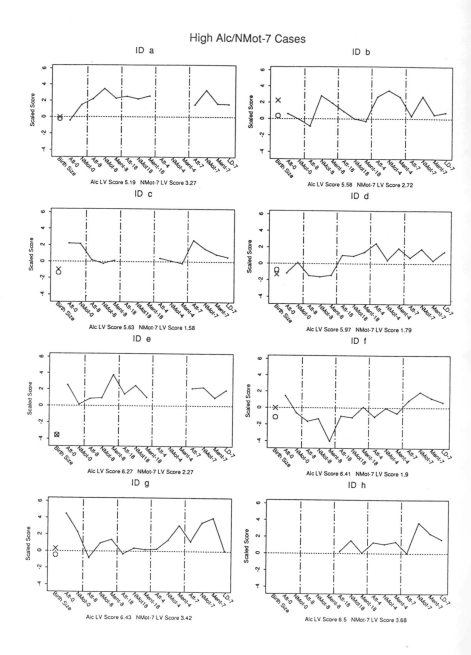

ID a

Alc LV Score 5.19 NMot-7 LV Score 3.27

ID b

Alc LV Score 5.58 NMot-7 LV Score 2.72

ID c

Alc LV Score 5.63 NMot-7 LV Score 1.58

ID d

Alc LV Score 5.97 NMot-7 LV Score 1.79

ID e

Alc LV Score 6.27 NMot-7 LV Score 2.27

ID f

Alc LV Score 6.41 NMot-7 LV Score 1.9

ID g

Alc LV Score 6.43 NMot-7 LV Score 3.42

ID h

Alc LV Score 6.5 NMot-7 LV Score 3.68

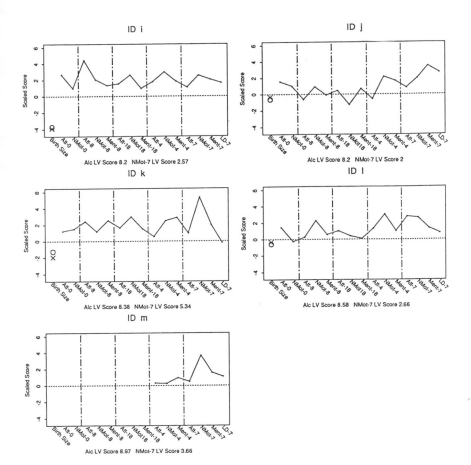

Figure 8.3a. Profiles of PLV scores for the 13 cases scoring high on both the first Alcohol LV and the NMot-7 PLV. (a) Profiles plotted individually for these 13 cases (in order of their scores on the Alcohol LV). The vertical axis of scores is as in Figure 8.1. "O" on the left margin indicates child's birthweight in standard scores from the population mean. "X" indicates deviations in head circumference at birth. Scores below the mean represent low birth weight and small head circumference.

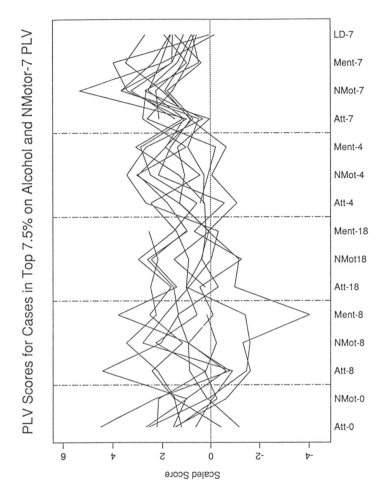

PLV Scores for Cases in Top 7.5% on Alcohol and NMotor-7 PLV

Figure 8.3b . Profiles plotted jointly for all 13 cases.   (See Figure 8.3a. description.)

frequencies of scores below the average line at zero. We see too few of those deviations here.

These analyses have suggested two subsets of children who could be called "affected by fetal alcohol" in a specific sense: 13 who were identified in childhood as having a 7-year alcohol-related neuromotor profile and 11 who were discernible at birth as having a neonatal alcohol-related attentional profile. Seven of the babies with deviant Att-0 scores at birth went on to have deviant NMot-7 scores. Of the remaining four, two appeared to have recovered by 8 months and had no subsequently deviant profiles up through 7 years. The other two also appeared to have recovered by 8 months, but then began to develop deviant attentional profiles by 4 and 7 years. Interestingly, eight of these 11 children did not have a deviant *mental* profile by 7 years, and eight did not have the profile of Alcohol-related LD-7.

In the most heavily exposed children, deviance on the neonatal attention profile was a better predictor of a deviant 7-year neuromotor profile than birthweight or head circumference at birth. Only three of the 13 children with deficient neuromotor profiles at age 7 years were two or more standard deviations below the mean on weight or head circumference at birth. (Of these, two were also deviant on neonatal attention.)

We interpret Figure 8.3 as evidence for the somewhat bold assertion that 11 of these 13 cases are *truly alcohol-affected.* We know they were exposed, and we know they showed the Alcohol-salient profile on the NMot-7 block; evidence from the other PLVs indicates patterns of earlier deviance as well.

We are not claiming, of course, that these 11 cases are the *only* subjects who are "fetal-alcohol-affected." There are 33 others in the higher-dose group; some might be identified by the other outcome blocks. Here we are asserting only that these 11 children *are* highly alcohol-affected. Similar results were reported in a large non-human primate study: while no single neurobehavioral test detected all the more heavily exposed young macaques, all of the more heavily exposed offspring had deviant performance on at least one of the tests in the battery (Clarren, Astley, & Bowden, 1988).

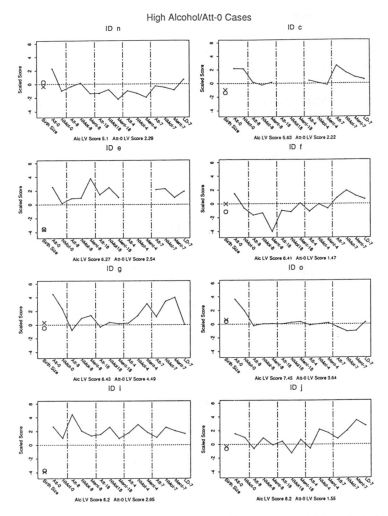

Figure 8.4. Profiles of PLV scores for the 11 cases scoring high on both the first Alcohol LV and the neonatal Attention PLV. (a) Profiles plotted individually for these 11 cases (in order of their scores on the Alcohol LV). "O" on the left margin indicates child's birthweight in standard scores from the population mean. "X" indicates deviations in head circumference at birth. Scores below the mean represent low birth weight and small head circumference. (b) Profiles plotted jointly for all 11 cases.

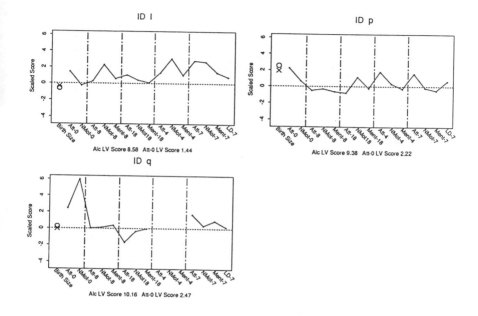

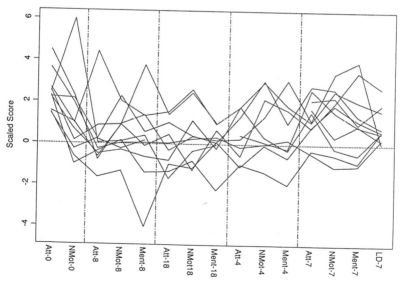

PLV Scores for Cases in Top 7.5% on Alcohol and Attention-0 PLV

Now we return to the other PLV that was described at the outset of this chapter as also highly correlated with Alcohol, namely, the Att-0 block. As with the NMot-7 PLV, the correlation of the Att-0 PLV with Alcohol is likewise 0.33, and 11 of the top 44 subjects for Att-0 were likewise in the top 7.5% of subjects for the Alcohol LV. However, a survey of the profiles of these 11 subjects, Figure 8.4, shows them to fall "below zero" much too frequently to serve as evidence of true deficit: more than half again as often as we found using the NMot-7 criterion, 37 times in 114 scores. We conclude that Att-0 and NMot-7, while equally correlated with the Alcohol LV, load differently on the (unmeasured) factor of "minimal brain damage" that we believe underlies all 15 of these PLVs and their successors at subsequent waves of the study. In other words, while of the high-Alc-high-Att-0 subjects nearly half "got better" (cases ID f, ID n, ID o, ID p, ID q), only two of the high-Alc-high-NMot-7 subjects (ID d and, again, ID f) got that way by "getting worse".

NMot-7 is the only one of the age-7 PLVs to which this approach is appropriate. The other PLVs correlate in the mid-teens with the Alcohol LV, vs. 0.33 for NMot-7. Within the subset of the 100 subjects of highest net deficit (first outcome LV score from Chapter 6, not partial but total), the correlation of Alcohol with NMot-7 is still 0.33; for the other three blocks it dips to or below 0.00, indicating the failure of the profiles to correlate with Alcohol at all within the high-"deficit" group.

In conclusion, examination of profiles of PLV scores for the 15 outcome blocks with respect to the Alcohol LV score shows that by using the 7-year Neuromotor block we may be able to identify 11 specific children manifesting "fetal alcohol effects." Among the 7.5% (44/581) of the children showing the greatest deficits on the NMot-7 PLV score, 30% (13/44) were among the top 7.5% in scores on the Alcohol LV; and of these 13 children, 11 show deficits on almost all of the other 14 PLV scores. These 11 children qualify as having been truly alcohol-affected. For no other block can we similarly identify a substantial fraction of the high-PLV children as both being most highly Alcohol-exposed and also showing general deficits across most of the outcome blocks.

These 11 children are certainly not the only cases who are alcohol-affected, but they do appear to represent a cluster of apparently homogeneously-affected children who could be identified individually at the beginning of the school years and for whom specific early interventions could be justified. The clinical relevance of this finding for detection of the individual 7-year-old with alcohol-related neurobehavioral deficits may be a breakthrough—up until now, identification of fetal alcohol affected children has been based primarily on morphology, not behavior. As this volume goes to press we have found strong evidence that most of these 11 cases continue to manifest deficits on attention and memory tasks at age 14. We hope other investigators will attempt to replicate and extend this finding as soon as possible.

## CHAPTER 9

Reflections on Study Design; Summary of Findings and Implications

In this chapter we present no new analyses of data and no new statistical methods. Instead we review our most important findings and then amplify implications for child development and public health. Recall that the purpose of this monograph is to examine the long-term effects of prenatal alcohol exposure – effects across all five exam ages (neonatal, 8 and 18 months, and 4 and 7 years). At each age the tests were intended to measure the emergence of deviations from normal development that might be attributable to alcohol. At most ages we could sort these tests into three "blocks" (primary domains of behavior): Attention (measured at all five ages), Neuromotor (all five), and Mental (all ages after the Neonatal). We also included a Learning Disabilities block at 7 years that incorporated "real-life" outcomes in the form of ratings, classifications, and performance measures. The Alcohol block contains 13 different aspects of dose as measured by maternal self-report during mid-pregnancy. We begin with some reflections on methodology, move to a summary of findings, discuss implications for public health, and conclude with a preview of things to come.

9.1 Reflections on Study Design

Had we used a "convenience" sample not specifically over-sampled for heavier drinkers and smokers or stratified for smoking across alcohol categories, and had we not selected a generally low-risk population, it is unlikely that our study would have been powerful enough to detect the enduring effects of prenatal alcohol, even though they are real. Had we carried out a conventional study, with one measure

of dose and one principal outcome score, we could not have learned
as much as we learned from the highly redundant measurement design
described in Chapters 2 and 3. Likewise, had we used more conventional statistical methods, we could not have adequately explored the
massive database produced by our redundant longitudinal design.
Partial Least Squares (PLS) was the tool which allowed us to capital-
ize on the redundancy inherent in the design for the detection of teratogenic insult across the first 7 years of life.

In this section we examine how the study design either constrained or enhanced the findings that were actually discovered.
While some of the following observations may be specific to research in behavioral teratology, others apply generally to a variety of
longitudinal studies in child development. Some are strengths of
this redundant longitudinal study design. Others are weaknesses, errors, or considered choices we wish in hindsight we could have or
would have made differently.

9.1.1 Interviewing Mid-Pregnancy

Interviewing the mothers during mid-pregnancy assured a more homogeneous sample not contaminated with high-risk mothers lacking
adequate prenatal care. Interviewing all mothers at exactly the same
time during pregnancy, regardless of when they began prenatal care,
standardized the gestational age of the fetus at the time that the measurement of dose was obtained and afforded us contemporaneous data
on drinking during mid-pregnancy even though the earlier history
was reconstructed retrospectively. Because we did not conduct a final
interview in the immediate postpartum period, information was lost
about drinking during the last half of pregnancy. Had we gathered
closely-spaced data on dose throughout pregnancy, we could have
studied the effects of timing of exposure on outcome in much more
detail. Either of these modifications would have increased the costs
of the study considerably. Our decision to focus our resources on
exposure during this earliest part of pregnancy (the period of organogenesis) was fortunate, as estimates of dose in the period prior to

pregnancy recognition proved the more important in predicting and accounting for prenatal alcohol effects through 7 years. Had we had more resources, a postpartum interview to cover third trimester drinking would have been worthwhile.

9.1.2 Identifying and Oversampling the High-Dose Group

Oversampling the high-dose group from the screening sample of 1529 pregnant women gave us a broader cohort of more highly-exposed children in a follow-up cohort of manageable size. This decision resulted in an efficient and cost-effective study design that we recommend highly.

Alcohol was used during pregnancy by most women in this population in 1974/75. Only 20% totally abstained from alcohol use during pregnancy—the same proportion who abstained prior to pregnancy recognition. By contrast, 75% of this population abstained from cigarette use during pregnancy (26). Apparently, this population of well-educated, low-risk mothers knew not to smoke cigarettes during pregnancy, but in 1974/75, did not yet know not to drink alcohol. Fewer than 1% (n=13) reported that they had any problems with alcohol (7), and fewer than 1% reported cocaine use (82). 89% of the mothers reported they were never intoxicated during pregnancy; 9% reported only one or two intoxications. Reports of being intoxicated had little relationship to the amount of alcohol reported consumed at the time of intoxication (7).

As a behavioral teratology study is primarily concerned with dose, it is important to pay careful attention to the "heavier" drinkers in the sample. Assessment of many different patterns of alcohol use, and utilization of these in selecting the follow-up cohort, were key factors in the ability of this study to detect alcohol effects. As our earlier work clearly demonstrated (7), women who get classified as "heavier" drinkers on one alcohol scale may not be classified so on another alcohol scale. For instance, the AA scale (average ounces of absolute alcohol per day), does poorly in selecting binge drinkers. Our cut-off of AA≥1.00 for recruiting a risk-level drinker would have missed 30% of the highest binge drinkers (VV-11) according to Cahalan's VV (Volume-Variability) Scale. Even lowering the cut-off to AA≥.75 would miss 10% of the heaviest binge drinkers (VV-11). Likewise, an AA≥1.00 cut-off would miss 40% of the women identified as "heavy drinkers" on Cahalan's QFV scale. As most women classified as "heavy drinkers" on the QFV scale qualify on the basis of only one type of beverage, an AA≥1.00 cut-off has a differential effect on subject loss as a function of type of beverage consumed and differences in patterns of drinking associated with these beverages. The AA≥1.00 cut-off would miss 20% of the women identified as "heavy" wine drinkers on the QFV, 35% of the "heavy" liquor drinkers, and a full 50% of the "heavy" beer drinkers. The complex guidelines for recruiting from the interview sample into the follow-up cohort assured that the group followed would be an appropriate constituency to detect alcohol effects on offspring, if they did in fact exist.

9.1.3 Designing the Study to Minimize the Confounding Effects of Covariates

Alcohol use and smoking are significantly correlated in the population, and both are predicted to have an adverse effect on pregnancy outcome. Our study design included an oversampling for heavy smoking at low levels of alcohol use. This made it possible to better separate the effects due to one or the other on the outcomes under consideration. Other potential confounders, associated with high-risk pregnancies, were partially controlled in the study design by eliminating all mothers not in prenatal care by the fifth month of pregnancy. If most of the heavier drinkers had received no prenatal care, no amount of later statistical adjustment could reveal alcohol effects (even if real) when adjusting for prenatal visits. The same holds for other SES-type variables. The unusual window in time which permitted us to find a population in which 80% of the women drank during pregnancy, and in which the group with the highest number of "risk level" drinkers was the group with the lowest pregnancy risk (namely, well-educated career women), necessitated some additional stratification of the cohort for college-educated women who were very light drinkers. Thus, these study design features permitted relatively easy separation of the alcohol effects from the effects due to poverty, maternal education, smoking, and so forth.

9.1.4 Developing the Battery Based on Knowledge of FAS

Observing a multitude of outcome measures proved to be a fortunate decision, as it permitted the examination of multiple latent variables as potential outcome summaries. The choice of tests was based on our clinical experience with patients of all ages with Fetal Alcohol Syndrome. Thus, sets of outcome variables were "aimed" at particular behavioral anomalies, rather than being scattered in a non-directed survey. This proved a particularly good strategy for the Neonatal exam. The absence of many such "specifically aimed" tests at the 8- and 18-month exams may have contributed to the paucity of strong findings from these periods. Among the outcome variables, general mental and motor scales and IQ test scores did not prove to be as sensitive as those which were specifically targeted to alcohol effects observed in patients with FAS at appropriate ages.

9.1.5 Changing Test Batteries During Data Collection

While for all exam waves the battery of tests was selected according to our clinical knowledge of infants and children with FAS, occasionally changes were made in the midst of an exam phase. For example, at the 7-year exam, the Stroop Test had been included in the original battery because children with FAS have difficulty shifting cognitive set (46). The decision to replace the Stroop with language tests (in the interest of getting a more comprehensive 7-year battery) and neurologic tests (because of the availability of new information) may have been, in retrospect, a mistake. Within its half of the sample, the Stroop Test revealed slower central processing time to be salient for prenatal alcohol exposure, but as the sample size was small, we did not include it in the present longitudinal analyses. Our original idea of a focused battery based on differences observed in children with FAS was indeed an appropriate strategy for a study of alcohol teratogenesis.

9.1.6 Combining Objective and Subjective Measurements

Our decision to combine real test data from performance tasks with subjective ratings of behavior provided a much richer array of outcomes than would have been possible from either set alone. Scores from objective tests were most salient for the long-term effects of prenatal alcohol exposure, as would be expected if a primary biologic cause is postulated. On the other hand, the subjective ratings from examiners, teachers, and parents provide the basis for understanding the qualitative aspects of these behavioral deficits, and permit generalizability of the findings to a wider variety of settings.

9.1.7 Developing Specialized Coding Systems

We developed far more specialized coding systems to accompany the standardized tests than we were able to include in these longitudinal analyses. This was due to a 500-item software constraint on the size of the variable pool when these analyses began (newer technology would not be so restrictive). Nevertheless, some specialized scoring systems were particularly useful in this analysis, particularly those developed for the Brazelton Scale. A simple threshold score was developed that revealed the trial at which the baby first gave a scorable reflex. As Section 6.3 shows, two of these were among the best individual outcomes in terms of their salience for alcohol. On the other hand, failure to include the many specialized qualitative codes developed for the 8- and 18-month Bayley Exams in this longitudinal analysis may have contributed to the poor showing of these exam ages compared to the others. The prominence of these specialized qualitative codes is also observable at the 7-year exam, where more of the "process" scores developed for the CMT were salient for Alcohol than were the quantitative scores originally part of the CMT Scoring System (see Section 7.1). These findings support the importance of qualitative dimensions of performance in assessing minimal brain damage, including that caused by alcohol.

9.1.8 Excluding and Including Nutrition

The original nutritional component of our design was not funded. This was unfortunate, as information about blood levels of essential minerals and vitamins might have helped us sort out the persisting influences of maternal prenatal nutrition on the development of the children through 7 years of age. All of these "effects" derive from a single 24-hour recall in 1975. While the nutritional measures don't appear to confound alcohol in this data set, their independent contributions would nevertheless have been important to investigate with greater breadth and precision. On the other hand, incorporating a blood-drawing component could have seriously impaired the excellent compliance that characterized this study.

9.1.9 Omitting Parental IQ

Omitting parental IQ was a calculated decision made at the outset. The cost of scheduling and administering 1000 additional IQ tests was an important factor, but commitment of our well-educated, busy parents was another. We reasoned that excellence of follow-up and parental collaboration were too important to the long-term goals of the longitudinal study design to risk the alienation of the parents through IQ testing, as had been implied in the Collaborative Perinatal Study (Broman, Nichols, & Kennedy, 1975). In retrospect, this decision was a good one. Follow-up has been excellent and the correlations we find in our study between parental education and child IQ (0.43 to 0.46) are at least as strong as typical parent-child IQ correlations reported in the literature (0.38 to 0.46 [Bouchard & McGue, 1981; Smith et al., 1983]). The omission of the parental IQ scores may have decreased the precision with which this interesting covariate can be controlled, but we doubt that it has induced any biases in the findings.

9.1.10 Succeeding in Following up the Cohort

The excellent overall follow-up rate of 86% since birth attests to our strenuous efforts in this regard (see Chapter 2) and to the develop-

ment of a successful methodology for longitudinal research (90).
Indeed, in the absence of the expected differential loss of the more
highly exposed children, we have been able to observe the continuing
effects of prenatal alcohol exposure up through 7 years. The wisdom
of our funding agency in continuing to fund outreach activities even
during periods of data analysis has made this success possible. One
problem that continues to vex us concerns the dissemination of information from the study. Our policy of sending occasional letters
about some of the findings to interested mothers was a successful
strategy until the study received increased media attention for its contributions to public policy. Occasionally a parent's commitment to
the study has changed dramatically following media coverage of the
findings.

9.1.11 Budgeting for Success

The costs of redundant longitudinal research are large at every phase.
Selection of the correct tests for each anticipated finding and the correct exam age for each wave of data collection is important and delicate, requiring not only a good knowledge of child development and
of the target teratogen but also expensive pilot testing. Cohort trac-
ing and contact are recurrent tasks requiring great skill and determi-
nation (57, 90). Data acquisition requires a highly motivated and co-
hesive team of examiners who are reliable in scoring and similar in
their approaches to children and in their compulsive attention to detail. Data analysis begins with repeated editing of the data by several
levels of statistical clerks. The "final" longitudinal analysis takes
many years to prepare even after all the data are coded and cleaned.
(The present monograph is being written in years 17 and 18 of the
study. The 106 papers on the study and/or on FAS listed in
Appendix I were written in the interim.)

The cost of this study (direct and indirect costs) over the 17 years
of uninterrupted funding since its inception has been $3,307,417, or
$6,862 per child in the follow-up cohort. While these figures in-
clude the costs incurred in developing and conducting an adolescent
follow-up wave, they do not include the $234,107 in additional funds
(direct and indirect costs) from other sources necessary to keep the

study operating over this time, or the costs of analyzing the data from the adolescent follow-up.

9.2 Summary and Interpretation

We now turn our attention to a nonquantitative summary of the main findings from these longitudinal analyses. What is the longitudinal impact of prenatal alcohol exposure on these children across their first seven years?

The review that follows begins with the PLS findings for the relationships among the Outcome Blocks at five waves of exams as they are predicted or accounted for by the Alcohol block. (Recall that we use the word "prediction" in the context of regression on scores case by case, while the word "accounting" refers to the way that PLS models matrices of correlations.) Next we discuss findings relative to the causal pathway of Alcohol as it affects the three types of Outcome blocks separately across time. Finally, we review how we used the latent variable scores to determine profiles for the detection of individual subjects affected by prenatal alcohol exposure. Unless otherwise stated, all effects are in the anticipated direction, as was generally observable from Appendices III and IVb.

9.2.1 There is No "Gold Standard" for Measuring Alcohol Dose that Predicts to the Breadth of Child Outcomes Assessed in this Study

As Figure 5.1 shows, the individual alcohol scores are extended along a straight line as they account for correlations with the 474 individual outcome scores. The full gamut of alcohol scores is necessary for fully assessing the teratogenic effects of alcohol. These scores range from pure monthly drinking occasions (MOCC) to average ounces alcohol per day (AA), through the maximum drinks per occasion (MAX), to the average number of drinks per occasion (ADOCC). All these alcohol scores affect outcomes—but they don't all affect the *same* outcomes. In fact, two main Alcohol latent variables appear sufficient to account for correlations with the Outcome variables. The principal dimension of dose includes nearly all the alcohol scores in a mildly binge-weighted combination (the horizontal axis in Figures 5.1–5.3). The other dimension refers to variations around this profile of correlation, some outcomes salient for a more binge-weighted profile, others for a less binge-weighted profile or even for the contrast between the ADOCC-type and MOCC-type drinking patterns. The alcohol block sorted exposures by two important periods of gestation: embryogenesis ("P" scores, prior to pregnancy recognition) and during mid-pregnancy ("D" scores). In our analyses the P scores are more salient than the D scores in accounting for the typical outcome. Still, each of the 13 alcohol scores contributes something to the explanation of outcomes in almost every block.

The degree to which these consequences of prenatal alcohol exposure are generalizable to prenatal exposure to other drugs, such as cocaine, that are ingested during pregnancy cannot be directly determined from this study. However, as most cocaine users also use alcohol (82), it is obvious that careful maternal drinking histories during pregnancy must be obtained on all mothers whose children are participating in studies of "drug babies." The level of alcohol exposure associated with child outcomes in the present study would never be detected in cursory questions about a history of alcohol problems or dependence. The results obtained are dependent on careful and redundant measurement of dose.

9.2.2 There Is No Simple "Gold Standard" Outcome for the Long-Term Behavioral Consequences of Alcohol, At Least Up Through Age 7 Years

As Figure 5.2 shows, the two Alcohol latent variables explode the 474 outcomes into an elliptical array. Those most strongly affected by alcohol have been ejected furthest from the center. They lie along all points of the compass, some reflecting predominant influences from one type of alcohol score, others most highly associated with another, as Figure 5.3 shows.

Several of the individual outcomes with the highest saliences for alcohol are from the Brazelton Neonatal Examination: Habituation to light, Incurvation threshold, Moro reflex, and State changes.

Habituation to light is the single most salient item in the group of 474 outcomes for prediction by Alcohol. No items from the 8-month exam, one from the 18-month, and only two from the 4-year exam are among the 24 items most sensitive to Alcohol according to one or another profile of dose. However, 17 items from the 7-year exam are among the top 24. These include three from the tasks of drawing and copying designs (generally the qualitative aspects of performance rather than the quantitative: especially reversals, poor integration, and quality of drawings); two different measures of Arithmetic (from the WISC-R and the WRAT-R); several ratings from the Myklebust Pupil Rating Scale (Cooperation/impulsivity, Follows instructions, and the MPRS total score); teachers' ratings of reading problems; mothers' ratings of children's academic adjustment problems; the WISC-R FULLIQ7, VERBIQ7, and Vocabulary Scaled Score; and false alarms or errors of commission from the AX vigilance task. The fact that these most Alcohol-salient outcomes at 7 years reflect data obtained by laboratory tests, by parental report, and by teacher report, indicates the broad general impact of prenatal alcohol exposure on the neurobehavioral functioning of the school-age child. This pattern of findings strengthens the conclusions that (a) the prenatal alcohol effects were biologically determined, as they were manifest already on day one of life, and (b) that the prenatal alcohol effects are definitely not "washing out" over time.

9.2.3 There Seem to be No Significant Covariates that Explain Away These Results

In Chapter 6 we developed methods for examining the possible effects of about 150 covariates on our outcome variables. The findings do not assign to Alcohol any effects of other causes of neurobehavioral problems in these children. While many other causes of behavioral problems exist, ranging from poor prenatal nutrition to poverty or divorce, adjustment for any or all of these covariates leaves most of the effects of Alcohol more or less unchanged. It is particularly notable that the effects of prenatal drug exposures such as nicotine disappear almost wholly after the neonatal wave of observations. At no age do they confound any of the Alcohol effects we are reporting here.

Furthermore, there seem to be no significant interactions involving Alcohol, that is, no dependence of the estimated effects of Alcohol on environmental variables, either prenatal or postnatal. In other words, the Alcohol effects were neither dependent upon nor enhanced by maternal smoking of cigarettes or marijuana, by poor nutrition during pregnancy, or by the other covariates examined in these analyses. Likewise, the Alcohol effects were neither dependent upon nor enhanced by a poor postnatal social environment or a poorly educated mother. This is not to say that such interactions do not exist, but only that they were not observed in this particular data set using the 150 or so covariates we measured and involving children followed only to 7 years, from primarily intact middle class families, whose mothers were primarily social drinkers. A previous report (76) of interactions of prenatal alcohol with poorer father education and larger family size applied to only one outcome (7-year IQ) and one dichotomous alcohol predictor; they are not replicated in the multitude of Alcohol patterns and potential outcomes examined in these analyses. This is consistent with the current understanding of the statistics of interaction terms in the behavioral sciences (cf. Wahlsten, 1990), which acknowledges their unreliability except under conditions of strong theory and excellent measurement precision.

9.2.4 The Longitudinal Effect of Prenatal Alcohol Exposure Is Like an Alcohol Drip into the Mental Causal Chain, with Some Infusion at Each Age, Up through 7 Years

In examining the longitudinal structure of these data, we found that the series of Mental blocks (from 8 months through 7 years) seems to be a true causal chain. These Mental blocks include not only standardized IQ and mental tests at each age of assessment, but also various examiner ratings and global assessments of mental and language function. The sequence of scores that results has a clear longitudinal structure, predicting from one age to another as shown in Figure 5.5. In fact, the predictability of the Mental block from one age to the next is nearly as good as the age-to-age correlations of the standardized tests alone, but these mental block PLV scores are considerably more sensitive to Alcohol and so more useful for this teratology study. The presence of this causal chain for the Mental block permits at least one formal examination of the strictly longitudinal effects of alcohol on the developing child.

Although the alcohol exposure occurred only prenatally, the impact of that exposure can be observed anew at each exam age as the child's maturity permits the measurement of yet more difficult tasks. As Figure 5.5 indicates, the amount of the "new" Alcohol effect is relatively constant across the four measurement ages: the Alcohol effect thus accumulates with age over the whole Mental causal chain. The cumulative effects of prenatal alcohol on mental development across the first seven years of the child's life are quite substantial, especially for tasks like Arithmetic that require attention to detail.

While the net PLVs (Partial outcome Latent Variables, wave by wave) do not form a causal chain in the way the Mental blocks do separately, the finding of a "steady Alcohol drip" nevertheless continues to be true. At every wave, the net outcome LV, not just its Mental component, incorporates Alcohol-related signal not predictable by any combination of latent scores from earlier waves.

9.2.5 The Attention Block at Birth and the Neuromotor Block at 7 Years Are the Outcome Blocks Most Strongly Predicted by Prenatal Alcohol Exposure

These two outcome blocks, one from the neonatal assessment and one from the 7-year assessment, yield the latent variables most highly correlated with the pooled Alcohol LV. As Figure 8.2 indicates, the Alcohol LV is correlated 0.33 with both the Att-0 LV and the NMot-7 LV, but these two outcome LVs are not further correlated with each other. This suggests that these outcomes are reflecting different channels of exposure.

The PLS analysis also examines saliences of individual outcomes for prediction by the block-specific Alcohol profiles. Of all the variables in the Att-0 Block, the six most salient for alcohol are Habituation to light, Incurvation threshold, Self-quieting, Neonatal state changes, Placing threshold, and Walking threshold. Clinically, this profile of alcohol damage suggests a baby who makes frequent state changes from asleep to awake, has atypical reflex thresholds, and has difficulty tuning out redundant stimuli (i.e., is over-reactive to stimulation).

Of the 12 variables most salient for Alcohol from the 7-year Neuromotor Block, six are from our modification of the Szatmari neurological screening test, five from our modification of the Children's Memory Test, and one from our modification of Seashore's standardized neuropsychological test for older children and adults. The items from the Szatmari indicate that right-left differentiation items are particularly salient for Alcohol at 7 years (Touch your nose with your *left* hand; Touch your *left* ear with your *right* hand). On the other hand, alcohol exposure at the levels measured in this study did not appear to affect fine motor coordination per se (performance on successive finger movements, thumb/finger alternation, pronation/supination of hand), although deficits on these items were reported in an unpublished dissertation on learning disabled children of alcohol-abusing mothers (Horowitz, 1984).

Although two memory items (one visual and one verbal) were in the top group of 7-year Neuromotor variables, three of the top items were qualitative aspects of perceptual-motor performance deriving from process scores adapted for this study from Koppitz (1964) (reversals, integration, and general quality of drawing). In retrospect, a Bender-Gestalt Test, scored by the Koppitz system, might have been a simpler and more expedient method for capturing this aspect of neuromotor functioning than the CMT or other Memory for Designs tests, which focus on quantitative scoring systems. One would conclude in examining these top outcomes salient for Alcohol at 7 years that it is the "Neuro" rather than the "Motor" aspect of the Neuromotor Block that represents the best teratogenic endpoints at this age. These were, indeed, the targeted behaviors at the 7-year exam.

9.2.6 Both the Learning Disabilities Block and the Neuromotor-7 Block are Well Accounted for by Alcohol in the PLS Analysis, But They are Salient for Different Patterns of Alcohol

As pointed out in Chapter 7, the fraction of correlation explained by PLS is quite high for both of these blocks. However they are accounted for by different Alcohol latent variables (compare Figures 7.2 and 7.3); as it happens, only the NMot-7 LV is predicted well by Alcohol at the level of individual scores. NMot-7 is related to the "mostly volume" pattern of alcohol while the LD-7 LV is more related to the contrast between bingeing and occasions. Because bingeing is intermittent, there is much more variability in the latter pattern. The variation of times and amounts induces variability in the exposure of different fetuses. Lower reliability results in lower predictability, so that, even though the effects of binge drinking may be worse for some individual babies, the effects on the group are harder to detect by ordinary correlational methods.

The most Alcohol-salient items of the LD-7 block are Math remediation placement, parent ratings of more academic and social adjustment problems, teacher ratings of poor reading or spelling skills, Myklebust teacher ratings for poor performance on Cooperation/impulsivity, Comprehends Words, Retains Information, Grammar, and Tactfulness, and the Myklebust Total PRS (Learning Disabilities) score. While the pattern in the correlation matrix is clear, the lack of correlation at the level of individual scores is somewhat disappointing. It may be that by the end of the first grade there has not yet been enough "baseline" learning for the expression of learning disabilities. Full behavioral manifestations of learning disabilities might have been better measured in the third or fourth grade when the consequences of the neuromotor deficits observed here would have had time to become manifest.

9.2.7 There are Profiles of Alcohol Effects on WISC Scaled Scores and Myklebust Ratings which are Both Accounted for and Predicted By Alcohol Better Than Full Scale IQ or Myklebust Total Score

These contrast LVs were derived in Section 7.2 by centering two raw PLS salience profiles, that for the 11 WISC subtests and that for the 24 Myklebust items.

The profiled WISC LV is the contrast of three subscales against the rest of the WISC-R. The three subscales particularly sensitive to prenatal alcohol exposure are Arithmetic, Digit Span, and Block Design; they contrast principally with Object Assembly, Vocabulary and Comprehension. This pattern of Alcohol-related deficits was reported in our papers on the cross-sectional analyses of the 7-year neurobehavioral data (65-67), but the analyses in Chapter 7 sharpen the clinical picture of a useful contrast.

The contrast between good verbal skills and poor memory and problem-solving skills poses a dilemma for these children. Expectations for their performance are based on their verbal skills, while their ability to follow through on expectations are compromised by problems with memory, attention, and problem-solving.

While the magnitude of deficit is obviously not severe in these children with basically normal intelligence, whose mothers were primarily social drinkers, the *pattern* of deficit is particularly interesting in that it replicates our clinical studies in older patients with FAS/FAE.

Problems with arithmetic, memory, attention, and problem-solving are typical of adolescents and adults with FAS (48, 53, 61, 62, 83). These patients, who are much more disabled intellectually than the children in the present study, nevertheless show the same behavioral paradoxes. They function better in the verbal realm but have more problems with arithmetic, memory, and problem-solving. They "talk a good line" but can't follow through. This pattern of contrasting abilities sets them up for an increasing incidence of psychosocial problems as they get older. Further waves of examination will be needed to understand the long-term implications of these more subtle functional deficits in the children under investigation here.

The Myklebust Pupil Rating Scale also revealed a profile of classroom behaviors that was both accounted for and predicted by prenatal alcohol exposure. The most salient indicators for this classroom profile are seen in Figure 7.6: Problems with cooperation/impulsivity, Comprehends Words, Retains Information, Grammar, and Tactfulness, as they contrast with such items as Coordination and Balance. As the Myklebust scores derive from the ratings of hundreds of classroom teachers on 469 children attending different schools, it is remarkable that these profile scores are as predictable by Alcohol as those obtained from a standardized IQ test administered in the laboratory by one or two psychometrists. The contrast with Coordination and Balance is surprising in that we have recently described problems with balance and fine-motor coordination as alcohol-related outcomes in a paper on the cross-sectional analyses of the 4-year motor outcomes (69). At 7 years, we do not find that laboratory measures of coordination discriminate children at the level of prenatal alcohol exposure measured here. In children with FAS, kinetic tremor, axial ataxia, and dysdiadochokinesia have been reported clinically in school-age children (Marcus, 1984). Motor coordination in normal children with lower exposure histories may be better measured in the laboratory at age 4, when these skills are emerging, than via the casual observations of second-grade teachers. Nevertheless, the contrast is of interest: these findings show that teachers do not identify these alcohol-affected children as having the kind of sensory-motor problems (such as those associated with mild cerebral palsy) that might target them for special consideration in the schools.

The behavioral deficits that these teachers do identify—problems with cooperation/impulsivity, comprehension and memory—have broad implications for the functioning of these alcohol-affected children in society. Here we may see the full impact of prenatal alcohol exposure in its earliest social appearance. In the child who doesn't remember what he's told and doesn't understand what is expected of him or her, yet has no physical or language disability, the stage is set for classroom behavior problems (through poor cooperation/high impulsivity) and peer rejection (through poor tactfulness). There is an analogous finding, again, for children with FAS and FAE: particularly for those with nearly normal IQ, major difficulties with classroom behavior and peer rejection are often present, sometimes entailing such major dislocations in later years as school drop-out or even expulsion.

Further understanding of the adolescent consequences of social drinking during pregnancy await further follow-up of the cohort. We already know, from cross-sectional analyses of an 11-year-old questionnaire for teachers, that alcohol-related classroom behavior problems and continuing difficulty with arithmetic are still observable at age 11 in this cohort at about the same levels of correlation reported here (95).

9.2.8 Language Disabilities are Generally Absent from the Lists of Fetal Alcohol Effects Revealed by these Analyses

Our clinical experience, which directed the selection of outcomes for this study, did not suggest that language problems per se represent an explicit area of disability for patients with FAS and FAE, beyond whatever language delays might be expected from their general levels of functioning. Instead, we have often seen how good but superficial language skills can mask early neuromotor deficits that foreshadow later school problems. Young children who talk a lot, who ask a lot of questions, and who are uninhibited, friendly, and outgoing may seem more functional as preschoolers than they turn out to be in the controlled classroom setting. These behaviors are characteristic of young children with FAS/FAE. Therefore, the original longitudinal design for our social drinking study did not include any specific language tests other than those involved in assessment of IQ and memory. However, in order to examine the language area more fully, we changed the 7-year protocol midway during the gathering of that wave to include some specific tests developed from clinical assessments used by Johnson and Blalock (1987). As originally anticipated, specific deficits in spoken and written language at the end of

Grade 1 were not as strongly associated with prenatal alcohol exposure as the other items measured at this age.

9.2.9 Arithmetic Disabilities in the Second Grade are Predicted by Prenatal Alcohol Exposure, Particularly a Binge Pattern of Consumption

In our intentionally redundant study design we had several different measures of arithmetic skill. Regardless of whether measured directly in paper and pencil arithmetic tests, mental computations, teacher report, or parental report, arithmetic disabilities were related to prenatal alcohol exposure, particularly the various measures of massed drinking, such as ever drinking five or more drinks per occasion, average drinks per occasion, and maximum drinks any occasion.

The prominence of these early arithmetic deficits is in complete accord with our clinical experience of the more severe arithmetic disabilities observed in older patients with FAS/FAE (83). We have proposed that these arithmetic deficits represent the early manifestation of difficulties with problem solving, generalization, and abstract thinking, skills that adults with FAS seldom achieve (cf. Dorris, 1989).

Our own cultural myopia regarding the importance of early mathematics achievement relative to reading has been eloquently described by Stevenson and Stigler (1992) in contrasting American and Japanese/Taiwanese pedagogic methods and attitudes. Such factors may put alcohol-affected children in our society at even greater risk. On the other hand, recognition of the biologic roots of alcohol-related arithmetic disabilities in young children should facilitate early detection of affected individuals as well as earlier and perhaps more effective remedial programming.

9.2.10 The Neurobehavioral Outcomes Predicted Here by Alcohol were from Drinking in the Social Drinking Range

Fewer than 1% of these mothers reported any major problems with alcohol. Our findings are in no way restricted to this 1% of the sample, but extend from the top of our Alcohol LV downward across many patterns of alcohol use. The curves in Figure 4.1, for instance, show vertical displacements down to fairly low doses. That is, our findings apply not to some sort of "category" of drinking that is called "social drinking," but "across the social drinking range," from just above abstinence into the range of the heaviest drinkers.

Recall that our findings are in the form of a dose-response relationship: not the effect "at" a particular level of dose, but the incremental effect of an increment of dose all across this range. To the extent that the curves in Figure 4.1 are nearly straight, these slopes might be reported in ordinary units: e.g., "so many IQ points per drink per occasion." We have not emphasized this form of report in this monograph because reports in terms of the PLS analyses lead to a much clearer understanding of patterns. For a discussion regarding a "risk-free" or "threshold" level for these effects, see Section 9.3.2.

9.2.11 At Least 11 Individual Children with Fetal Alcohol Effects Were Detected Using Exclusively Behavioral Assessments

Chapter 8 (Fig. 8.3) embodies the most practical of all the study's specific aims: the empirical detection of school-age children with clear alcohol-related deficits. That figure portrays the longitudinal profile of part of the cohort across all waves of examination: the individual LV profiles, from birth to 7 years, of the children who were characterized by the specific pattern of NMot-7 deficit that is most strongly associated with alcohol. Each of these children had been worse than the mean on almost every single previous evaluation; also, most of them had had clear deficits (two standard deviations worse than the mean) on at least one previous block at at least one previous age. We concluded that alcohol caused the NMot-7 deficits. That it was the Neuromotor block that detected these truly alcohol-affected children is not surprising. The items in this block are more biologic, more easily measurable, and more objectively measured than those in the Learning Disabilities block, for which we must rely on judgments owing to the dearth of specific criteria at this early age. Many different patterns of earlier deficit preceded the NMot-7 deficits. The success of this detection task at 7 years suggests that it may be possible to eventually develop a neurobehavioral screening test for alcohol-related minimal brain damage. These longitudinal analyses indicate that 7 years would be better than any younger age for conducting such an examination, and that neurobehavioral, rather than mental, or language, or learning disabilities tests, would be the most likely candidates for screening. The profile of Alcohol correlations associated with this NMot-7 detection criterion is the most reliable "mostly-volume" or "AAP-type," to which all of the 13 indicators contribute nearly equally.

9.3 Fetal Alcohol Effects and the Public Interest

In this section we speculate on some matters that go beyond the limits of our study design, our data, and our analyses.

9.3.1 Cost of Prenatal Alcohol Exposure

There has been a considerable recent increase in public awareness of FAS (cf. Dorris' bestseller of 1989) and, in consequence, attempts to estimate the "cost" to society of FAS at its current prevalence rates. Our analyses indicate that FAS is one end of a continuous dose-response relationship reaching far into the "normal" range on a great variety of neurobehavioral outcomes. It follows that the net social cost of prenatal exposure to alcohol is far higher than the costs incurred for patients with FAS alone. In Chapter 8, for instance, we identified 11 children as FAE based exclusively on our Neuromotor Block (versus two identified as FAS in this cohort at birth). Then, in terms of special programming, behavioral problems, lost productivity, and so on, the net cost of alcohol exposure must be considerably more than the cost of FAS alone. Nor can one place a dollar value on the shift of the normal mean corresponding to the diminution of arithmetic skills, abstract thinking, problem solving and impulse control in the 50th through 90th percentiles of dose. How can one figure the costs of losing 1 or 2 IQ subtest points in half the population, or the extent to which prenatal alcohol exposure contributes to the lack of vigilance that kills 50,000 of us annually by automobile?

9.3.2 "Safe" Levels of Alcohol to the Fetus

There is no statistical evidence here for any "risk-free" or "threshold" level of prenatal alcohol exposure in the context of this dose-response analysis. One final figure (Figure 9.1) depicts this most clearly. It is an extension of one of the frames in Figure 4.1, which showed the transformations of our alcohol variables most consistent

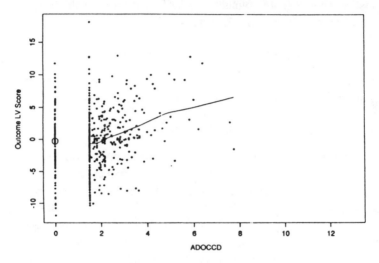

Figure 9.1 Extension of one frame from Figure 4.1: Outcome LV1 against the raw alcohol indicator ADOCCD (average drinks per occasion during mid-pregnancy). ADOCCD is a weighted average deriving from the quantity-frequency-variability interview from which the smallest "quantity" coded is "1-2 drinks" which is scored 1.5 drinks. Thus, no positive score can be less than 1.5. ADOCC scores of exactly 1.50 correspond to the mothers who drank, but who never drank more than 1–2 drinks of any alcoholic beverage. Scores just above 1.5 come from mothers who almost always have only 1–2, but infrequently have 3 or more drinks. The abstainer mean is shown by the "O"; data for "1-2" drinks or more have been smoothed by the "lowess" scatterplot smoother available in the S language (Becker et al., 1988). There is no evidence at all in this smoothing function of a threshold below which an additional drink is not harmful. The effect of "additional" drinks per occasion begins at the very leftmost point of the curve, as soon as there are more than "1-2" drinks of any alcohol beverage. The outlying case at far right is the one omitted from all of our correlational analysis.

with our model of linear effects (based on the data and analysis in [67]). The plot is of the sample scores on ADOCCD, average drinks per occasion during mid-pregnancy, against our main outcome LV. ADOCC scores of exactly 1.50 correspond to the mothers who drank, but who never drank more than 1–2 drinks of any alcoholic beverage. Scores just above 1.5 come from mothers who almost always have only 1–2, but infrequently have 3 or more drinks.

The biometrics of searching for thresholds is quite technical. In the typical analysis of experimental animal data, a "threshold" is a dose below which groups appear to show mean response equivalent to that for the nondrinkers. The equivalent in this study would be a dose on each alcohol score below which the curve of Figure 4.1 is flat. Our scatterplot smoothing technique would slightly erode such flat sections, and PLS itself further linearizes plots like Figure 9.1. Still, the best estimates of dose-response relationships for some of our most powerful predictors do not include flat spots. Furthermore, issues of threshold cannot be tested as nested hypotheses, as the "explained variance" is nonlinear in the location of the threshold, and there seems to be no straightforward extension to models in which both dose and response are measured with error. Furthermore, variations in susceptibility cannot be circumvented in human studies. Real biologic thresholds are best studied by precise calibrations of dose-response relationships in controlled (animal) populations. Within the limits of our measurement of dose, however, the assertion emphasized above is in accord with the best calibration of the dose-response curve available to this study.

9.4 Preview of Things to Come

Our clinical work suggests that for many children with FAS, particularly those with approximately normal intelligence, the end of first grade is a fairly benign time. By third or fourth grades children with FAS often begin to suffer as a result of major problems with arithmetic, abstract thinking, attention, and organization. Behavioral problems usually escalate at middle school or junior high when they are expected to regulate themselves as they move from teacher to teacher, classroom to classroom, day after day. Social adjustment problems are manifest in adolescence, leading to crises around the time of leaving school. Problems with judgment, self-direction and independence are then frequently observed (83). These clinical insights have guided our plans for succeeding waves of data collection with the present study.

It is our hope to continue the Seattle Longitudinal Study into adulthood for our cohort of 500. One wave of additional data was gathered from teacher report when the children were 11 years old (95), and preliminary analyses are described in Section 9.2.7. At this writing, an eighth, full-scale wave of data is being analyzed. This represents a 4-hour battery of attentional, cognitive and motor tests of the 14-year-olds, and general interview data from them and their parents. The scores of this battery should provide a final benchmark for the underlying cognitive/neurobehavioral developmental processes that we have traced through the lives of these children. The first papers from this wave are indicating continuing prenatal alcohol effects at 14 years, on attention, memory, and Arithmetic and Word Attack performance (104, 105). On the other hand, growth parameters show little association with prenatal alcohol after 8 months of age (106). In the next full wave of examinations, we hope to measure IQ once more, academic achievement once more, and psychopathology. By this next exam, we will have traced the impact of prenatal alcohol exposure on these children up to the end of adolescence.

We hope also that work will begin soon on an FAE screening inventory making use of the findings from this study. We see our work to date as a first step in identifying the behavioral phenotype of alcohol teratogenesis. The central nervous system and behavioral consequences of prenatal alcohol exposure (rather than the physical and morphologic manifestations) are ultimately the most debilitating. Delineating the behavioral phenotype should be an important step in screening for affected children and developing appropriate interventions.

Papers from the Seattle Longitudinal Prospective Study on Alcohol and Pregnancy and from the Fetal Alcohol and Drug Unit (a, b)

1976

1. Streissguth, A. P. (1976). Maternal alcoholism and the outcome of pregnancy: A review of the Fetal Alcohol Syndrome. In M. Greenblatt & M. A. Schuckit (Eds.), *Alcohol problems in women and children* (pp. 251-274). New York: Grune and Stratton.

2. Streissguth, A. P. (1976). Psychologic handicaps in children with Fetal Alcohol Syndrome. In F. A. Seixas & S. Eggleston (Eds.), *Work in progress in alcoholism* (Vol. 273, pp. 140-145). New York: Annals of the New York Academy of Sciences.

3. Streissguth, A. P., Martin, D. C., & Buffington, V. E. (1976). Test-retest reliability of three scales derived from a quantity-frequency-variability assessment of self-reported alcohol consumption. In F. A. Seixas & S. Eggleston (Eds.), *Work in progress in alcoholism* (Vol. 273, pp. 458-466). New York: Annals of the New York Academy of Sciences.

4. Lund, C. (1976). A reliable, inexpensive device for recording head-turning. *Journal of Experimental Child Psychology, 21,* 361-362.

1977

5. Martin, J. C., Martin, D. C., Lund, C. A., & Streissguth, A. P. (1977). Maternal alcohol ingestion and cigarette smoking and their effects on newborn conditioning. *Alcoholism: Clinical and Experimental Research, 1(3),* 243-247.

Note: Clinical papers on fetal alcohol syndrome and patient management are designated '‡'. Papers on public policy and prevention are designated '†'.

6.   Streissguth, A. P. (1977). Maternal drinking and the outcome of
        pregnancy: Implications for child mental health. *American
        Journal of Orthopsychiatry, 47(3)*, 422-431.

7.   Streissguth, A. P., Martin, D. C., & Buffington, V. E. (1977).
        Identifying heavy drinkers: A comparison of eight alcohol
        scores obtained on the same sample. In F. A. Seixas (Ed.),
        Currents in alcoholism (Vol. 2, pp. 395-420). New York: Grune
        & Stratton.

8.   Streissguth, A. P., Martin, D. C., & Barr, H. M. (1977). *Factor
        structure of the Brazelton Neonatal Assessment Scale and
        experimental design considerations in the use of the Brazelton
        for outcome research.* (Tech. Report No. 77-01). Seattle:
        University of Washington, Pregnancy and Health Study.

1978

9.   Clarren, S. K., Alvord, E. C., Jr., Sumi, S. M., Streissguth, A. P.,
        & Smith, D. W. (1978). Brain malformations related to prenatal
        exposure to ethanol. *Journal of Pediatrics, 92*, 64-67.

10.   Hanson, J. W., Streissguth, A. P., & Smith, D. W. (1978). The
        effects of moderate alcohol consumption during pregnancy on
        fetal growth and morphogenesis. *Journal of Pediatrics, 92(3)*,
        457-460.

11.   Landesman-Dwyer, S., Keller, L. S., & Streissguth, A. P. (1978).
        Naturalistic observations of newborns: Effects of maternal
        alcohol intake. *Alcoholism: Clinical and Experimental
        Research, 2(2)*, 171-177.

12.   Ragozin, A. S., Landesman-Dwyer, S., & Streissguth, A. P.
        (1978). The relationship between mothers' drinking habits and
        children's home environments. In F. A. Seixas (Ed.), *Currents in
        alcoholism* (Vol. 4, pp. 39-49). New York: Grune & Stratton.

13.   Streissguth, A. P. (1978). Fetal Alcohol Syndrome: An
        epidemiologic perspective. *American Journal of Epidemiology,
        107(6)*, 467-478.

14.   Streissguth, A. P., Herman, C. S., & Smith, D. W. (1978a).
        Intelligence, behavior, and dysmorphogenesis in the Fetal
        Alcohol Syndrome: A report on 20 patients. *Journal of
        Pediatrics, 92(3)*, 363-367.

15.   Streissguth, A. P., Herman, C. S., & Smith, D. W. (1978b).
        Stability of intelligence in the Fetal Alcohol Syndrome: A

preliminary report. *Alcoholism: Clinical and Experimental Research, 2(2)*, 165-170.

16. Streissguth, A. P., Martin, J. C., & Martin, D. C. (1978). *Experimental design considerations and methodological problems in the study of the effects of social drinking on the outcome of pregnancy* (Tech. Rep. No. 78-01). Seattle: University of Washington, Department of Psychiatry & Behavioral Sciences, Fetal Alcohol and Drug Unit.

17. Landesman-Dwyer, S., Keller, L., & Streissguth, A. P. (1978). Reply to Drs. Sanders, Haynes, and Emde's review. *Sleep Reviews, 169*, 36-39.

17a.‡ Little, R. E. & Streissguth, A. P. (1978). Drinking during pregnancy in alcoholic women. *Alcoholism: Clinical and Experimental Research, 2(2)*, 179-183.

1979

18. Martin, D. C., Martin, J. C., Streissguth, A. P., and Lund, C. A. (1979). Sucking frequency and amplitude in newborns as a function of maternal drinking and smoking. In M. Galanter (Ed.), *Currents in alcoholism* (Vol. V, pp. 359-366). New York: Grune & Stratton.

19. Streissguth, A. P. (1979). Fetal Alcohol Syndrome: Where are we in 1978? *Women and Health, 4(3)*, 223-237.

19a.‡ Little, R. E., Streissguth, A. P., & Page, E. L. (1979). Techniques for recruiting special types of persons for research: Pitfalls and successes in enlisting recovered alcoholic women. *Public Health Reports, 94(4)*, 332-335.

1980

20. Streissguth, A. P., Barr, H. M., Martin, D. C., & Herman, C. S. (1980). Effects of maternal alcohol, nicotine and caffeine use during pregnancy on infant mental and motor development at eight months. *Alcoholism: Clinical & Experimental Research, 4(2)*, 152-164.

21. Streissguth, A. P. (1980). Introduction: Female alcoholism: Impacts on women and children. In M. Galanter (Ed.), *Currents in alcoholism* (Vol. VII, 429-434). New York: Grune & Stratton.

22. Streissguth, A. P., Landesman-Dwyer, S., Martin, J. C., & Smith, D. W. (1980). Teratogenic effects of alcohol in humans and laboratory animals. *Science, 209*, 353-361.

23.   Herman, C. S., Kirchner, G. L., Streissguth, A. P., & Little, R. E.
       (1980). Vigilance paradigm for preschool children used to relate
       vigilance behavior to IQ and prenatal exposure to alcohol.
       Perceptual & Motor Skills, 50, 863-867.

24.   Streissguth, A. P. (1980). Alcool como agente teratogênico: a
       sindrome do alcoolismo fetal. *Revista da Associacao Brasileira
       de Psiquiatria, 2(2)*, 121-130.

25.   Kaminski, M., Rumeau-Rouquette, L., & Streissguth, A. P.
       (1980). Tabac, alcool et grossesse: Apport des etudes
       epidemiologiques. In G. Barrier & G. M. Thoulon (Eds.),
       Medecine Perinatales (pp. 169-191). Deauville, France: 10es
       Journee Nationales, Societe Francaise de Medecine Perinatale.

25a.† Little, R. E., Streissguth, A. P., & Guzinski, G. M. (1980).
       Prevention of fetal alcohol syndrome: A model program.
       Alcoholism: Clinical and Experimental Research, 4(2), 185-
       189.

25b.† Little, R. E., Streissguth, A. P., Barr, H. M., & Herman, C. S.
       (1980). Decreased birth weight in infants of alcoholic women
       who abstained during pregnancy. *Journal of Pedicatrics, 96(6)*,
       974-976.

                                    1981

26.   Streissguth, A. P., Martin, D. C., Martin, J. C., & Barr, H. M.
       (1981). The Seattle longitudinal prospective study on alcohol
       and pregnancy. *Neurobehavioral Toxicology and Teratology, 3*,
       223-233.

27.   Streissguth, A. P. (1981). Summary and recommendations:
       Epidemiologic and human studies on alcohol and pregnancy,
       Neurobehavioral Toxicology and Teratology, 3, 241-242.

28.   Darby, B. L., Streissguth, A. P., & Smith, D. W. (1981). A
       preliminary follow-up of 8 children diagnosed Fetal Alcohol
       Syndrome in infancy. *Neurobehavioral Toxicology and
       Teratology, 3(2)*, 157-159.

29.   Barr, H. M., Streissguth, A. P., Martin, D. C., & Horst, T. E.
       (1981) Methodological issues in assessment of caffeine intake:
       A method for quantifying consumption and a test-retest
       reliability study. In L. F. Soyka & G. P. Redmond (Eds.), *Drug
       metabolism in the immature human* (pp. 265-280). New York:
       Raven Press.

30.   Buffington, V., Martin, D. C., Streissguth, A. P., & Smith, D.
       W. (1981). Contingent negative variation in the Fetal Alcohol
       Syndrome: A preliminary report. *Neurobehavioral Toxicology
       and Teratology, 3(2)*, 183-185.

31. † Streissguth, A. P. (1981). Offspring effects of different levels of
       alcohol consumption during pregnancy. In C. Perris, G. Struwe,
       & B. Jansson (Eds.), *Biological Psychiatry* (pp. 916-991).
       Elsevier: North-Holland Biomedical Press.

31a.† Little, R. E., Grathwohl, H. L., Streissguth, A. P., & McIntyre,
       C. (1981). Public awareness and knowledge about the risks of
       drinking during pregnancy in Multnomah County, Oregon.
       American Journal of Public Health, 71(3), 312-314.

31b.† Little, R. E. & Streissguth, A. P. (1981). Effects of alcohol on
       the fetus: Impact and prevention. *Canadian Medical Association
       Journal, 125*, 159-164.

1982

32.   Streissguth, A. P., Barr, H. M., & Martin, D. C. (1982).
       Offspring effects and pregnancy complications related to self-
       reported maternal alcohol use. *Developmental Pharmacology &
       Therapeutics, 5*, 21-32.

32a.   Little, R. E. & Streissguth, A. P. (1982). Alcohol: Pregnancy
       and the fetal alcohol syndrome. Unit 5 of *Alcohol Use and its
       Medical Consequences: A Comprehensive Slide Teaching
       Program for Biomedical Education,* Project Cork Institute of
       Dartmouth Medical School. (A slide/teaching unit available from
       Milner-Fenwick, Inc., 2125 Greenspring Drive, Timonium, MD
       21093.)

1983

33.   Streissguth, A. P., & Martin, J. C. (1983). Prenatal effects of
       alcohol abuse in humans and laboratory animals. In B. Kissin &
       H. Begleiter (Eds.), *The pathogenesis of alcoholism,* (Vol. 7, pp.
       539-589). New York: Plenum.

34.   Streissguth, A. P., Darby, B. L., Barr, H. M., Smith, J. R., &
       Martin, D. C. (1983). Comparison of drinking and smoking
       patterns during pregnancy over a 6-year interval. *American
       Journal of Obstetrics and Gynecology, 145(6)*, 716-724.

35.   Streissguth, A. P., Barr, H. M., & Martin, D. C. (1983). Maternal alcohol use and neonatal habituation assessed with the Brazelton Scale. *Child Development, 54,* 1109-1118.

36.   Streissguth, A. P. (1983). Alcohol and pregnancy: An overview and an update. *Substance and Alcohol Actions/Misuse, 4,* 149-173.

36a. Streissguth, A. P., Barr, H. M., Labbe, R. F., Smith, J. R., Darby, B. L., Smith, N. J., Martin, D. C., & Doan, R. N. (1983). Alcohol use and iron status in pregnant women. *Alcoholism: Clinical and Experimental Research, 7(2),* 227-230.

36b.† Little, R. E., Streissguth, A. P., Guzinski, G. M., Grathwohl, H. L., Blumhagen, J. M., & McIntyre, C. E. (1983). Change in obstetrician advice following a two-year community educational program on alcohol use and pregnancy. *American Journal of Obstetrics and Gynecology, 146(1),* 23-28.

1984

37.   Streissguth, A. P., Barr, H. M., & Martin, D. C. (1984). Alcohol exposure *in utero* and functional deficits in children during the first four years of life. In: R. Porter, M. O'Connor, & J. Whelan (Eds). *Mechanisms of Alcohol Damage in Utero. (CIBA Foundation Symposium #105*:176-196). London:Pitman.

38.   Streissguth, A. P., Martin, D. C., Barr, H. M., Sandman, B. M., Kirchner, G. L., & Darby, B. L. (1984). Intrauterine alcohol and nicotine exposure: Attention and reaction time in 4-year-old children. *Developmental Psychology, 20(4),* 533-541.

39.   Streissguth, A. P., Martin, D. C., Martin, J. C., & Barr, H. M. (1984). A longitudinal prospective study on the effects of intrauterine alcohol exposure in humans. In S. P. Mednick, M. Harway, & K. M. Finello (Eds.), *Handbook of longitudinal research: Birth and childhood cohorts* (Vol. 1, pp. 448-469). New York: Praeger.

40.   Barr, H. M., Streissguth, A. P., Martin, D. C., & Herman, C. S. (1984). Infant size at 8 months of age: Relation ahip to maternal use of alcohol, nicotine, and caffeine during pregnancy. *Pediatrics, 74(3),* 336-341.

40a.† Little, R. E., Young, A., Streissguth, A. P., & Uhl, C. N. (1984). Preventing fetal alcohol effects: Effectiveness of a demonstration project. In R. Porter, M. O'Connor, & J. Whelen

(Eds.), CIBA Foundation Symposium 105: *Mechanisms of Alcohol Damage in Utero* (pp. 254-274). London: Pitman.

40b.‡ Ervin, C. S., Little, R. E., Streissguth, A. P., & Bcck, D. E. (1984). Alcoholic fathering and its relation to child's intellectual development: A pilot investigation. *Alcoholism: Clinical and Experimental Research, 8(4),* 362-365.

1985

41. Stock, D. L., Streissguth, A. P., & Martin, D. C. (1985). Neonatal sucking as an outcome variable: Comparison of quantitative and clinical assessments. *Early Human Development, 10,* 273-278.

42. Streissguth, A. P., & Little, R. E. (1985). Alcohol-related morbidity and mortality in offspring of drinking women: Methodological issues and a review of pertinent studies. In M. A. Schuckit (Ed.), *Alcohol patterns and problems* (Vol. 5, pp. 113-155). New Brunswick: Rutgers University Press.

43.‡ Streissguth, A. P., Clarren, S. K., & Jones, K. L. (1985). Natural history of the Fetal Alcohol Syndrome: A 10-year follow-up of eleven patients. *Lancet, 2,* 85-91.

44. Streissguth, A. P., & LaDue, R. A. (1985). Alteraciones psicológicas y del comportamiento en niños expuestos al alcohol antes del nacimiento. In *Proceedings of jornadas internacionales sindrome alcoholico fetal* (pp. 111-129). Madrid, Spain: Fundacion Valgrande.

44a.† Little, R. E., Streissguth, A. P., Guzinski, G. M., Uhl, C. N., Paulozzi, L., Mann, S. L., Young, A., Clarren, S. K., & Grathwol, H. L. (1985). A evaluation of the pregnancy and health program. *Alcohol Health and Research World. 10(1),* 44-53, 75.

1986

45. Streissguth, A. P. (1986). Fetal Alcohol Syndrome: An overview and implications for patient management. In N. J. Estes and M. E. Heinemann (Eds.), *Alcoholism: Development, Consequences, and Interventions* (pp. 195-206). St. Louis: Mosby.

46. Streissguth, A. P., Barr, H. M., Martin, D. C., & Darby, B. L. (1986) The Fetal Alcohol Syndrome as a model for the study of the behavioral teratology of alcohol. In N. A. Krasnegor, D. B.

Gray, & T. Thompson (Eds.), *Developmental behavioral pharmacology* (Vol. 5, pp. 265-291). Hillsdale, NJ: Erlbaum.

47.   Streissguth, A. P. (1986). Smoking and drinking during pregnancy and offspring learning disabilities: A review of the literature and development of a research strategy. In M. Lewis (Ed.), *Learning disabilities and prenatal risk* (pp. 28-67). Urbana-Champaign, IL: University of Illinois Press.

48.   Streissguth, A. P. (1986). The behavioral teratology of alcohol: Performance, behavioral, and intellectual deficits in prenatally exposed children: A review of the literature. In J. R. West (Ed.), *Alcohol and brain development* (pp. 3-44). New York: Oxford University Press.

49.   Streissguth, A. P., Barr, H. M., Sampson, P. D., Parrish-Johnson, J. C., Kirchner, G. L., & Martin, D. C. (1986). Attention, distraction and reaction time at age 7 years and prenatal alcohol exposure. *Neurobehavioral Toxicology and Teratology, 8(6),* 717-725.

50.   Streissguth, A. P., Sampson, P. D., Barr, H. M., Clarren, S. K., & Martin, D. C. (1986). Studying alcohol teratogenesis from the perspective of the Fetal Alcohol Syndrome: Methodological and statistical issues. In H. M. Wisniewski & D. A. Snider (Eds.), *Mental retardation: Research, education, & technology transfer* (Vol. 477, pp. 63-86). New York: New York Academy of Sciences.

51.   Sampson, P. D., Bookstein, F. L., Clarren, S. K., & Streissguth, A. P. (1986). *Tensor biometric analysis of landmark data in dysmorphology* (Report No. 92). Seattle: University of Washington, Department of Statistics.

51a.‡ Streissguth, A. P., LaDue, R. A., & Randels, S. (1986). A Manual on Adolescents and Adults with Fetal Alcohol Syndrome and Fetal Alcohol Effects with Special Reference to American Indians. Published by the Indian Health Service, U. S. Department of Health and Human Services, Public Health Service. Available free from Indian Health Service, Headquarters West, 300 San Mateo NE, Suite 500, Albuquerque, New Mexico 87108; Attn: Lisa K. Snyder, M.H.R.

51b.† Streissguth, A. P. (1986). Alcohol and motherhood: Physiological findings and the fetal alcohol syndrome. *Women and Alcohol: Health-Related Issues* (Research Monograph No. 16, pp. 215-225). Rockville, MD: U.S. Department of Health & Human Services.

1987

52.   Clarren, S. K., Sampson, P. D., Larsen, J., Donnell, D., Barr, H.
       M., Bookstein, F. L., Martin, D. C., & Streissguth, A. P. (1987).
       Facial effects of fetal alcohol exposure: Assessment by
       photographs and morphometric analysis. *American Journal of
       Medical Genetics, 26(3)*, 651-666.

53.   Streissguth, A. P., & LaDue, R. A. (1987). Fetal alcohol:
       Teratogenic causes of developmental disabilities. In S. Schroeder
       (Ed.), *Toxic substances and mental retardation* (pp. 1-32).
       Washington, DC: American Association on Mental Deficiency.

54.   Streissguth, A. P., Treder, R. P., Barr, H. M., Shepard, T. H.,
       Bleyer, W. A., Sampson, P. D., & Martin, D. C. (1987). Aspirin
       and acetaminophen use by pregnant women and subsequent child
       IQ and attention decrements. *Teratology, 35(2)*, 211-219.

55.   Streissguth, A. P. (1987, September). FAS: Only the tip of the
       iceberg. *U. S. Journal of Drug and Alcohol Dependence*, pg. 8.

56.   Sampson, P. D., Streissguth, A. P., Vega-Gonzales, S. C., Barr,
       H. M., & Bookstein, F. L. (1987). *Predicting classroom
       behavior ratings by prenatal alcohol exposure: Latent variable
       modeling and non-linear scaling* (Tech. Report No. 103). Seattle:
       University of Washington, Department of Statistics.

57.   Giunta, C. T., Barr, H. M., Gillespie, J. M., & Streissguth, A. P.
       (1987) *Techniques for minimizing subject attrition in
       longitudinal research* (Tech. Report No. 87-01). Seattle:
       University of Washington, Pregnancy and Health Study.

58.   Darby, B. L., & Streissguth, A. P. (1987). *The children's memory
       task scoring manual (CMT)* (Tech. Rep. No. 87-03). Seattle:
       University of Washington, Pregnancy and Health Study.

59.   Streissguth, A. P., Barr, H. M., Darby, B. L., & Ervin, C. H.
       (1987, 1991) *The MIIS, a simple and reliable method of
       assessing mother-infant interactions which predict 4 year I. Q.*
       (Tech. Rep. No. 87-02). Seattle: University of Washington,
       Pregnancy and Health Study.

59a.† Streissguth, A. P., LaDue, R. A., & Randels, S. P. (1987). Indian
       adolescents and adults with fetal alcohol syndrome: Findings and
       recommendations. *The IHS Primary Care Provider, 12(11)*, 89-
       91.

59b.† Little, R. E. & Streissguth, A. P. (1987). Reducing fetal alcohol
       effects: The Seattle pregnancy and health program. In F.

Majewski (Ed.), *Die Alkohol-Embryopathie* (pp. 197-203). Frankfurt/Main: Umwelt & Medizin Verlagsgessellschaft mbH.

1988

60.   Graham, J. M., Hanson, J. W., Darby, B. L., Barr, H. M., & Streissguth, A.P. (1988). Independent dysmorphology evaluations at birth and 4 years of age for children exposed to varying amounts of alcohol in utero. *Pediatrics, 81*(6), 772-778.

61.‡   Streissguth, A. P., & Randels, S. P. (1988). Long term effects of Fetal Alcohol Syndrome. In G. C. Robinson & R. W. Armstrong (Eds.), *Alcohol and child/family health* (pp. 135-151). Vancouver, BC: University of British Columbia.

61a.‡ Giunta, C. T. & Streissguth, A. P. (1988). Patients with fetal alcohol syndrome and their caretakers. *Social Casework: The Journal of Contemporary Social Work, 69(7),* 453-459.

61b.‡ Streissguth, A. P. & Giunta, C. T. (1988). Mental health and health needs of infants and preschool children with fetal alcohol syndrome. *International Journal of Family Psychiatry, 9(1),* 29-47.

1989

62.‡   Streissguth, A. P. (1989). Fetal Alcohol Syndrome: Public health implications and recent findings. *Washington Public Health, 7(1),* 5-7.

63.   Streissguth, A. P., Barr, H. M., Sampson, P. D., Darby, B. L. & Martin, D. C. (1989). IQ at age 4 in relation to maternal alcohol use and smoking during pregnancy. *Developmental Psychology, 25(1),* 3-11.

64.   Streissguth, A. P., Sampson, P. D., & Barr, H. M. (1989). Neurobehavioral dose-response effects of prenatal alcohol exposure in humans from infancy to adulthood. In D. E. Hutchings (Ed.), *Prenatal abuse of licit and illicit drugs* (Vol. 562, pp.145-158). New York: Annals of the New York Academy of Sciences.

65.   Streissguth, A. P., Barr, H. M., Sampson, P. D., Bookstein, F. L., & Darby, B. L. (1989). Neurobehavioral effects of prenatal alcohol. Part I: Literature review and research strategy. *Neurotoxicology and Teratology, 11(5),* 461-476.

66.   Sampson, P. D., Streissguth, A. P., Barr, H. M., & Bookstein, F. L. (1989). Neurobehavioral effects of prenatal alcohol. Part II:

Partial Least Squares analysis. *Neurotoxicology and Teratology, 11(5),* 477-491.

67.   Streissguth, A. P., Bookstein, F. L., Sampson, P. D., & Barr, H. M. (1989). Neurobehavioral effects of prenatal alcohol. Part III: PLS analyses of neuropsychological tests. *Neurotoxicology and Teratology, 11(5),* 493-507.

68.   Ketterlinus, R. D., Bookstein, F. L., Sampson, P. D., & Lamb, M. E. (1989). Partial least squares analysis in developmental psychopathology. *Development and Psychopathology, 1,* 351-371.

1990

69.   Barr, H. M., Streissguth, A. P., Darby, B. L., & Sampson, P. D. (1990). Prenatal exposure to alcohol, caffeine, tobacco and aspirin: Effects on fine and gross motor performance in 4-year old children. *Developmental Psychology, 26(3),* 339-348.

70.   Driscoll, C. D., Streissguth, A. P., & Riley, E. P. (1990). Prenatal alcohol exposure: Comparability of effects in humans and animal models. *Neurotoxicology and Teratology, 12(3),* 231-237.

71.   Bookstein, F. L., & Sampson, P. D. (1990). Statistical models for geometric components of shape change. *Communications in Statistics, 19(5),* 1939-1972.

72.   Bookstein, F. L., Sampson, P. D., Streissguth, A. P., & Barr, H. M. (1990). Measuring "dose" and "response" with multivariate data using Partial Least Squares Techniques. *Communications in Statistics, 19(3),* 765-804.

73.†‡ Streissguth, A. P. (1990). Fetal Alcohol Syndrome and the teratogenicity of alcohol: Policy implications. *King County Medical Society Bulletin, 69(5),* 32-39.

74.†   Streissguth, A. P. (1990). What we can do about Fetal Alcohol Syndrome. *Dispatch International,* 1-4.

75.   Streissguth, A. P. (1990). Prenatal alcohol-induced brain damage and long term postnatal consequences: Introduction to the symposium. *Alcoholism: Clinical and Experimental Research, 14*(5), 648-649.

76.   Streissguth, A. P., Barr, H. M., & Sampson, P. D. (1990). Moderate prenatal alcohol exposure: Effects on child IQ and learning problems at age 7 1/2 years. *Alcoholism: Clinical and Experimental Research, 14(5),* 662-669.

77.† Streissguth, A. P. (1990). Today I visited an Aleut village: Observations on preventing fetal alcohol syndrome. *The IHS Provider, 15(7),* 125-127.

78. Martin, D. C., Borg-Breen, D., Martin, J. C., & Streissguth, A. P. (1990). Microcomputer measurement and analysis of newborn sucking. *Behavior Research Methods, Instruments, & Computers, 22(4),* 393-401.

79.‡ Burgess, D. M., & Streissguth, A. P. (1990). Educating students with fetal alcohol syndrome or fetal alcohol effects. *Pennsylvania Reporter, 22(1),* 1-3.

80. Streissguth, A. P. (1990). Fetal alcohol syndrome and the teratogenicity of alcohol. In C. N. Stefanis, A. D. Rabavilas, & C. R. Soldatos (Eds.), *Psychiatry: A world perspective, Volume 1: Classification and psychopathology; child psychiatry; substance use.* Proceedings of the VIII World Congress of Psychiatry, Athens, 12-19 October, 1989. Amsterdam; New York: Excerpts Medica; New York, USA: Elsevier Science Publishers.

1991

81. Barr, H. M., & Streissguth, A. P. (1991). Caffeine use during pregnancy and child outcome: A 7-year prospective study. *Neurotoxicology & Teratology, 13(4),* 441-448.

82. Streissguth, A. P., Grant, T. M., Barr, H. M., Brown, Z. A., Martin, J. C., Mayock, D. E., Ramey, S. L., Moore, L. (1991). Cocaine and the use of alcohol and other drugs during pregnancy. *American Journal of Obstetrics & Gynecology, 164(5):*1239-1243.

83.‡ Streissguth, A. P., Aase, J. M., Clarren, S. K., Randels, S. P., LaDue, R. A., & Smith, D. F. (1991). Fetal alcohol syndrome in adolescents and adults. *Journal of the American Medical Association, 265(15),* 1961-1967.

84.‡ Streissguth, A. P., Randels, S. P., & Smith, D. F. (1991). A test-retest study of intelligence in patients with fetal alcohol syndrome: Implications for care. *Journal of the American Academy of Child and Adolescent Psychiatry, 30(4),* 584-587.

85.† Streissguth, A. P. (1991). Neonatal effects of alcohol use. In J. Kinney *Clinical Manual of Substance Abuse* (part II, chapter 14, pp. 202-206). St. Louis, Missouri: Mosby Year Book.

86.† Streissguth, A. P. (1991). The 1990 Betty Ford Lecture, What every community should know about drinking during pregnancy and the lifelong consequences for society. *Substance Abuse, 12*(3), 114-127.

1992

87.‡ LaDue, R. A., Streissguth, A. P., & Randels, S. P. (1992). Clinical considerations pertaining to adolescents and adults with Fetal Alcohol Syndrome. In T. B. Sonderegger (Ed.), *Perinatal substance abuse: Research findings and clinical implications* (pp. 104–131). Baltimore: The Johns Hopkins University Press.

88. Streissguth, A. P. (1992). Fetal alcohol syndrome: Early and long-term consequences. In L.Harris (Ed.), *Problems of drug dependence 1991: Proceeding of the 53rd annual scientific meeting* (National Institute on Drug Abuse Research Monograph No. 119). Rockville, MD: U.S. Department of Health and Human Services.

89.‡ Randels, S. P., & Streissguth, A. P. (1992). Fetal alcohol syndrome and nutrition issues. *Nutrition Focus, 7(3)*, 1-6.

90. Streissguth, A. P., & Giunta, C. T. (1992). Subject recruitment and retention for longitudinal research: Practical considerations for a nonintervention model . In M. M. Kilbey & K. Asghar (Eds.), *Methodological issues in epidemiological, prevention, and treatment research on drug-exposed women and their children.* [National Institute on Drug Abuse Monograph No. 117]. Rockville, Maryland: U.S. Department of Health and Human Services, Public Health Service.

91.‡ Carmichael Olson, H., Burgess, D. M., & Streissguth, A. P. (1992). Fetal alcohol syndrome (FAS) and fetal alcohol effects (FAE): A lifespan view, with implications for early intervention. *ZERO TO THREE / National Center for Clinical Infant Programs, 13(1)*, 24-29.

92.‡ Streissguth, A. P. (1992). Fetal alcohol syndrome and fetal alcohol effects: A clinical perspective of later developmental consequences. In I. S. Zagon & T. A. Slotkin (Eds.) *Maternal substance abuse and the developing nervous system* (pp. 5–25). San Diego, CA: Academic Press, Inc.

93.‡ Burgess, D. M. & Streissguth, A. P. (1992). Fetal alcohol syndrome and fetal alcohol effects: Principles for educators. *Phi Delta Kappan, 74(1)*, 24-29.

94.   Streissguth, A. P., Barr, H. M., & Sampson, P. D. (1992). Alcohol use during pregnancy on child development: Report on a longitudinal, prospective study of human behavioral teratology. In C. W. Greenbaum & J. G. Auerbach (Eds.), *Longitudinal studies of children at psychological risk: Cross-national perspectives* (pp.174-200). Norwood, NJ: Ablex.

95.   Carmichael Olson, H., Sampson, P. D., Barr, H., Streissguth, A. P., & Bookstein, F. L. (1992). Prenatal exposure to alcohol and school problems in late childhood: A longitudinal prospective study. *Development and Psychopathology, 4,* 341-359.

95a.‡ LaDue, R. A., O'Hara, B.A. (1992). Documentation of critical issues related to the comprehensive Indian Fetal Alcohol Syndrome (FAS) Prevention and Treatment Act. *Focus: Dislocation and Relocation of American Indians and Japanese Americans, 6(2),* 8-9. [Official publication of Division 45 of the American Psychological Association. Centennial Convention Issue].

96.   Streissguth, A. P. (1992). Fetal alcohol syndrome in older patients. *Proceedings of 6th ISBRA Congress,* A & A, Suppl 1.

97.‡   Burgess, D. M., Lasswell, S. L., & Streissguth, A. P. (1992) *Educating Children Prenatally Exposed to Alcohol and Other Drugs.* The Planning for Learning Project. Sponsored by the Washington State Legislature and the Fetal Alcohol & Drug Unit, University of Washington, Seattle.

98.   Feldman J., Kerr B., & Streissguth A. P. (1992). *Correlational analyses of procedural and declarative learning performance* (Tech. Rep. No. 92-06). Seattle: University of Washington, Pregnancy & Health Study.

Manuscripts in Press and Submitted

99.†   Streissguth, A. P. (in press). Developmental neurotoxicity of alcohol: State of the research and implications for public policy and future directions. In G. Melton, T. Sonderegger, and S. Schroeder (Eds.), *Behavioral toxicology of childhood and adolescence.* Lincoln, NE: University of Nebraska Press.

100.‡ Streissguth, A. P., Sampson, P. D., Barr, H. M., Bookstein, F. L., & Carmichael Olson, H. (in press). Effects of prenatal alcohol vs. tobacco on children: Contributions from the Seattle longitudinal prospective study and implications for public policy. In H. L. Needleman and D. Bellinger (Eds.) *Prenatal Exposure to Toxicants: Developmental Consequences.* Johns Hopkins University Press.

101. Carmichael Olson, H. Streissguth, A.P., Bookstein, F.L., Barr H.M, Sampson, P.D. (in press). Developmental research in behavioral teratology: The impact of prenatal alcohol exposure on child development. In S. L. Friedman and H. C. Haywood (Eds.). *Developmental Follow-up: Concepts, Domains, and Methods.* Orlando, FL, Academic Press.

102. Kopera-Frye, K. & Streissguth, A. P. (in press) Fetal alcohol syndrome: Clinical implications, effects on development, and prevention. In Lieber, C. S., & Seltz, H. K. (Eds.) *Alkoholismus und Alkoholische Organischaden* .

103. Streissguth, A.P., & Dehaene, P. (in press). Fetal alcohol syndrome in twins of alcoholic mothers: Concordance of diagnosis and IQ. Journal of American Human Genetics.

104. Streissguth, A. P, Sampson, P. D., Carmichael Olson, H., Bookstein, F. L., Barr, H. M., Scott, M., Feldman, J., & Mirsky, A. F. (in press). Maternal drinking during pregnancy: Attention and and short-term memory performance in 14-year-old offspring: A longitudinal prospective study. *Alcoholism: Clinical & Experimental Research.*

105. Streissguth, A. P., Barr, H. M., Carmichael Olson, H., Sampson, P. D., Bookstein, F. L., & Burgess, D. M. (submitted) *Drinking during pregnancy decreases Word Attack and arithmetic scores on standardized tests: Adolescent data from a population-based prospective study.*

106. Sampson, P. D., Bookstein, F. L., Barr, H. M., & Streissguth, A. P. (submitted) *Prenatal alcohol exposure, birthweight and measures of child size from birth to age 14 years*

Outline: Seattle Study Maternal Prenatal Interview

1.	Personal data and pregnancy history:	29 questions
2.	Smoking habits:	8 questions
3.	Beverage consumption during pregnancy (5 months):	
	Coffee:	5 questions
	Tea:	5 questions
	Wine:	5 questions
	Beer:	5 questions
	Liquor:	5 questions
	Colas, soft drinks and diet drinks:	5 questions
4.	Beverage use in month or so prior to pregnancy or pregnancy recognition:	
	Same as above categories:	5 questions in each category
5.	Overconsumption:	
	Attempts to control consumption:	4 questions
	Number of intoxications during pregnancy:	5 questions
	Problems due to drinking	4 questions
6.	Reasons for drinking:	27 questions, with yes/no answers
7.	Changes in beverage consumption during pregnancy:	8 questions
8.	Drug and medicine usage during pregnancy:	26 questions
9.	Diet during pregnancy:	15 questions

Seattle Study Maternal Prenatal Interview: Quantity-Frequency-Variability Questions for Beverage Consumption

(Identical questions asked for coffee, tea, wine, beer, liquor, and cola soft drinks)

(Same questions asked for the month or so prior to pregnancy or prior to pregnancy recognition)

During this pregnancy, how often have you been drinking wine? Choose one of the statements from the blue sheet to describe how often you drink wine. (Read statements aloud, beginning at top—while subject looks at identical list on blue sheet.)

- (8) 3 or more times a day
- (7) 2 times a day
- (6) about once a day
- (5) 3 or 4 times a week
- (4) once or twice a week
- (3) 2 or 3 times a month
- (2) about once a month
- (1) less than once a month
- (0) not at all

Think of all the times you've had wine recently. When you do drink wine, how often do you have 5 glasses or more? Choose one of the statements from the pink sheet to describe how often. (Read statements aloud—while subject looks at identical list on pink sheet.)

- (4) nearly every time
- (3) more than half the time
- (2) less than half the time
- (1) once in a while
- (0) never

When you do drink wine, how often do you have 3 or 4 glasses? (Read statements aloud—while subject looks at identical list on pink sheet.)

- (4) nearly every time
- (3) more than half the time
- (2) less than half the time
- (1) once in a while
- (0) never

How often do you have only 1 or 2 glasses? (Read statements aloud—while subject looks at identical list on pink sheet.)

- (4) nearly every time
- (3) more than half the time
- (2) less than half the time
- (1) once in a while
- (0) never

Seattle Study Maternal Prenatal Interview: Supplemental Alcohol Questions

(Same questions asked for the month or so prior to pregnancy or prior to pregnancy recognition)

Any subject who reported ingesting 5 or more drinks on an occasion was given "supplemental" alcohol questions which asked the number of times that 5–7, 8–11, or 12-or-more drinks were ingested. Questions were asked of each time period (the month prior to pregnancy recognition and during pregnancy; see Room, 1970).

1. About how many times since you have been pregnant would you say you had at least 12 drinks (see the pink band on the card)? That's about a pint of whiskey or other liquor, 5 quarts (or 15 cans) of beer, a fifth of sherry or 2 fifths (or bottles) of table wine—or some combination that's roughly equivalent to that much alcohol.

    (Code number of times, code "0" if none). _____

    Types of beverage: _____

2. About how many times since you have been pregnant would you say you had between 8 and 11 drinks (see the green band on the card)? That's about 3/4 a pint of whiskey or other liquor, or 4 quarts (or 10 cans) of beer, or 3/4 of a bottle of sherry or sweet wine—or 1 1-2 bottles of table wine—or some combination that's roughly equivalent to that much alcohol.

    (Code number of times, code "0" if none). _____

    Types of beverage: _____

3. About how many times since you have been pregnant would you
   say you had between 5 and 7 drinks (see the yellow band on the
   card)? That is about a half pint of whiskey or other liquor, 3
   quarts (or 7 cans) of beer, or about a half bottle of sherry or 1
   bottle of table wine—or some combination that's roughly
   equivalent to that much alcohol.

   (Code number of times, code "0" if none).   _____
   Types of beverage: _____

Chronological Listing of Outcome Variables (Birth Through 7 Years) Arranged by Outcome Blocks for Data Analysis: Distribution Statistics, Correlations with IQ, and Means by Binge Drinking in Early Pregnancy

	Alcohol Exposure (Mean Scores)			Total Sample				
Items by Outcome Blocks	Binge P	No Binge	N	M	±	SD	Min	Max
Block 1. Attention in Neonates (Att-0)								
1. Habituation Light - NBAS	4.58	5.23	400	5.06	±	1.58	1 - 9	
2. Habituation Rattle - NBAS	5.19	5.71	369	5.57	±	1.99	1 - 9	
3. Habituation Bell - NBAS	5.42	5.49	347	5.47	±	1.98	1 - 9	
4. Habituation Pinprick - NBAS	3.48	3.62	284	3.58	±	1.52	1 - 9	
5. Orientation Ball - NBAS	5.40	5.49	380	5.47	±	2.17	1 - 9	
6. Orientation Rattle - NBAS	6.26	6.32	401	6.30	±	1.69	1 - 9	
7. Orientation Face - NBAS	5.79	5.68	372	5.71	±	1.94	1 - 9	
8. Orientation Voice - NBAS	6.91	7.07	393	7.03	±	1.78	1 - 9	
9. Orientation Voice & Face - NBAS	6.02	5.94	367	5.96	±	1.91	1 - 9	
10. Alertness - NBAS	4.82	4.92	402	4.89	±	2.12	1 - 9	

(Appendix IIIa continues on next page)

227

	Alcohol Exposure (Mean Scores)		Total Sample					
Items by Outcome Blocks	Binge P	No Binge	N	M	±	SD	Min	Max
11. Consolability - NBAS	6.81	6.94	309	6.91	±	1.55	1 -	9
12. Peak of Excitement - NBAS	6.42	6.62	416	6.56	±	1.30	3 -	9
13. Rapidity of Buildup - NBAS	4.37	4.59	415	4.53	±	1.72	1 -	9
14. Irritability - NBAS	4.85	4.91	415	4.89	±	2.09	1 -	9
15. Activity - NBAS	4.89	4.68	414	4.73	±	1.23	2 -	8
16. Lability of States - NBAS	3.44	3.57	407	3.54	±	1.83	1 -	9
17. Self-quieting - NBAS	5.95	6.07	400	6.04	±	2.25	1 -	9
18. Number of Smiles - NBAS	.20	.36	416	.32	±	.88	0 -	7
19. Glabella - Reflex	2.09	2.06	410	2.07	±	.40	0 -	3
20. Abnormal Glabella - Reflex	.15	.14	410	.15			0 -	1
21. Rotation of eyes - Reflex	3.72	3.75	403	3.74	±	.84	0 -	4
22. Abn Eye Rotation L or R - Reflex	.10	.10	403	.10			0 -	1
23. Nystagmus - Reflex	.10	.12	399	.11			0 -	1
24. Clonus Threshold	3.95	3.94	416	3.94	±	.38	1 -	4
25. Plantar Threshold	1.13	1.14	416	1.13	±	.39	1 -	3
26. Babinski Threshold	1.23	1.22	416	1.23	±	.52	1 -	4
27. Passive Arms Threshold	1.18	1.30	412	1.27	±	.56	1 -	4
28. Passive Legs Threshold	1.16	1.18	411	1.17	±	.47	1 -	4

29.	Rooting Threshold	1.56	1.58	416	1.58 ± .85	1 - 4
30.	Sucking Threshold	1.17	1.27	415	1.24 ± .53	1 - 4
31.	Palmar Threshold	1.33	1.27	413	1.29 ± .57	1 - 4
32.	Standing Threshold	1.44	1.30	414	1.34 ± .68	1 - 4
33.	Walking Threshold	1.66	1.45	412	1.50 ± .92	1 - 4
34.	Placing Threshold	1.46	1.35	411	1.38 ± .64	1 - 4
35.	Incurvation Threshold	1.71	1.83	416	1.80 ± 1.06	1 - 4
36.	Prone Head Mvt Threshold	2.18	2.31	413	2.28 ± .69	2 - 4
37.	Spontaneous Crawl Threshold	1.26	1.22	415	1.23 ± .59	1 - 4
38.	Stimulated Crawl Threshold	1.35	1.37	415	1.37 ± .79	1 - 4
39.	Glabella Threshold	1.09	1.10	410	1.10 ± .42	1 - 4
40.	Rotation Head Threshold	1.35	1.23	416	1.26 ± .76	1 - 4
41.	Rotation Eyes Threshold	1.17	1.14	404	1.15 ± .57	1 - 4
42.	TNR Threshold	2.28	2.16	415	2.19 ± 1.44	1 - 4
43.	Moro Threshold	1.25	1.19	415	1.21 ± .47	1 - 4
44.	Neonatal State	3.80	4.20	361	4.10 ± 3.47	0 - 8

Block 2. Neuromotor in Neonates (NMot-0)

45.	General Tonus - NBAS	5.43	5.19	415	5.25 ± 1.43	1 - 9
46.	Motor Maturity - NBAS	4.70	4.78	415	4.76 ± 1.30	1 - 8
47.	Pull-to-Sit - NBAS	5.05	5.10	412	5.09 ± 1.93	1 - 9
48.	Cuddliness - NBAS	5.44	5.73	415	5.65 ± 1.73	1 - 9

(Appendix III-a continues on next page)

Items by Outcome Blocks	Alcohol Exposure (Mean Scores)		Total Sample					
	Binge P	No Binge	N	M	±	SD	Min	Max
49. Defensive Movements - NBAS	6.41	6.40	414	6.40	±	1.93	1	9
50. Tremulousness - NBAS	5.72	5.76	416	5.75	±	2.47	1	9
51. Startle - NBAS	3.09	3.40	415	3.32	±	1.73	1	9
52. Lability Skin Color - NBAS	4.89	5.06	416	5.02	±	1.54	1	9
53. Hand-Mouth Behavior - NBAS	5.77	5.62	412	5.66	±	2.35	1	9
54. L & R Clonus - Reflex	4.04	4.03	416	4.03	±	.24	4	6
55. L & R Plantar - Reflex	4.01	4.00	416	4.00	±	.53	2	6
56. L & R Babinski - Reflex	3.87	3.90	416	3.89	±	.56	0	6
57. L & R Passive Arms - Reflex	3.88	3.80	412	3.82	±	1.04	0	6
58. L & R Passive Legs - Reflex	4.39	4.23	411	4.27	±	1.00	0	6
59. L & R Rooting - Reflex	3.70	3.48	416	3.54	±	1.33	0	6
60. Sucking Reflex - Reflex	1.91	1.93	415	1.93	±	.37	0	3
61. L & R Palmar - Reflex	4.00	4.02	412	4.02	±	.88	0	6
62. L & R Standing - Reflex	4.00	3.99	415	3.99	±	1.29	0	6
63. L & R Walking - Reflex	3.19	3.43	413	3.37	±	1.74	0	6
64. L & R Placing - Reflex	3.85	3.84	411	3.84	±	.80	0	6
65. L & R Incurvation - Reflex	2.99	2.89	416	2.92	±	1.60	0	6
66. Prone/Head Movement - Reflex	1.94	1.75	413	1.80	±	.77	0	3

					Range
67.	L & R Spont Crawl - Reflex	3.54	3.72	415	3.67 ± 1.02	0 - 6
68.	L & R Stimulated Crawl - Reflex	3.63	3.61	415	3.61 ± 1.02	0 - 4
69.	L & R Rotation of Head - Reflex	3.55	3.68	416	3.65 ± 1.03	0 - 4
70.	L & R TNR - Reflex	4.12	4.12	415	4.12 ± .44	4 - 6
71.	L & R Moro - Reflex	3.82	4.04	415	3.98 ± 1.00	0 - 6
72.	Abnormal Clonus - Reflex	.02	.02	416	.02	0 - 1
73.	Abnormal Plantar - Reflex	.07	.10	416	.09	0 - 1
74.	Abnormal Babinski - Reflex	.14	.10	416	.11	0 - 1
75.	Abnormal Passive Arms - Reflex	.31	.27	412	.28	0 - 1
76.	Abnormal Passive Legs - Reflex	.30	.27	411	.27	0 - 1
77.	Abnormal Rooting - Reflex	.39	.35	416	.36	0 - 1
78.	Weak Suck - Reflex	.16	.13	415	.14	0 - 1
79.	Abnormal Palmar - Reflex	.25	.24	412	.24	0 - 1
80.	Abnormal Standing - Reflex	.39	.36	415	.37	0 - 1
81.	Abnormal Walking - Reflex	.47	.49	413	.49	0 - 1
82.	Abnormal Placing - Reflex	.21	.22	411	.22	0 - 1
83.	Abnormal Incurvation - Reflex	.50	.54	415	.53	0 - 1
84.	Abnormal Head Movement - Reflex	.19	.23	413	.22	0 - 1
85.	Abnormal Spont Crawl - Reflex	.21	.25	415	.24	0 - 1
86.	Abnormal Stimulated Crawl - Reflex	.17	.14	415	.15	0 - 1
87.	Abnormal Rotation/Head - Reflex	.14	.11	416	.12	0 - 1

(Appendix III-a continues on next page)

Items by Outcome Blocks	Alcohol Exposure (Mean Scores)		Total Sample					
	Binge P	No Binge	N	M	±	SD	Min	Max
88. Abnormal TNR - Reflex	.08	.08	415	.08			0 -	1
89. Abnormal Moro - Reflex	.27	.28	415	.27			0 -	1
90. Number of Tremors - BO	25.17	25.52	416	25.43	±	27.82	0 -	99
91. Global Impression - GR	3.49	3.52	400	3.52	±	.97	1 -	6
Block 3. Attention at 8 months of age (Att-8)								
92. Cooperativeness - IBR	5.86	5.85	460	5.85	±	1.44	1 -	9
93. Object Exploitation - IBR	6.52	6.31	459	6.37	±	.91	3 -	9
94. Goal Directedness - IBR	5.32	5.12	460	5.17	±	1.45	2 -	8
95. Attention Span - IBR	6.05	5.84	460	5.90	±	1.01	3 -	9
96. Endurance - IBR	5.93	5.78	460	5.82	±	1.46	1 -	9
97. Activity - IBR	5.33	5.24	460	5.26	±	1.36	1 -	9
98. Reactivity - IBR	6.23	6.12	460	6.15	±	1.27	2 -	9
99. Focus, Self-Organization - IBR	5.27	5.28	428	5.28	±	1.51	1 -	9
100. The With-it Scale - IBR	5.54	5.58	427	5.57	±	1.56	2 -	9
101. Intense Periods of Excitement - BO	.08	.04	427	.05			0 -	1
102. Excessive Crying - BO	.04	.02	430	.03			0 -	1
103. Responsive to Social Situation - GR	4.23	4.21	431	4.21	±	.92	2 -	7

Block 4. Neuromotor at 8 Months of Age (NMot-8)

#				N	Mean ± SD	Range
104.	Psychomotor Dev Index - BSID	107.47	108.50	461	108.21 ± 14.50	60 - 150
105.	Fine Motor Development - GR	3.86	3.98	433	3.95 ± 1.15	1 - 7
106.	Gross Motor Development - GR	4.39	4.36	433	4.37 ± 1.03	2 - 7
107.	Any Unusual Hand Behaviors - BO	.19	.14	402	.15	0 - 1
108.	Any Clear Tremor - BO	.06	.05	429	.06	0 - 1
109.	Any Other Unusual Behaviors - BO	.13	.13	384	.13	0 - 1
110.	General Body Tension - IBR	4.40	4.18	460	4.24 ± 1.36	1 - 8
111.	General Body Tone - IBR	5.29	5.10	402	5.15 ± .78	2 - 9
112.	Poor Quality Performance - IBR	4.76	4.63	427	4.67 ± 1.33	1 - 9

Block 5. Mental/Language at 8 Months of Age (Ment-8)

#				N	Mean ± SD	Range
113.	Mental Dev Index - BSID	115.57	115.62	461	115.60 ± 16.32	64 - 151
114.	General Mental Dev - GR	4.12	4.19	417	4.17 ± .86	2 - 7
115.	Overall Impression - GR	3.99	4.10	430	4.07 ± .96	1 - 7

Block 6. Attention at 18 months of age (Att-18)

#				N	Mean ± SD	Range
116.	Cooperativeness - IBR	4.92	5.14	489	5.08 ± 1.81	2 - 9
117.	Object Exploitation - IBR	5.73	5.71	488	5.72 ± 1.00	2 - 9
118.	Goal Directedness - IBR	4.71	5.07	489	4.97 ± 1.37	2 - 9
119.	Attention Span - IBR	5.27	5.35	489	5.33 ± 1.09	1 - 9
120.	Endurance - IBR	4.63	4.78	488	4.73 ± 1.75	1 - 9

(Appendix III-a continues on next page)

	Alcohol Exposure (Mean Scores)		Total Sample					
Items by Outcome Blocks	Binge P	No Binge	N	M	±	SD	Min	Max
121. Activity at Table - IBR	5.49	5.30	489	5.36	±	1.25	3	9
122. Activity on Floor - IBR	6.05	5.81	458	5.88	±	1.10	3	9
123. Reactivity - IBR	5.72	5.65	487	5.67	±	1.17	2	9
124. Focus, Self-Organization - IBR	5.18	5.36	488	5.31	±	1.40	2	9
125. The With-it Scale - IBR	5.78	6.01	474	5.95	±	1.44	2	9
126. Enthusiastic Approach to Obj - IBR	.83	.86	468	.85			0	1
127. Intense Periods of Excitement - BO	.06	.04	489	.05			0	1
128. Excessive Crying - BO	.05	.05	488	.05			0	1
129. Responsive to Social Situation - GR	4.10	4.21	488	4.18	±	.97	2	7
130. Distracted by Noises - BR	1.07	.99	475	1.01	±	.61	0	3
131. Distracted by Sights - BR	1.08	1.23	476	1.19	±	.71	0	3
132. Inattention to Tasks - BR	1.49	1.49	476	1.49	±	.82	0	4
133. Unfocused Quality - BR	1.06	1.01	476	1.03	±	.90	0	4
134. Refuses to Cooperate - BR	1.17	1.02	475	1.06	±	.94	0	4
135. Hyperactive, Intense Motion - BR	.49	.39	476	.42	±	.78	0	4
Block 7. Neuromotor at 18 Months of Age (NMot-18)								
136. Psychomotor Dev Index - BSID	98.65	97.84	(486)	98.07	±	12.21	62	143
137. Fine Motor Development - GR	3.70	3.91	(488)	3.85	±	.76	2	6

				(N)	Mean ± SD	Range
138.	Gross Motor Development - GR	3.99	4.00	(488)	4.00 ± .78	1 - 7
139.	Any Unusual Hand Behaviors - BO	.02	.04	(488)	.03	0 - 1
140.	Any Clear Tremor - BO	.05	.06	(489)	.06	0 - 1
141.	Any Other Unusual Behaviors - BO	.04	.05	(486)	.05	0 - 1
142.	General Body Tension - IBR	4.91	4.91	(489)	4.91 ± .81	3 - 9
143.	General Body Tone - IBR	5.09	5.12	(487)	5.11 ± .53	3 - 8
144.	Poor Quality Performance - IBR	4.22	3.87	(480)	3.97 ± 1.50	1 - 8

Block 8. Mental/Language at 18 Months of Age (Ment-18)

				(N)	Mean ± SD	Range
145.	Mental Dev Index - BSID	104.24	106.05	(487)	105.53 ± 15.90	58 - 151
146.	Receptive Verbalization - BSID	3.15	3.15	(487)	3.15 ± 1.24	1 - 8
147.	Expressive Verbalization - BSID	3.86	3.94	(487)	3.91 ± 2.58	0 - 10
148.	Unclassified Verbalizations - BSID	1.54	1.48	(487)	1.49 ± .90	0 - 4
149.	General Mental Development - GR	4.08	4.29	(488)	4.23 ± 1.08	1 - 7
150.	Language Production - Quantity-GR	2.93	2.94	(487)	2.94 ± .85	1 - 5
151.	Language Production - Quality-GR	3.03	3.17	(487)	3.13 ± 1.00	0 - 5
152.	Lang Production - Spontaneity-GR	3.82	3.80	(469)	3.80 ± .83	0 - 5
153.	Overall Impression - GR	4.01	4.16	(488)	4.12 ± .97	2 - 7

(Appendix III-a continues on next page)

	Alcohol Exposure (Mean Scores)		Total Sample					
Items by Outcome Blocks	Binge P	No Binge	N	M	±	SD	Min	Max
Block 9. Attention at 4 years of age (Att-4)								
154. Cooperativeness - BR	5.49	5.99	456	5.84	±	2.14	1 -	9
155. Activity at Table - BR	4.89	4.58	456	4.68	±	1.43	1 -	9
156. Activity on Floor - BR	5.21	5.04	456	5.09	±	1.43	2 -	9
157. Reactivity - BR	5.88	5.76	452	5.80	±	1.61	1 -	9
158. Attention Span - BR	5.64	6.17	450	6.01	±	1.60	1 -	9
159. Goal Directedness - BR	5.46	5.91	456	5.77	±	1.66	2 -	9
160. Endurance - BR	5.80	6.18	455	6.06	±	1.96	1 -	9
161. Frustration Tolerance - BR	5.93	6.31	455	6.20	±	1.86	1 -	9
162. The With-it Scale - BR	5.99	6.15	455	6.10	±	1.71	1 -	9
163. Focus, Self-Organization - BR	5.96	6.48	456	6.32	±	2.05	1 -	9
164. Impulsivity-Reflectivity - BR	5.17	5.43	456	5.35	±	1.64	1 -	9
165. Intense Periods of Excitement - BO	.02	.02	456	.02			0 -	1
166. Responsive to Social Situation - GR	4.35	4.53	456	4.48	±	1.35	1 -	7
167. Errors of Omission - Vigilance	12.33	12.72	360	12.60	±	6.14	0 -	25
168. Errors of Commission - Vigilance	126.95	155.12	360	146.51	±	138.83	0 -	866
169. Log Ratio Correct Responses - Vig	.16	.15	360	.15	±	.16	0 -	0.69
170. Log Time in Motion - Vig	4.57	4.57	370	4.57	±	.67	3 -	6.19

#					
171.	Log Time Not Oriented - Vig	3.95	3.95	372	3.95 ± 1.57	0 - 6.58
172.	Talking During Vigilance - BO	2.57	2.40	374	2.45 ± 1.31	1 - 5
173.	Out of Seat During Vigilance - BO	1.58	1.39	374	1.45 ± .87	1 - 5
174.	Attempts to Converse Dur Vig - BO	2.06	1.93	374	1.97 ± 1.22	1 - 5
175.	Hyperactive Diagn. Now/Past - PRS	.07	.06	451	.06	0 - 1
176.	Easy to Care For - PRS	2.22	2.23	453	2.23 ± .97	1 - 5
177.	Overactivity (Psych Checklist) - PRS	.16	.11	453	.13	0 - 1
178.	Attention (Psych Checklist) - PRS	.07	.03	453	.05	0 - 1
179.	Impulsivity (Psych Checklist) - PRS	.07	.06	453	.06	0 - 1
180.	Excitable, Impulsive - PRS	1.05	.90	449	.95 ± .80	0 - 3
181.	Fails to Finish Things - PRS	.68	.59	451	.62 ± .63	0 - 3
182.	Restless, Squirmy - PRS	.76	.56	449	.62 ± .75	0 - 3
183.	Restless, Always Up & Going - PRS	1.01	.84	450	.89 ± .88	0 - 3
184.	Distractible - PRS	.37	.32	449	.34 ± .61	0 - 3
185.	Easily Frustrated - PRS	.81	.62	451	.68 ± .66	0 - 3
186.	Wiggles, Fiddles, Squirms - PRS	12.27	10.81	396	11.24 ± 7.02	0 - 51
187.	Verbal Interrup & Excess Talk - PRS	6.68	5.73	417	6.01 ± 4.52	0 - 20

Block 10. Neuromotor at 4 Years of Age (NMot-4)

#					
188.	WPPSI Mazes Scaled Score	10.82	11.52	452	11.30 ± 2.95	4 - 19
189.	WPPSI Geometric Design 1 Score	1.25	1.29	452	1.28 ± .50	0 - 2
190.	WPPSI Geometric Design 2 Score	.69	.68	452	.69 ± .58	0 - 2

(Appendix III-a continues on next page)

Items by Outcome Blocks	Alcohol Exposure (Mean Scores)		Total Sample					
	Binge P	No Binge	N	M	±	SD	Min	Max
191. WPPSI Geometric Design 3 Score	.83	.89	452	.87	±	.60	0 - 2	
192. WPPSI Geometric Design 4 Score	.26	.25	452	.25	±	.49	0 - 2	
193. WPPSI Geometric Design 5 Score	.27	.42	452	.38	±	.58	0 - 2	
194. WPPSI Geometric Design 6 Score	.06	.11	452	.10	±	.34	0 - 2	
195. WPPSI Geometric Design 7 Score	.04	.08	452	.06	±	.29	0 - 2	
196. WPPSI Geometric Design 8 Score	.01	.05	452	.04	±	.23	0 - 2	
197. WPPSI Geometric Design 9 Score	0.00	.01	452	.01	±	.08	0 - 1	
198. WPPSI Geometric Design 10 Score	.01	.01	452	.01	±	.15	0 - 2	
199. Unusual Line Direction (Torque)	.34	.35	410	.35			0 - 1	
200. Clockwise Circle (Torque)	.66	.62	443	.63			0 - 1	
201. Fine Motor Development - GR	4.22	4.40	454	4.35	±	.96	1 - 7	
202. Gross Motor Development - GR	4.04	4.20	455	4.15	±	1.05	1 - 7	
203. General Body Tone - BR	5.06	4.84	453	4.91	±	1.07	1 - 9	
204. Body Tension - BR	4.66	4.57	451	4.60	±	1.36	1 - 9	
205. Any Unusual Hand Behaviors - BO	.01	.00	456	.00			0 - 1	
206. Any Clear Tremor - BO	.04	.03	456	.03			0 - 1	
207. Any Other Unusual Behaviors- BO	.02	.02	456	.02			0 - 1	
208. Right Handedness- BO	.82	.88	455	.86			0 - 1	

#				N	Mean ± SD	Range
209.	Vert GB Errors - Dom - WMSB	27.28	25.05	429	25.73 ± 11.15	6 - 84
210.	Vert GB Errors - ND - WMSB	30.21	30.38	428	30.33 ± 13.15	3 - 94
211.	Vert GB Time in Err - Dom - WMSB	1.77	1.61	429	1.66 ± .44	0.53 - 3.31
212.	Vert GB Time in Err - ND - WMSB	1.90	1.83	428	1.85 ± .38	0.74 - 2.99
213.	Horz GB Errors - Dom - WMSB	18.57	17.46	430	17.80 ± 7.11	2 - 57
214.	Horz GB Errors - ND - WMSB	21.85	20.46	429	20.88 ± 8.45	2 - 54
215.	Horz GB Time in Err - Dom - WMSB	1.61	1.49	430	1.52 ± .37	0.41 - 2.62
216.	Horz GB Time in Err - ND - WMSB	1.72	1.65	429	1.67 ± .35	0.69 - 2.84
217.	Maze GB Errors - Dom - WMSB	46.09	43.28	431	44.13 ± 12.25	10 - 155
218.	Maze GB Errors - ND - WMSB	49.92	50.36	430	50.22 ± 11.75	26 - 130
219.	Maze GB Time in Err - Dom - WMSB	2.33	2.18	431	2.22 ± .38	0.59 - 3.03
220.	Maze GB Time in Err - ND - WMSB	2.43	2.37	430	2.39 ± .27	0.64 - 3.10
221.	1.3 cm RS Errors - Dom - WMSB	1.22	.99	430	1.06 ± 1.98	0 - 14
222.	1.3 cm RS Errors - ND - WMSB	1.96	1.81	429	1.85 ± 2.86	0 - 16
223.	1.3 cm RS Time in Err-Dom-WMSB	.15	.11	430	.12 ± .24	0 - 1.57
224.	1.3 cm RS Time in Err -ND-WMSB	.24	.21	429	.22 ± .34	0 - 2.54
225.	0.3 cm RS Errors - Dom - WMSB	4.82	3.82	430	4.13 ± 5.41	0 - 32
226.	0.3 cm RS Errors - ND - WMSB	6.28	5.11	429	5.47 ± 5.93	0 - 35
227.	0.3 cm RS Time in Err-Dom-WMSB	.48	.37	429	.40 ± .47	0 - 2.55
228.	0.3 cm RS Time in Err -ND-WMSB	.65	.56	428	.59 ± .54	0 - 2.46
229.	# Finger Taps - Trial 1 - Dom	13.98	14.10	451	14.06 ± 1.80	10 - 20

(Appendix III-a continues on next page)

Items by Outcome Blocks	Alcohol Exposure (Mean Scores)		Total Sample				
	Binge P	No Binge	N	M	± SD	Min	Max
230. # Finger Taps - Trial 2 - Dom	13.50	13.47	451	13.48	± 1.71	9	- 20
231. # Finger Taps - Trial 3 - Dom	13.17	13.17	451	13.17	± 1.73	9	- 18
232. # Finger Taps - Trial 1 - ND	13.23	13.18	449	13.19	± 1.73	8	- 19
233. # Finger Taps - Trial 2 - ND	12.39	12.52	449	12.48	± 1.67	8	- 17
234. # Finger Taps - Trial 3 - ND	12.37	12.26	449	12.29	± 1.60	7	- 18
235. Finger Tapping Fatigue - Dom	.81	.93	451	.89	± 1.09	-3	- 4
236. Finger Tapping Fatigue - ND	.87	.91	449	.90	± 1.05	-2	- 4
237. Log GB Time - Dom - WMSB	4.27	4.21	452	4.23	± .29	3.61	- 5.63
238. Log GB Time - ND - WMSB	4.32	4.29	450	4.30	± .33	3.58	- 5.83
239. Log # Pegs Dropped - Dom - WMSB	.29	.23	452	.24	± .42	0	- 1.95
240. Log # Pegs Dropped - ND - WMSB	.37	.37	450	.37	± .49	0	- 2.40
241. GB Strategy - Dom - WMSB	.06	.04	452	.05		0	- 1
242. GB Strategy - ND - WMSB	.09	.11	450	.11		0	- 1
243. Grip Strength - Dom	4.87	4.97	447	4.94	± 1.64	0.50	- 11
244. Grip Strength - ND	4.26	4.31	445	4.29	± 1.58	1	- 9
245. TPT - Incomplete - Dom	.07	.04	439	.05		0	- 1
246. TPT - Time - Dom	95.77	96.40	439	96.21	± 68.28	8	- 300
247. TPT - Incomplete - ND	.05	.03	436	.04		0	- 1

				Mean	±	SD	Range
248.	TPT - Time - ND	72.63	71.37	436	71.75	±	59.27	2 - 300
249.	TPT - Incomplete - Both	.02	.02	437	.02			0 - 1
250.	TPT - Time - Both	60.93	54.05	436	56.13	±	53.03	0 - 300
251.	Balance - GMB	63.85	64.41	454	64.24	±	10.26	8 - 94
252.	Distance Summary Score - GMB	50.07	50.03	442	50.05	±	17.85	9 - 96
253.	Stopping Accuracy - GMB	18.15	17.58	442	17.75	±	6.22	3 - 40
254.	Skipping: Arm - GMB	4.58	4.84	248	4.76	±	2.33	1 - 7
255.	Running: Arm - GMB	1.66	1.58	452	1.60	±	1.24	1 - 5
256.	Running: Torso - GMB	2.22	2.15	452	2.17	±	.75	1 - 3
257.	Small Ball Throw: Method - GMB	1.64	1.67	453	1.66	±	.94	1 - 5
258.	Small Ball Throw: Aim - GMB	1.96	1.98	439	1.97	±	.79	1 - 3
259.	Large Ball Throw - GMB	1.96	2.04	439	2.01	±	.78	1 - 3
260.	Large Ball Catch - GMB	3.04	3.02	449	3.03	±	.94	1 - 5
261.	Upstairs: Method - GMB	1.08	1.12	455	1.11	±	.38	1 - 2.50
262.	Downstairs: Method - GMB	1.90	1.87	455	1.88	±	.74	1 - 2.50
263.	Skipping: Method - GMB	2.81	2.69	444	2.73	±	1.29	1 - 4
264.	Large Ball Kick: Coordination-GMB	2.12	2.12	452	2.12	±	1.20	1 - 5

Block 11. Mental/Language at 4 Years of Age (Ment-4)

				Mean	±	SD	Range
265.	WPPSI Full Scale IQ	107.64	111.10	452	110.03	±	14.81	59 - 151
266.	WPPSI Verbal Scale IQ	107.88	110.51	452	109.69	±	15.89	61 - 150
267.	WPPSI Performance Scale IQ	105.74	109.61	452	108.41	±	13.38	64 - 148

(Appendix III-a continues on next page)

Items by Outcome Blocks	Alcohol Exposure (Mean Scores)		Total Sample					
	Binge P	No Binge	N	M	±	SD	Min	Max
268. WPPSI Information	12.11	12.41	452	12.32	±	2.95	3 - 19	
269. WPPSI Vocabulary	10.76	11.32	451	11.14	±	2.94	3 - 19	
270. WPPSI Arithmetic	11.24	12.14	451	11.86	±	3.14	4 - 19	
271. WPPSI Similarities	11.24	11.44	452	11.38	±	3.19	4 - 19	
272. WPPSI Comprehension	11.16	11.21	451	11.19	±	3.47	1 - 19	
273. WPPSI Animal House	11.05	11.56	452	11.40	±	3.19	1 - 18	
274. WPPSI Pictures Completion	11.56	12.16	452	11.98	±	2.67	4 - 19	
275. WPPSI Geometric Design	9.81	10.30	452	10.15	±	2.55	3 - 18	
276. WPPSI Block Design	11.01	11.52	451	11.36	±	2.83	4 - 19	
277. General Mental Development - GR	4.34	4.49	455	4.44	±	1.17	1 - 7	
278. Language Development - GR	4.16	4.14	426	4.15	±	1.17	1 - 7	
279. Overall Impression - GR	4.26	4.38	456	4.34	±	1.14	1 - 7	
280. Predict Acad Adjust Problems - PRS	2.26	2.16	452	2.19	±	1.13	1 - 5	
281. Concerns about Starting School-PRS	.22	.19	453	.20			0 - 1	
282. Difficulty Learning - PRS	.12	.12	447	.12	±	.38	0 - 3	
283. Different Speech for Age - PRS	.23	.26	451	.25	±	.56	0 - 3	

Block 12. Attention at 7 Years of Age (Att-7)

284.	CPT Log Err of Omission X-Task	1.35	1.31	454	1.32	±	.83	0 - 3.47
285.	CPT Log Err of Omission AX-Task	1.63	1.43	454	1.49	±	.79	0 - 3.30
286.	CPT Log Err of Commission X	1.94	1.80	454	1.84	±	.87	0 - 4.55
287.	CPT Log Err of Commission AX	1.76	1.38	454	1.49	±	.90	0 - 4.39
288.	CPT Ratio Correct Responses X	.84	.86	454	.86	±	.13	0.27 - 1.00
289.	CPT Ratio Correct Responses AX	.86	.90	454	.89	±	.12	0.27 - 1.00
290.	CPT Mean Reaction Time X	71.53	71.43	454	71.46	±	6.02	54 - 91
291.	CPT Log % Time in Motion X	1.98	1.86	410	1.89	±	.87	0 - 3.93
292.	CPT Log % Time in Motion AX	2.50	2.33	412)	2.37	±	.90	0 - 4.26
293.	CPT Attention to Screen X	.99	.81	428	.86	±	.93	0 - 3
294.	CPT Attention to Screen AX	1.11	.98	425	1.02	±	.98	0 - 4
295.	CPT Awareness of Errors X	1.72	1.71	424	1.71	±	.95	0 - 4
296.	CPT Awareness of Errors AX	1.44	1.33	419	1.36	±	.75	0 - 4
297.	Responsive to Social Situation-GR	4.14	4.24	474	4.21	±	1.34	1 - 7
298.	Auditory Attention Span - Errors	75.28	74.99	238	75.07	±	14.41	40 - 108
299.	Diagnosed Hyperactivity - PRS	.01	.01	459	.01			0 - 1
300.	Diagnosed/Suspected Hyperact.-PRS	.08	.06	459	.07			0 - 1
301.	Severity of Child's Hyperactivity-PRS	.10	.07	456	.08	±	.34	0 - 3

(Appendix III-a continues on next page)

Block 13. Neuromotor at 7 Years of Age (NMot-7)

Items by Outcome Blocks	Alcohol Exposure (Mean Scores)		Total Sample					
	Binge P	No Binge	N	M	±	SD	Min	Max
302. CMT Process Score M&C - GR	.36	.29	486	.31			0	1
303. Seashore Rhythm Test C Errors	4.48	3.84	482	4.02	±	1.75	0	9
304. CMTV. Story D Poor Sequence	1.57	1.41	478	1.45	±	.65	1	3
305. CMT.Copy Des #1 Reversals	.12	.03	447	.06	±	.25	0	2
306. CMT.Copy Des #4 Poor Integration	.29	.21	448	.24			0	1
307. CMT.Copy Des #3 Poor Quality	.15	.08	448	.10	±	.37	0	3
308. CMT.Copy Des #4 Poor Magnitude	.13	.08	448	.10	±	.41	0	2
309. CMTV. Story B Poor Sequence	1.74	1.61	474	1.65	±	.69	1	3
310. Progressive Figures Log Time	.60	.56	483	.57	±	.28	0.21	1.88
311. MFF.# Responses Before Probe	9.24	9.46	453	9.40	±	4.03	0	25
312. CMTV. Story D Elements Recalled	13.62	14.59	484	14.31	±	4.07	0	20
313. MFF.# Correct Before Probe	5.56	5.75	453	5.70	±	2.17	0	12
314. CMT.Mem Des #3 Poor Quality	.37	.25	486	.29	±	.55	0	3
315. CMT.Mem Des #3 Poor Integration	.01	.00	486	.00			0	1
316. CMT.Mem Des #5 Recalled	5.10	5.32	448	5.25	±	1.40	0	8
317. CMT.Mem Des #2 Poor Integration	.13	.08	485	.09			0	1
318. CMT.Mem Des #1 Poor Integration	.26	.15	485	.18			0	1

#				n	Mean	± SD	Range
319.	CMTV. Story C Extra Idea	.50	.46	484	.47		0 - 1
320.	Torque Inconsistency ND	.09	.12	463	.11		0 - 1
321.	Seashore Rhythm Test A Errors	2.17	1.87	482	1.95	± 1.83	0 - 9
322.	Seashore Rhythm Test B Errors	2.99	2.89	482	2.92	± 1.87	0 - 10
323.	Blueberries: # Said	6.86	7.04	479	6.99	± 2.34	0.50 - 14
324.	Audiovisual Integration Errors	3.98	3.58	442	3.70	± 2.36	0 - 9
325.	Left Handedness	.14	.11	480	.12		0 - 1
326.	Legibility & Neatness of Writing	2.75	2.92	235	2.87	± .82	1 - 5
327.	Fine Motor Development -GR	1.13	1.14	469	1.13	± .36	1 - 3
328.	Gross Motor Development -GR	1.02	1.02	459	1.02	± .17	1 - 3
329.	Clear Unusual Hand Behaviors - BO	.02	.01	475	.02		0 - 1
330.	Clear Tremor - BO	.01	.01	475	.01		0 - 1
331.	Other Unusual Behaviors - BO	.06	.10	475	.09		0 - 1
332.	Neuro Touch Nose with Left Hand	.93	.98	208	.97		0 - 1
333.	Neuro.R Hand to L Ear - Sc#1	.89	.95	207	.93		0 - 1
334.	Neuro.R Hand to L Ear - Sc#2	.95	.97	206	.97		0 - 1
335.	Neuro.Touch E's Left Hand	.44	.45	208	.45		0 - 1
336.	Neuro.E's R Hand - Arms Crossed	.46	.43	208	.44		0 - 1
337.	Neuro.E's L Hand - Arms Crossed	.46	.45	206	.45		0 - 1
338.	Neuro.Point to Wall to the Left	.88	.91	208	.90		0 - 1
339.	Neuro.R Hand to E's L Hand - Sc#1	.39	.32	208	.34		0 - 1

(Appendix III-a continues on next page)

| | Alcohol Exposure (Mean Scores) | | Total Sample | | | | |
Items by Outcome Blocks	Binge P	No Binge	N	M	± SD	Min - - Max
340. Neuro.R Hand to E's L Hand - Sc#2	.88	.89	208	.88		0 - 1
341. Neuro.L Hand to E's L Hand - Sc#1	.37	.30	208	.32		0 - 1
342. Neuro.L Hand to E's L Hand - Sc#2	.86	.90	208	.89		0 - 1
343. Neuro.L Hand/E's R-Arms Crs-Sc#1	.42	.39	208	.40		0 - 1
344. Neuro.L Hand/E's R-Arms Crs-Sc#2	.86	.89	208	.88		0 - 1
345. Neuro.R Hand/E's L-Arms Crs-Sc#1	.47	.47	208	.47		0 - 1
346. Neuro.R Hand/E's L-Arms Crs-Sc#2	.91	.91	208	.91		0 - 1
347. Neuro.Th/Index: ln(Time) - Dom	1.98	2.00	208	1.99	± .17	1.47 - 2.55
348. Neuro.Th/Index: ln(Time) - ND	2.04	2.08	209	2.06	± .16	1.70 - 2.74
349. Neuro.Th/Index: Diff - Dom	.11	.24	209	.20	± .42	0 - 2
350. Neuro.Th/Index: Diff - ND	.14	.29	209	.25	± .48	0 - 2
351. Neuro.Suc.Fing Mvmt:ln(Time)-Dom	2.64	2.63	208	2.63	± .24	1.94 - 3.46
352. Neuro.Suc.Fing Mvmt: ln(Time)-ND	2.65	2.63	208	2.64	± .22	2.02 - 3.38
353. Neuro.Suc.Finger Mvmt: Diff - Dom	.65	.83	207	.78	± .69	0 - 2
354. Neuro.Suc.Finger Mvmt: Diff - ND	.71	.82	207	.79	± .68	0 - 2
355. Neuro.Sup/Pro: ln(Time) - Dom	2.16	2.16	209	2.16	± .19	1.65 - 3.14
356. Neuro.Sup/Pro: ln(Time) - ND	2.26	2.28	209	2.27	± .18	1.83 - 2.92
357. Neuro.Sup/Pro: Diff - Dom	.33	.44	209	.41	± .62	0 - 2

#	Variable			N	Mean	±	SD	Range	
358.	Neuro.Sup/Pro: Diff - ND	.49	.73	209	.67	±	.67	0 -	2
359.	Neuro.Toe Tap: Log(Time) - Dom	2.20	2.20	209	2.20	±	.26	1.65 -	3.51
360.	Neuro.Toe Tap: Log(Time) - ND	2.24	2.26	208	2.25	±	.25	1.72 -	3.10
361.	Neuro.Toe Tap: Diff - Dom	.42	.44	206	.44	±	.64	0 -	2
362.	Neuro.Toe Tap: Diff - ND	.46	.54	206	.51	±	.68	0 -	2
363.	Neuro.Heel-Toe Tap: Log(Time) - Dom	2.57	2.60	207	2.59	±	.27	1.82 -	3.58
364.	Neuro.Heel-Toe Tap: Log(Time) - ND	2.62	2.64	207	2.64	±	.28	1.75 -	3.63
365.	Neuro.Heel-Toe Tap: Diff - Dom	.88	1.03	207	.99	±	.69	0 -	2
366.	Neuro.Heel-Toe Tap: Diff - ND	1.02	1.13	207	1.10	±	.66	0 -	2

Block 14. Mental/Language at 7 Years of Age (Ment-7)

#	Variable			N	Mean	±	SD	Range	
367.	WISC-R: Full Scale IQ	104.78	108.72	482	107.58	±	14.45	54	-152
368.	WISC-R: Verbal Scale IQ	103.55	107.19	482	106.13	±	15.48	52	-155
369.	WISC-R: Performance Scale IQ	105.28	108.82	482	107.79	±	13.94	64	-145
370.	WISC-R: Information	10.37	10.97	482	10.79	±	2.93	2	- 19
371.	WISC-R: Similarities	11.46	11.90	482	11.77	±	3.22	2	- 19
372.	WISC-R: Arithmetic	9.19	10.46	481	10.10	±	3.05	2	- 19
373.	WISC-R: Vocabulary	11.31	11.54	482	11.47	±	3.18	2	- 19
374.	WISC-R: Comprehension	10.79	11.10	482	11.01	±	3.11	1	- 19
375.	WISC-R: Digit Span	9.51	10.30	482	10.07	±	2.66	1	- 19
376.	WISC-R: Picture Completion	10.84	11.30	482	11.17	±	2.53	4	- 18
377.	WISC-R: Picture Arrangement	11.34	11.83	482	11.68	±	3.00	2	- 19

(Appendix III-a continues on next page)

Items by Outcome Blocks	Alcohol Exposure (Mean Scores)		Total Sample						
	Binge P	No Binge	N	M	±	SD	Min	- -	Max
378. WISC-R: Block Design	11.16	12.15	482	11.86	±	3.21	1	-	19
379. WISC-R: Object Assembly	11.20	11.34	482	11.30	±	2.62	2	-	19
380. WISC-R: Coding	9.34	9.86	482	9.71	±	3.13	2	-	19
381. WRAT-R Reading Standard Score	108.66	114.73	482)	112.96	±	17.52	57	-	156
382. WRAT-R Spelling Standard Score	102.89	107.60	482	106.23	±	16.28	48	-	155
383. WRAT-R Arithmetic Stand Score	100.47	105.59	482	104.10	±	10.93	52	-	152
384. General Mental Development - GR	4.03	4.27	473	4.20	±	1.25	1	-	7
385. Language Development - GR	4.15	4.17	473	4.17	±	1.19	1	-	7
386. Overall Impression - GR	3.87	4.14	473	4.06	±	1.24	1	-	7
387. Oral Length of Utterance (SBT)	5.25	5.18	235	5.20	±	1.14	2.25	-	9.44
388. Written Length of Utterance (SBT)	4.00	4.23	232	4.16	±	1.06	1	-	9.67
389. DSS Score (SBT)	5.22	5.12	235	5.15	±	1.82	0.67	-	10.56
390. Misspelled Words (SBT)	.14	.14	233	.14	±	.12	0	-	0.59
391. Phonetically Misspelled Words (SBT)	.49	.53	216	.52	±	.34	0	-	1
392. Oral Syntax Errors (SBT)	.49	.50	235	.50	±	1.02	0	-	6
393. Written Syntax Errors (SBT)	1.62	1.21	233	1.33	±	1.60	0	-	8

Block 15. Learning Disability Assessed at 7 Years of Age (LD-7)

				N	Mean	±	SD	Range
394.	Full IQ7 minus WRAT Reading	-3.88	-6.00	482	-5.39	±	15.19	-48 - 39
395.	Full IQ7 minus WRAT Spelling	1.89	1.13	482	1.35	±	14.29	-41 - 46
396.	Full IQ7 minus WRAT Arithmetic	4.31	3.13	482	3.48	±	11.90	-31 - 44
397.	Distractibility - BR	3.05	2.67	480	2.78	±	1.85	1 - 7
398.	Cooperation - BR	5.11	5.42	481	5.33	±	1.49	1 - 7
399.	Inappropriately Persistent - BR	.06	.03	486	.04			0 - 1
400.	Reassurance Seeking - BR	3.28	3.18	483	3.21	±	1.76	1 - 7
401.	Organization - BR	4.82	5.01	479	4.96	±	1.65	1 - 7
402.	Delayed Speech - PRS	.01	.04	479	.03			0 - 1
403.	Stuttering, Stammering - PRS	.06	.05	479	.05			0 - 1
404.	Poor Articulation - PRS	.14	.14	480	.14			0 - 1
405.	Difficulty Using Sentences - PRS	.03	.05	479	.04			0 - 1
406.	Unwillingness to Talk - PRS	.02	.03	398	.03			0 - 1
407.	Other Speech/Lang. Problems - PRS	.06	.05	470	.06			0 - 1
408.	Difficulty of Caring for Child - PRS	2.17	2.12	479	2.14	±	1.05	1 - 5
409.	Learning Problem at School - PRS	.28	.22	480	.24			0 - 1
410.	Behavior Problem at School - PRS	.22	.19	480	.20			0 - 1
411.	Social Problem at School - PRS	.17	.11	480	.12			0 - 1
412.	Other Problem at School - PRS	.09	.07	478	.08			0 - 1
413.	Special Remedial Prog - PRS	.25	.16	473	.19			0 - 1

(Appendix III-a continues on next page)

| | Alcohol Exposure (Mean Scores) | | Total Sample | | | |
Items by Outcome Blocks	Binge P	No Binge	N	M	± SD	Min - - Max
414. Program for Exceptional Child - PRS	.07	.12	478	.11		0 - 1
415. Program for Specific LD - PRS	.08	.04	469	.05		0 - 1
416. Program for Remedial Reading - PRS	.12	.10	479	.10		0 - 1
417. Program for Remedial Math - PRS	.03	.01	213	.02		0 - 1
418. Tutoring - PRS	.02	.02	481	.02		0 - 1
419. Physical Therapy - PRS	.01	.01	481	.01		0 - 1
420. Perceptual Motor Training - PRS	.00	.01	481	.00		0 - 1
421. Speech Therapy - PRS	.05	.04	465	.05		0 - 1
422. Other Special Programs - PRS	.03	.04	475	.04		0 - 1
423. Social Adj Problems in School - PRS	2.35	1.82	480	1.98	± 1.18	1 - 6
424. Acad Adj Problems in School - PRS	2.74	2.14	479	2.31	± 1.27	1 - 6
425. Child Seems Clumsy for Age - PRS	1.82	1.82	207	1.82	± 1.11	1 - 6
426. Repeated Grade - PRS/TQ	.09	.07	485	.08		0 - 1
427. Skipped Grade - PRS/TQ	.03	.02	485	.02		0 - 1
428. Grade Appropriate for Birthdate	-.07	-.03	486	-.04	± .32	-1 - 1
429. Grade Appropriate Scale Score	-.12	-.06	486	-.07	± .40	-1 - 1
430. Conduct Problems (Conners)	4.26	3.60	476	3.79	± 3.01	0 - 20
431. Learning Problems (Conners)	3.07	2.39	476	2.58	± 2.17	0 - 12

#	Variable			N	Mean ± SD	Range
432.	Psychosomatic Probs (Conners)	.87	.77	476	.80 ± 1.14	0 - 5
433.	Impulsive Hyperactive (Conners)	4.48	3.70	475	3.93 ± 2.47	0 - 12
434.	Anxiety Problems (Conners)	1.61	1.57	473	1.58 ± 1.25	0 - 6
435.	Hyperkinesis Index (Conners)	7.79	6.40	476	6.80 ± 4.61	0 - 28
436.	ECBI Intensity Score	99.20	93.76	461	95.32 ± 24.77	36 - 193
437.	ECBI Intensity Score < 127	.11	.09	461	.10	0 - 1
438.	MPRS.Comprehending Words	3.22	3.48	469	3.41 ± .76	1 - 5
439.	MPRS.Cooperation / Impulsivity	3.21	3.63	469	3.51 ± 1.11	1 - 5
440.	MPRS.Attention	3.17	3.45	469	3.37 ± 1.00	1 - 5
441.	MPRS.Organization	2.99	3.23	469	3.16 ± .96	1 - 5
442.	MPRS.Adapts to New Situations	3.14	3.34	469	3.28 ± .90	1 - 5
443.	MPRS.Social Acceptance	3.33	3.42	469	3.40 ± .82	1 - 5
444.	MPRS.Following Instructions	3.25	3.43	469	3.38 ± .86	1 - 5
445.	MPRS.Comprehends Class Disc.	3.34	3.50	469	3.45 ± .96	1 - 5
446.	MPRS.Retains Information	3.22	3.53	468	3.44 ± .82	1 - 5
447.	MPRS.Vocabulary	3.22	3.38	469	3.34 ± .68	1 - 5
448.	MPRS.Grammar	3.17	3.40	469	3.34 ± .79	2 - 5
449.	MPRS.Word Recall	3.24	3.50	469	3.43 ± .79	1 - 5
450.	MPRS.Relating Experiences	3.30	3.47	467	3.42 ± .81	1 - 5
451.	MPRS.Formulating Ideas	3.15	3.39	469	3.32 ± .77	1 - 5
452.	MPRS.Judging Time	3.22	3.38	469	3.33 ± .98	1 - 5

(Appendix III-a continues on next page)

Items by Outcome Blocks	Alcohol Exposure (Mean Scores)		Total Sample					
	Binge P	No Binge	N	M	±	SD	Min	Max
453. MPRS.Spatial Orientation	3.57	3.70	469	3.67	±	.77	2	- 5
454. MPRS.Judging Size Relationships	3.50	3.66	469	3.61	±	.91	1	- 5
455. MPRS.Knowing Directions	3.21	3.32	469	3.29	±	.88	1	- 5
456. MPRS.Coordination	3.21	3.29	469	3.27	±	.76	1	- 5
457. MPRS.Balance	3.24	3.29	469	3.28	±	.61	1	- 5
458. MPRS.Manual Dexterity	3.08	3.28	469	3.22	±	.80	1	- 5
459. MPRS.Responsibility	3.17	3.32	469	3.28	±	.83	1	- 5
460. MPRS.Completion of Assignments	3.26	3.56	469	3.48	±	.95	1	- 5
461. MPRS.Tactfulness	3.44	3.68	469	3.62	±	.87	1	- 5
462. Classroom Skills-Reading - TQ	3.12	3.42	468	3.33	±	1.23	1	- 5
463. Classroom Skills-Spelling - TQ	2.99	3.37	468	3.26	±	1.12	1	- 5
464. Classroom Skills-Arithmetic - TQ	3.17	3.51	468	3.41	±	.98	1	- 5
465. Handwriting-Penmanship - TQ	2.99	3.22	468	3.16	±	1.06	1	- 5
466. Sentence Writing - TQ	2.99	3.27	468	3.19	±	1.10	1	- 5
467. Speech Articulation - TQ	3.34	3.44	469	3.41	±	.98	1	- 5
468. Frustration Tolerance - TQ	3.17	3.46	469	3.38	±	1.13	1	- 5
469. Impulsivity - TQ	3.21	3.40	469	3.34	±	1.13	1	- 5
470. Rigidity - TQ	3.29	3.42	467	3.39	±	1.01	1	- 5

471. LD Program This Year - TQ	.08	.06	465	.06	0 - 1
472. Is or Should be in LD Class - TQ	.10	.08	465	.08	0 - 1
473. MPRS.Total Score	77.72	82.54	465	81.19 ± 14.76	42 - 116
474. MPRS.Total Score <65	.18	.11	465	.13	0 - 1

Notes: Abbreviations are listed below in the order of their appearance in the table. The capitalized computer names in parentheses correspond to those in Appendix III-b, the 99 outcomes most salient for some alcohol pattern. Standard deviations are not prointed for the binary categorizations.

NBAS = Neurobehavioral Assessment Scale (Brazelton, 1973)

Reflex = reflex scores from the NBAS

Threshold = threshold scores from Reflex items of the NBAS

IBR = Infant Behavior Ratings from the BSID - by examiners

BSID = Bayley Scales of Infant Development (Bayley, 1969)

BO = Behavior Observations by examiners

GR = Global Ratings by examiners

BR = Behavior Ratings by examiners

Vig = Vigilance Test

PRS = Parent Ratings Scales (Conners Parent Rating Scale; Werry, Weiss & Peters Rating Scale; Eyeberg Child Behavioral Inventory; Psychiatric Checklist; study questionnaire)

WPPSI = Wechsler Preschool and Primary Scale of Intelligence (Wechsler, 1976)

Dom = Dominant Hand

ND = Non Dominant Hand

WMSB = Wisconsin Motor Steadiness Battery (Matthews & Klove, 1978)

Vert GB = Vertical Groove Board

Horiz GB = Horizontal Groove Board

Maze GB = Maze Coordination Groove Board

Err = Error

Notes (continued):

RS = Resting Steadiness

Log = Natural Logarithm

TPT = Tactual Performance Test (Reitan & Davison, 1974; Trites & Price, 1978)

GMB = Gross Motor Battery

Coord = Coordination

CPT = Continuous Performance Test (a Vigilance Test) (Rosvold, Mirsky, Sarason, Bransome & Beck, 1956)

X-Task = press to all "X"

AX-Task = press only to an "X" preceded by an "A" (Response/Inhibition – Impulse control)

CMT = Children's Memory Test (Dodrill & Miller, 1982)

CMTM = CMT Memory for Designs

CMTC = CMT Copy Designs

CMTV = CMT Verbal Memory

Des = design

Mem = memory

MFF = Memory for Faces (Milner, 1968)

Neuro = Neurological Exam (Szatmari & Taylor, 1984). Binary scores: 0=no; 1=yes

R = Right

L = Left

E's = examiner's

Sc#1=child gets to right destination

Sc#2=child uses correct hand

Crs = crossed

Th/Index = Thumb and Index finger opposition (# seconds to do 20 times)

Suc Finger Mvmt = Successive Finger Movements (# seconds to do 5 times)

Diff = Difficulty – Behavior Rating

Sup/Pro = Supinate/pronate Arm Alternatingly (# seconds to do 10 times)

Toe Tap = Repetitive toe tapping (# seconds to do 20 times)

Heel-Toe = Alternating Heel/Toe Tapping (# seconds to do 10 times)

WISC-R = Wechsler Intelligence Scale for Children - Revised (Wechsler, 1974)

WRAT-R = Wide Range Achievement Test - Revised (Jastak & Jastak, 1978)

SBT = Sentence Building Test of Johnson & Blalock (1987)

DSS = Developmental Sentence Scoring of L. Lee (1987)

TQ = Teacher Questionnaire

Conners = Parent Rating Scale of C. K. Conners (1969) - (Parent Report)

ECBI = Eyeberg Child Behavior Inventory (Eyeberg & Ross, 1978) - (Parent Report)

MPRS = Myklebust Pupil Rating Scale (1981) - (Teacher Report)

Appendix III-b

Alphabetized List of 474 Outcome Variables Used for the Longitudinal Analyses

Index numbers are sequence numbers for Appendix III-a.

280	ACADADJ4	296	AWERRAX	124	BR18M20	154	BR4Y4
424	ACADADJ7	295	AWERRX	125	BR18M21	155	BR4Y7A
15	ACTIV	289	AXRATCOR	142	BR18M4	156	BR4Y7B
428	AGEGRADE	56	BABIN	117	BR18M6	157	BR4Y8
365	AHTDDOM	26	BABINTH	118	BR18M7	92	BR8M1
366	AHTDND	251	BAL	119	BR18M8	97	BR8M10
10	ALERT	457	BAL7	120	BR18M9	98	BR8M11
273	ANH4	276	BLKD4	203	BR4Y1	111	BR8M12
434	ANXIETY	378	BLKD7	158	BR4Y10	112	BR8M19
270	ARITH4	323	BLUSAID	159	BR4Y11	99	BR8M2
372	ARITH7	116	BR18M1	160	BR4Y12	100	BR8M21
464	ARITHTQ	122	BR18M10F	161	BR4Y13	110	BR8M4
178	ATTEN4Y	121	BR18M10T	162	BR4Y14	93	BR8M6
440	ATTEN7	123	BR18M11	163	BR4Y15	94	BR8M7
298	AUDATTER	143	BR18M12	164	BR4Y16		
324	AVINT	144	BR18M19	204	BR4Y2		(Appendix continues)

257

No.	Code	No.	Code	No.	Code	No.	Code
190	G2SCOR	138	GMSS18M	301	HYPSEV7	285	LAXEO50
191	G3SCOR	202	GMSS4Y	433	IMPHYP	287	LAXFA50
192	G4SCOR	328	GMSS7Y	179	IMPULS4Y	471	LDPRG1
193	G5SCOR	106	GMSS8M	469	IMPULSCR	472	LDPRG2
194	G6SCOR	261	GMUPME	65	INCURV	326	LEGIB
195	G7SCOR	448	GRAMMAR	35	INCURVTH	431	LERNPROB
196	G8SCOR	429	GRDPROP	268	INFO4	239	LFMGPDPD
197	G9SCOR	243	GRIPD4	370	INFO7	240	LFMGPDPN
275	GEOM4	244	GRIPND4	437	INTEN127	215	LFMHORTD
19	GLAB	45	GTONUS	436	INTENSIT	216	LFMHORTN
39	GLABTH	3	HABBELL	396	IQWRATA	219	LFMMAZTD
91	GLOBIMP	1	HABLIT	394	IQWRATR	220	LFMMAZTN
262	GMDNME	4	HABPIN	395	IQWRATS	223	LFMRS1TD
260	GMLBCA	2	HABRAT	14	IRRITAB	224	LFMRS1TN
264	GMLBCO	66	HEADMV	452	JUDGTIME	227	LFMRS2TD
259	GMLBTH	36	HEADMVTH	455	KNWDIR	228	LFMRS2TN
255	GMRAR	53	HNDMOUTH	52	LABSKIN	211	LFMVERTD
256	GMRTOR	465	HNDWRT	16	LABSTAT	212	LFMVERTN
258	GMSBAM	300	HYP12D7	363	LAHTTD	351	LFSMTD
257	GMSBME	299	HYP2D7	364	LAHTTND	352	LFSMTND
254	GMSKAR	175	HYPER4Y	278	LANG4Y		
263	GMSKME	435	HYPERKIN	385	LANG7Y		

(Appendix continues)

84	RHEADMV	21	ROTEYE	131	SB18M3	37	SPCRWLTH
208	RIGHTHND	41	ROTEYETH	132	SB18M4	414	SPEC1
470	RIGID	69	ROTHD	133	SB18M5	415	SPEC2
83	RINCURV	40	ROTHDTH	134	SB18M7	416	SPECMATH
346	RL10C	79	RPALM	294	SCRENAX	418	SPEC5
345	RL10E	75	RPARM	293	SCRENX	419	SPEC6
332	RL1C	82	RPLAC	466	SENWRT	420	SPEC7
334	RL2C	73	RPLANT	309	SEQB	421	SPEC8
333	RL2E	76	RPLEG	304	SEQD	422	SPEC9
335	RL3E	77	RROOT	271	SIM4	417	SPECMATH
336	RL4E	22	RROTEYE	371	SIM7	413	SPECPROG
337	RL5E	87	RROTHD	427	SKIPPED	467	SPEECH
338	RL6C	85	RSPCRWL	18	SMILES	283	SPEKDF
340	RL7C	80	RSTAND	443	SOCACP	463	SPELLING
339	RL7E	86	RSTCRWL	423	SOCADJ	402	SPLANG1
342	RL8C	78	RSUCK	129	SOCSIT18	403	SPLANG2
341	RL8E	88	RTNR	166	SOCSIT4Y	404	SPLANG3
344	RL9C	361	RTTDDOM	297	SOCSIT7Y	405	SPLANG4
343	RL9E	362	RTTDND	103	SOCSIT8M	406	SPLANG5
89	RMORO	81	RWALK	357	SPADDOM	407	SPLANG6
59	ROOT	135	SB18M18	358	SPADND		
29	ROOTTH	130	SB18M2	67	SPCRWL		

(Appendix continues)

Appendix IV-a Scatterplot of 99 Outcomes Most Salient for Some Pattern of Alcohol Exposure

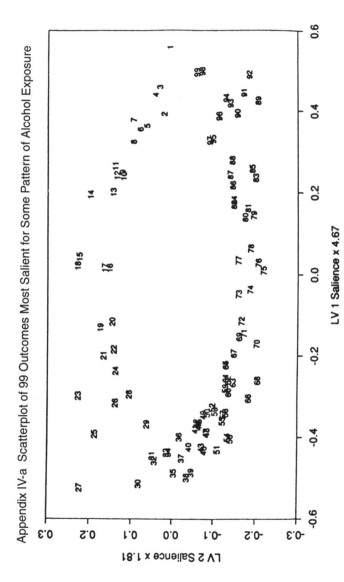

Outcomes related to all the primary alcohol exposure patterns are represented; scores farthest from the center of the matrix have the strongest relationship to some alcohol exposure pattern. Index numbers proceeding counterclockwise from the East are identified in Appendix IV-b. Please refer to Figure 5.3 for a diagram of the alcohol patterns represented by each compass direction.

Appendix IV-b

Listing of the 99 Outcomes Most Salient for Some Pattern of Alcohol Exposure

(The index numbers below correspond to those in Appendix IV-a and are numbered consecutively around the Appendix IV-a matrix in a counterclockwise direction, beginning in the East.)
The variable names can be used with Appendix IV-a to key into the variable descriptions in Appendix IV-b.

Index #	Variable Name	Block	LV1 Salience x 4.67	LV2 Salience x 1.81	Net Summed Squared Correlation	Description
1	ACADADJ7	LD-7	.56	.01	.31	Academic Adjustment Problems in School – Parent Rept - 7 years
2	CSHORC	NMot-7	.39	.02	.15	Seashore Rhythm Test Trial C, # Errors
3	SOCADJ	LD-7	.46	.04	.21	Social Adjustment in School – Parent Rept
4	MWSYNERR	Ment-7	.44	.04	.19	Mean Written Syntax Errors per Sentence Produced - Johnson SBT
5	LERNPROB	LD-7	.36	.07	.14	Sum of Learning Problems – Conners Scale – Parent Rept
6	VERBX4Y	Att-4	.35	.08	.13	Verbal Interruption and Talking Excessively – Parent Report
7	SPECREAD	LD-7	.38	.10	.15	Remedial Reading Either Last or Next
8	HYPERKIN	LD-7	.32	.10	.11	Hyperkinesis Index – Conners Scale – Parent Report

(Appendix IV-b continues)

Index #	Variable Name	Block	LV1 Salience x 4.67	LV2 Salience x 1.81	Net Summed Squared Correlation	Description
9	VGSEAT	Att-4	.25	.12	.08	Child Out of Seat During 4-Year Vigilance – Examiner Rating
10	SPECPROG	LD-7	.24	.12	.07	Any Special Programs in School: Pre-sch to 2nd grade
11	PRS<65	LD-7	.26	.14	.09	Total MPRS < 65 – Myklebust Scale – Teacher Report
12	LXFA50	Att-7	.24	.13	.08	Log Errors of Commission – X Task – 7-Year Vigilance
13	CONPROB	LD-7	.20	.14	.06	Sum of Conduct Problems – Conners Scale – Parent Report
14	CSHORA	NMot-7	.19	.20	.08	Seashore Rhythm Test Trial A, # Errors
15	CSHORB	NMot-7	.04	.22	.05	Seashore Rhythm Test Trial B, # Errors
16	GMLBCO	NMot-4	.01	.15	.02	Large Ball Kick: Coordination – Gross Motor Battery
17	BR18M8	Att-18	.02	.16	.03	Inattention to Tasks – Examiner Rating
18	ACADADJ4	Ment-4	.02	.23	.05	Predicted Academic Adjustment Problems – Parent Rept
19	FTNDFAT	NMot-4	–.13	.17	.05	Finger Tapping Fatigue Nondominant Trial 1-3
20	TORQNDIN	NMot-7	–.12	.15	.04	Nondominant Torque Inconsistency
21	SB18M3	Att-18	–.20	.17	.07	Distracted by Sights - Examiner Rating

#	Code	Description				
22	FACBTOT	Faces: Memory Before Probe, Total Responses	NMot-7	-.19	.14	.05
23	INCURVTH	Incurvation Threshold – Brazelton	Att-0	-.30	.23	.14
24	GMSKAR	Maturity of Use of Arms while Skipping – Gross Motor Battery	NMot-4	-.24	.14	.08
25	MORO	Left and Right Moro – Brazelton	NMot-0	-.39	.19	.19
26	TIDDOM	Difficulty with Dom – Thumb & Index Finger Opposition	NMot-7	-.32	.14	.12
27	HABLIT	Habituation to Light – Brazelton Scale	Att-0	-.52	.22	.32
28	FSMDND	Difficulty with Nondominant - Finger Successive Mvmt	NMot-7	-.29	.11	.10
29	D5MEM	Total Elements Remembered From Memory, Design #5	NMot-7	-.37	.06	.14
30	SPADND	Difficulty with Nondominant – Alt/Supinate-Pronate	NMot-7	-.51	.08	.27
31	DIG7	Digit Span Scaled Score, WISC-R	Ment-7	-.45	.05	.20
32	AXRATCOR	Ratio of Correct to Total Button Presses – AX Vigilance	Att-7	-.46	.04	.21
33	TACTFUL	Tactfulness – Teacher Rept	LD-7	-.44	.01	.19
34	GRAMMAR	Grammar – Teacher Rept	LD-7	-.44	.01	.19
35	COOPRTQ	Cooperation/Impulsivity – Teacher Rept	LD-7	-.49	-.00	.24
36	BLKD7	Block Design Scaled Score, WISC-R	Ment-7	-.40	-.02	.16
37	SPELLING	Classroom Skills – Spelling –Teacher Rept	LD-7	-.45	-.02	.20

(Appendix IV-b continues)

Index #	Variable Name	Block	LV1 Salience x 4.67	LV2 Salience x 1.81	Net Summed Squared Correlation	Description
38	WRATASS	Ment-7	-.50	-.04	.25	Arithmetic Standard Score – WRAT
39	ARITH7	Ment-7	-.49	-.05	.24	Arithmetic Scaled Score, WISC-R
40	BR4Y10	Att-4	-.42	-.06	.18	Attention Span – Behavior Rating Scale – Examiner
41	BR4Y11	Att-4	-.38	-.06	.15	Goal Directedness – Behavior Rating Scale – Examiner
42	ARITH4	Ment-4	-.37	-.07	.14	Arithmetic Scaled Score, WPPSI-R
43	RETAIN	LD-7	-.42	-.07	.19	Retaining Information – Myklebust Scale – Teacher Rept
44	ARITHTQ	LD-7	-.37	-.06	.14	Classroom Skills - Arithmetic – Teacher Rept
45	WRATRSS	Ment-7	-.37	-.06	.14	Reading Standard Score – WRAT
46	COMPWD	LD-7	-.43	-.08	.19	Comprehending Word Meaning – Myklebust Scale – Teacher Rept
47	WORDRECL	LD-7	-.39	-.08	.16	Word Recall - Myklebust Scale – Teacher Rept
48	PERFIQ4	Ment-4	-.39	-.08	.16	Performance IQ Score, WPPSI-R
49	WMLU	Ment-7	-.34	-.07	.12	Mean Length of Utterance (Written) – Johnson SBT
50	STORY	LD-7	-.34	-.08	.12	Relating Experiences – Myklebust Scale – Teacher Rept

#	Variable	Group				Description
51	TOTALPRS	LD-7	−.43	−.11	.20	Total Pupil Rating Score – Myklebust Scale – Teacher Rept
52	INFO7	Ment-7	−.33	−.10	.12	Information Scaled Score, WISC-R
53	SIM7	Ment-7	−.34	−.10	.12	Similarities Scaled Score, WISC-R
54	FULLIQ7	Ment-7	−.40	−.13	.18	Full Scale IQ, WISC-R
55	PIC4	Ment-4	−.36	−.12	.14	Picture Completion, WPPSI-R
56	VERBIQ7	Ment-7	−.40	−.14	.18	Verbal Scale IQ, WISC-R
57	FULLIQ4	Ment-4	−.34	−.12	.13	Full IQ Score, WPPSI-R
58	TASKFINI	LD-7	−.34	−.13	.13	Finishes Tasks – Myklebust Scale – Teacher Rept
59	MENTSS7Y	Ment-7	−.28	−.12	.09	General Mental Development – Examiner Rating
60	OVRIMP7Y	Ment-7	−.29	−.13	.10	Overall Impression – Examiner Rating
61	GRDPROP	LD-7	−.25	−.13	.08	Grade in School: Behind, OK, or Ahead in Grade
62	VERBIQ4	Ment-4	−.26	−.13	.09	Verbal IQ Score, WPPSI-R
63	VOCAB	LD-7	−.27	−.14	.09	Vocabulary, WISC-R
64	OVRIMP4Y	Ment-4	−.22	−.13	.07	Overall Impression – Examiner Rating
65	MENTSS4Y	Ment-4	−.22	−.13	.07	General Mental Development – Examiner Rating
66	READING	LD-7	−.31	−.18	.13	Classroom Skills – Reading – Teacher Rept
67	JUDGTIME	LD-7	−.19	−.15	.06	Judging Time – Myklebust Scale – Teacher Rept

(Appendix IV-b continues)

Index #	Variable Name	Block	LV1 Salience x 4.67	LV2 Salience x 1.81	Net Summed Squared Correlation	Description
68	FOLINSTR	LD-7	-.26	-.20	.11	Follows Instructions – Myklebust Scale – Teacher Rept
69	LANG7Y	Ment-7	-.15	-.16	.05	Language Development – Examiner Rating
70	VOC7	Ment-7	-.17	-.20	.07	Vocabulary Scaled Score, WISC-R
71	INFO4	Ment-4	-.15	-.17	.05	Information Scaled Score, WPPSI-R
72	COMP4	Ment-4	-.12	-.16	.04	Comprehension Scaled Score, WPPSI-R
73	OBJ7	Ment-7	-.05	-.16	.03	Object Assembly Scaled Score, WISC-R
74	LANG4Y	Ment-4	-.04	-.18	.04	Language Development - Examiner Rating
75	NEOSTATE	Att-0	.01	-.22	.05	State Changes – Brazelton Scale
76	UNCLVERB	Ment-18	.03	-.20	.04	Unclassified Verbalizations Among Items 80-163 – Bayley Scale
77	FMVERCN	NMot-4	.03	-.15	.02	Fine Motor Errors, Vertical Grooved Test, NonD – Wisconsin MSB
78	SQUIETB	Att-0	.06	-.18	.04	Self-Quieting – Brazelton Scale
79	PULLTSIT	NMot-0	.14	-.19	.06	Pull-to-Sit – Brazelton Scale
80	RL5E	NMot-7	.14	-.17	.05	Touch My Left Hand - Arms Crossed – Szatmari
81	UBHND7	NMot-7	.16	-.18	.06	Unusual Hand Behavior – Examiner Rating

ID	Code	Description				
82	RROOT	Abnormal Rooting in Either Direction – Brazelton Scale	.05	–.14	.17	NMot-0
83	RL8E	Touch My Left Hand With Your Left Hand – Szatmari	.09	–.20	.24	NMot-7
84	RL7E	Touch My Left Hand With Your Right Hand – Szatmari	.05	–.14	.18	NMot-7
85	PLACTH	Placing Threshold – Brazelton Scale	.10	–.19	.26	Att-0
86	FMVERCD	Fine Motor Errors, Vertical Groove Test, Dom – Wisconsin MSB	.07	–.14	.22	NMot-4
87	D2INTMEM	Poor Integration of Drawing 2, Memory – CMT	.08	–.13	.24	NMot-7
88	HNDMOUTH	Hand-Mouth Behavior – Brazelton Scale	.10	–.14	.28	NMot-0
89	D3QULCOP	Quality of Drawing 3 Copy – CMT	.22	–.20	.42	NMot-7
90	LFMVERTD	Fine Motor Log Time in Error, Vertical Grooved Test, Dom – Wisconsin MSB	.18	–.15	.39	NMot-4
91	D1INTMEM	Poor Integration of Drawing 1, Memory – CMT	.22	–.17	.44	NMot-7
92	DIREVCOP	Reversals of Drawing 1, Copy – CMT	.27	–.18	.49	NMot-7
93	FMRES2CD	Fine Motor Errors, Resting Steadiness, Dom – Wisconsin MSB	.19	–.13	.42	NMot-4
94	LFMRS2TD	Fine Motor Log Time in Error, Resting Steadiness #2, Dom in out Hand– Wisconsin MSB	.20	–.12	.43	NMot-4

(Appendix IV-b continues)

Index #	Variable Name	Block	LV1 Salience x 4.67	LV2 Salience x 1.81	Net Summed Squared Correlation	Description
95	HEADMV	NMot-0	.33	−.09	.12	Prone - Head movement – Brazelton Scale
96	LFMMAZTN	NMot-4	.39	−.11	.16	Fine Motor Log Time in Error, Maze, NonD – Wisconsin MSB
97	BR4Y1	NMot-4	.33	−.08	.11	General Body Tone – Examiner Rating
98	LAXFA50	Att-7	.50	−.06	.25	Log Errors of Commission – AX Task, Vigilance Test
99	LFMMAZTD	NMot-4	.49	−.05	.25	Fine Motor Log Time in Error, Maze, Dom – Wisconsin MSB

Notes: The column labeled "Block" indicates the Block in which each outcome is categorized and the age administered. This permits direct access to the data in Appendix III regarding which test the outcome derives from and the distribution statistics from this study. See notes to Appendix III for full information on each test administered. These quantities are extracted from the full PLS Analysis reported in Section 5.2. For aid in the interpretation of this table and the associated figure, see Section 5.3. The magnitudes of the entries in columns 1 and 2 can be compared. The third column of numbers is the square of the distance from the middle in Appendix III-a, which indicates the importance of some pattern of alcohol exposure for this variable.

Summary of PLS Results

This book has two main themes: methods and findings. We chose to centralize the discussion of methods in Chapters 2 (study design), Chapter 3 (procedures) and 4 (statistical computations). But then the findings had to be disassembled and scattered across a narrative organized method by method: two-block PLS analysis of entire correlation matrices, then scatters and regressions involving latent variable scores, then detection of specific profiles of damage in individual children.

As we noted in the Introduction and Guide to Using This Monograph, this serves some of our intended readers better than others. In particular, readers who are most interested in our general findings might find a narrative more convenient in which we grouped together all the findings regarding the same block or battery of measures rather than discussing them separately method by method. In this Appendix we review all the findings of Chapters 4 through 8 in this reordering. We do not have the space to present each finding again in full detail. Instead, first for the Alcohol block and then for the outcomes, in various groupings, we assemble the primary findings from earlier in this book, restate each in a sentence or two, and cite the text sections, tables, and figures in which it was discussed in its original methodological context.

The Alcohol Block

- The Alcohol block contains thirteen measures sampling a variety of timings and patterns of self-reported dose (Section 2.2.1, Appendix II, Tables 2.3–2.5).

- Transforming (recoding) these 13 items improves the power of the PLS models to simplify the structure of their correlations with the outcomes. These recodes were gently nonlinear (Figure 4.1, Section 5.1).

- In spite of the care taken to oversample the heavier drinkers when selecting the follow-up cohort, the Alcohol LV, computed as a salience-weighted combination of the 13 scaled individual alcohol scores, remains long-tailed (Figure 6.1). Properly scaled, high dose remains an infrequent phenomenon.

- The pattern of correlations of the Alcohol block with a composite of all the outcome scores emphasizes drinking early in pregnancy over drinking in mid-pregnancy, and shows binge-related intake to be more salient than spaced drinking (Section 5.2, Table 5.1, Figure 5.2).

- A second pattern of correlations of outcomes with the alcohol block incorporates a dimension of massed vs. spaced drinking. It may be reported as a contrast of high ADOCC against high MOCC at the same level of dose, or in several other ways (Section 5.2, Table 5.1, Figure 5.2).

- The Alcohol score with the greatest salience (net predictive power) for our 474 outcomes is ADOCCP, average drinks per occasion prior to knowledge of pregnancy. The score with the most typical profile of outcome correlations is MAXD, maximum drinks any occasion in mid-pregnancy. But the scores on our two Alcohol LVs (two dimensions of latent Alcohol dose) predict the typical outcome more powerfully than any single self-reported score (Section 5.2, Figure 5.2, Figures 6.1 and 6.2).

The Outcome Blocks

All 474 Outcomes Together

- A single dimension of alcohol dose explains 75% of the total summed squared correlations of all 13 alcohol scores with all 474 outcomes in our very large two-block PLS analysis (Table 5.3). The second dimension of alcohol explains an additional 11% of this total summed squared correlation.

- The sample correlation of the first Alcohol LV score with the estimated score for the first Outcome LV is 0.29; for the second pair, 0.33. These do not "wash out," but drop only to 0.26 and 0.30, respectively, when adjusted for relevant covariates (Section 6.2, Tables 6.2 and 6.3). The adjusted effect of alcohol is at least as large as that of any single covariate except sex of child.

- The sample scatter of the first outcome LV against its PLS alcohol predictor is very well-behaved (Figure 6.1), with no noticeable nonlinearity or outliers. That for the second outcome LV is less well-behaved. As a contrast, it explains less of the pattern of correlations with Alcohol, and it has less variance as a latent alcohol score. The reduction in covariance of this second pair of dimensions owes to the reduction in variance of this second alcohol LV, which is much longer-tailed than the first (Section 6.1).

- We have sorted the 474 individual outcomes by net salience for any combination of these two dimensions of alcohol scores (Appendix III). In descending order, the first few of these are HABLIT (poor habituation to light, from the Brazelton neonatal exam); ACADADJ7 (parent's report of academic adjustment problems at school at 7 years), D1REVCOP (more reversals in copying design 1 from the CMT, 7 years), SPADND (less rated difficulty with supination-pronation sequences, non-dominant hand, 7 years), WRATASS (poor WRAT arithmetic scaled arithmetic score, 7 years), LAXFA50 (more errors of commission, AX task, vigilance battery, 7 years), LFMMAZTD (more time in error, grooveboard maze, dominant hand, Wisconsin battery, 4 years), COOPR7 (poor cooperation/high impulsivity by teacher's report, 7 years), and ARITH7 (poor WISC-R scaled arithmetic score, 7 years).

- Each wave of outcomes has tapped substantially new effects of prenatal alcohol not expressed in the outcomes of earlier waves and not attributable to covariates (Section 6.3 and

Table 6.5). These may represent effects that become observable only as the children mature.

The Mental Blocks

- The Mental blocks included six of the 24 (out of 474) outcomes most salient for the first Alcohol latent variable (Table 5.1 and Appendix III). All derive from the 7-year wave of measurement: WRATASS (poor WRAT scaled arithmetic score, 7 years), ARITH7 (poor WISC-R scaled arithmetic score, 7 years), FULLIQ7 (lower WISC-R Full Scale IQ score, 7 years), VERBIQ7 (lower WISC-R Verbal Scale IQ score, 7 years), MWSYNERR (more written syntax errors, sentence building test, 7 years), and DIG7 (poor WISC-R Digit Span scaled score, 7 years). Most of these are most salient for a mildly binge-weighted pattern of maternal drinking (Figures 5.2 and 5.3).

- The effect of Alcohol upon the sequence of four Mental latent variables can be modeled as a causal chain, with a steady "Alcohol drip" wave after wave (Section 5.5). For purposes of this analysis across time, the Mental LV at each age is a standardized combination of all the scores available at that age (Bayley Infant Scales; WPPSI and WISC-R IQ tests; and WRAT Achievement test; as appropriate for age).

- A two-block PLS analysis of the effect of Alcohol upon the 11 subtests of the 7-year WISC-R shows that the effect of alcohol is *not* aligned with the general factor of intelligence per se. Instead, two subtests of the WISC-R, Arithmetic and Digit Span, are particularly salient as consequences of prenatal alcohol exposure at 7 years (Section 4.1, Table 4.3).

- The IQ latent variable expressing this dependence upon alcohol is strongly confounded with paternal education and SES. Analysis of a "centered IQ LV" studying only the weighted contrast between the alcohol-salient WISC scores and the others results in a correlation with the Alcohol LV of –0.17, now with hardly any remaining covariate effects (Section 7.3, Figure 7.4).

The Learning Disability Block

- The two-block PLS analysis of 81 items of the LD-7 block against 13 alcohol indicators is reported in Table 7.1 and Figure 7.2. The LD items most salient for prenatal alcohol exposure include ACADADJ7 (parent's report of academic adjustment problems in school at 7 years), SOCADJ (parent's report of social adjustment problems at 7 years), SPECMATH (special remedial math programs in school at 7 years), and the total Myklebust PRS score evaluated by classroom teachers. Individual MPRS items that were particularly salient include lower total MPRS score, poor cooperation/high impulsivity, tactlessness, low retention of information, poor word comprehension and retention, poor grammar and spelling, and poor arithmetic skills. The correlation of the Alcohol LV with the LD LV is 0.19. The alcohol predictor for the LD block is somewhat more binge-weighted than that for the pool of all 474 outcomes as a group.

- Our findings suggest that the conventional definition of Learning Disability as a discrepancy between ability and achievement is not useful for studying the effects of alcohol on learning problems in children of this age.

The Attention Blocks

- The Attention block for newborns showed a promising relation to Alcohol, with LV scores correlating 0.33. The items most salient for prenatal exposure (Section 6.3) include HABLIT, HABRAT and SMILES (poorer habituation to light and rattle, and fewer smiles) on the Brazelton Neonatal Scale, and also WALKTH and INCURVTH (high threshold for accomplishing the neonatal walking reflex, and lower threshold for the neonatal incurvation threshold).

- The salience of the block as a whole decreases with age (Table 8.1). The Attention-0 LV score is not accurate enough to serve as a signal of permanent alcohol damage at later waves (Chapter 8 and Figure 8.4).

The Neuromotor Blocks

- PLS analysis of the 65-item Neuromotor-7 block against alcohol (Figure 7.3 and Table 7.2) explains 75% of the summed squared correlations between blocks by a single pair of LVs. The NMot-7 items particularly salient for prenatal alcohol exposure include D1REVCOP and D3QULCOP (more reversals and poor quality of designs in Copy Designs tasks), D1INTMEM and D5MEM (poorly integrated design and fewer design elements recalled in Memory for Designs tasks), ELEMD (fewer story elements recalled in a verbal memory task), CSHORC (more errors in discerning similarities and differences in rhythmic patterns on Seashore test), and two items from the Szatmari neurological test: RL2E and RL1C (less success in touching left hand to nose and right hand to left ear) and four subjective ratings: SPADND, SPADDOM, TIDDOM, FSMDND (less difficulty in alternating hand and finger movements, with dominant and nondominant hands). This NMot-7 LV score correlates 0.33 with our overall Alcohol LV score.

- The correlation of these two LVs is large enough to suggest the possibility of detecting alcohol-damaged children by their scores (Chapter 8). Of the 13 children who are both in the top 7.5% of alcohol exposure and in the top 7.5% of this NMot-7 LV score, 11 show clear evidence of that damage: they are at or below the median of performance on every single earlier block- and wave-specific LV (Figures 8.2 and 8.3).

Literature Cited

Abel, E. L. (1979). Prenatal effects of alcohol on adult learning in rats. *Pharmacology Biochemistry & Behavior, 10(2),* 239-243.

Abel, E. L. (1980). Fetal alcohol syndrome: Behavioral teratology. *Psychological Bulletin, 87*(1), 29-50.

Abel, E. L. (1981). Behavioral teratology of alcohol. *Psychological Bulletin, 90,* 564-581.

Abel, E. L., & Sokol, R. J. (1987). Incidence of fetal alcohol syndrome and economic impact of FAS-related anomalies. *Drug and Alcohol Dependence, 19(1),* 51-70.

Aronson, M. (1984). Children of alcoholic mothers. *Report from the Department of Applied Psychology,* University of Göteborg, Göteborg, Sweden.

Aronson, M., Kyllerman, M., Sabel, K. G., Sandin, B., & Olegård, R. (1985). Children of alcoholic mothers: Developmental, perceptual and behavioural characteristics as compared to matched controls. *Acta Paediatrica Scandinavica, 74(1),* 27-35.

Baker, H. J., & Leland, B. (1967). *Detroit tests of learning aptitude, revised.* Indianapolis: Bobbs-Merrill.

Bayley, N. (1969). *Bayley scales of infant development.* New York: Psychological Corporation.

Becker, R. A., Chambers, J. M., & Wilks, A. R. (1988). *The new S language: A programming environment for data analysis and graphics.* Pacific Grove, CA: Wadsworth & Brooks/Cole Advanced Books & Software.

Bellinger, D., Leviton, A., Waternaux, C., & Allred, E. (1985). Methodological issues in modeling the relationship between low-level lead exposure and infant development: Examples from the Boston lead study. *Environmental Research, 38(1),* 119-129.

Birch, H. G., & Belmont, L. (1964). Auditory-visual integration in normal and retarded readers. *American Journal of Orthopsychiatry, 34,* 852-861.

Birch, H. G., & Lefford, A. (1963). Intersensory development in children. *Monograph of Social Research on Child Development, 28*(5), 1-48.

279

Blau, T. H. (1977). Torque and schizophrenic vulnerability. As the world turns. *American Psychologist, 32(12)*, 997-1005.

Blau, P. M., & Duncan, O. D. (1967). *The American occupational structure*. New York: John Wiley.

Bookstein, F. L. (1982). The geometric meaning of soft modeling, with some generalizations. In: K. G. Jöreskog and H. Wold (Eds.), *Systems under indirect observation: Causality-structure-prediction, part II*. (pp. 55-74). Amsterdam: North-Holland Publishing Company.

Bookstein, F. L. (1986). The elements of latent variable models. In M. Lamb, A. L. Brown, & B. Rosoff (Eds), *Advances in Developmental Psychology, 4*, 203-230.

Bookstein, F. L. (1990). An interaction term is not a measurement. *Behavioral and Brain Sciences 13*, 121-122.

Bookstein, F. L. (1991). *Morphometric Tools for Landmark Data: Geometry and Biology*. New York: Cambridge University Press.

Bouchard, T. J., & McGue, M. (1981). Familial studies of intelligence: A review. *Science, 212(4498)*, 1055-1059.

Boyd, T. A., Ernhart, C. B., Green, T. H., Sokol, R. J. & Martier S. (1990). Prenatal alcohol exposure and sustained attention in the preschool years. *Neurotoxicol Teratology, 13*, 49-55.

Brazelton, T. B. (1973). Neonatal behavioral assessment scale. *Clinics in developmental medicine*, No. 50. London: William Heinemann Medical Books, Limited.

Breiman, L., & Friedman, J. H. (1985). Estimating optimal transformations for multiple regression and correlation. *Journal of the American Statistical Association, 80(*391), 580-598. Comments 590-619.

Broman, S. H., Nichols, P. L., Kennedy, W. A. (1975). *Preschool IQ: Prenatal and early developmental correlates*. Hillsdale, N.J.: Lawrence Erlbaum Assoc.

Brown, R. T., Coles, C. D., Smith, I. E., Platzman, K. A., Silverstein, J., Erickson, S. & Falek, A. (1991). Effects of prenatal alcohol exposure at school age. II: Attention and behavior. *Neurotoxicol Teratology 13*, 369-376.

Cahalan, D., Cissin, I. H., & Crossley, H. M. (1969). *American drinking practices: A national study of drinking behavior and attitudes*. Rutgers Center for Alcohol Studies Publication, Monograph # 6. (260 pages).

Chernick, V., Childiaeva, R., & Ioffe, S. (1983). Effects of maternal alcohol intake and smoking on neonatal electroencephalogram and anthropometric measurements. *American Journal of Obstetrics and Gynecology, 146*(1), 41-47.

Chernoff, G. F. (1980). The fetal alcohol syndrome in mice: Maternal variables. *Teratology, 22*, 71-75.

Clarren, S. K. (1986). Neuropathology in fetal alcohol syndrome. In J. R. West (Ed.), *Alcohol and brain development* (pp. 158-166). ew York, Oxford: Oxford University Press.

Clarren, S. K., Astley, S.J., & Bowden, D.M. (1988). Physical anomalies and developmental delays in nonhuman primate infants exposed to weekly doses of ethanol during gestation. *Teratology, 37(6)*, 561-569.

Clarren, S. K., Astley, S. J., Bowden, D. M., Lai, H., Milam, A. H., Rudeen, P. K., Shoemaker, W. J. (1990). Neuroanatomic and neurochemical abnormalities in non-human primates exposed to weekly doses of alcohol during gestation. *Alcoholism: Clinical, Experimental Research*, 14 (5), 674-683.

Clarren, S. K., & Smith, D. W. (1978). The fetal alcohol syndrome. *New England Journal of Medicine, 298(19)*, 1063-1067.

Clements, S. D., & Peters, J. E. (1962). Minimal brain dysfunction in school-age child. *Archives of General Psychiatry, 6*, 185-197.

Clements, S. D. (1966). *Minimal brain dysfunction in children, terminology and identification. Phase one of a three phase project.* U.S. Department of Health, Education & Welfare. Public Health Service Publication No. 1415. Washington, D.C.: U.S. Government Printing Office.

Cochran, W. G. (1983). *Planning and analysis of observational studies.* New York: John-Wiley & Sons.

Coles, C. D., Brown, R. T., Smith, I. E., Platzman, K. A., Erickson, S. & Falek, A. (1991). Effects of prenatal alcohol exposure at school age. I. Physical and cognitive development. *Neurotoxicol Teratology, 13*, 357-367.

Coles, C. D., Smith, I., Fernhoff, P. M., & Falek, A. (1985). Neonatal neurobehavioral characteristics as correlates of maternal alcohol use during gestation. *Alcoholism: Clinical and Experimental Research, 9(5)*, 454-460.

Coles, C. D., Smith, I., Lancaster, J., & Falek, A. (1987). Persistence over the first month of neurobehavioral differences in infants exposed to alcohol prenatally. *Infant Behavior and Development, 10(1)*, 23-37.

Conners, C. K. (1969). A teacher rating scale for use in drug studies with children. *American Journal of Psychiatry, 126(1)*, 884-888.

Conry J. (1990). Neuropsychological deficits in fetal alcohol syndrome and fetal alcohol effects. *Alcoholism: Clinical and Experimental Research, 14(5)*, 650-655.

Day, N. L. (1992). Effects of prenatal alcohol exposure. In Zagon, I.S. and Slotkin, T.A. (Eds.), *Maternal Substance Abuse and the Developing Nervous System* (pp. 27-43). San Diego: Academic Press.

Dehaene, P., Samaille-Villette, C., Samaille, P-P., Crépin, G., Walbaum, R., Deroubaix, P., Blanc-Garin, A-P. (1977a). Le syndrome d'alcoolisme fœtal dans le nord de la France. *La Revue de L'alcoolisme, 23(3),* 145-158.

Dehaene, P, Tritran, M., Samaille-Villette, C., Samaille, P. P., Crépin, G. Delahousse, G., Walbaum, R., Fasquelle, P. (1977b). Fréquence du syndrome d'alcoolisme fœtal. *Nouvelle Presse Médicale, 6(20),* 1763.

Dodrill, C., & Miller, B. (1982). *Children's memory test.* Seattle, Washington: Regional Epilepsy Center (private publication).

Dorris, M. (1989). *The Broken Cord.* New York: Harper & Row Publishers.

Efron, B., & Tibshirani, T. (1986). Bootstrap methods for standard errors, confidence intervals, and other measures of statistical accuracy. *Statistical Science, 1,* 54-77.

Elardo, R., Bradley, R., & Caldwell, B.M. (1975). The relation of infants' home environments to mental test performance from six to thirty-six months: A longitudinal analysis. *Child Development, 46(1),* 71-76.

Ernhart, C. B., Wolf, A. W., Linn, P. L., Sokol, R. J., Kennard, M. J., & Filipovitch, H. (1985). Alcohol-related birth defects: Syndromal anomalies, intrauterine growth retardation and neonatal behavioral assessment. *Alcohol: Clinical and Experimental Research. 9(5),* 447-453.

Eyberg, S. M., & Ross, A. W. (1978). Assessment of child behavior problems: The validation of a new inventory, *Journal of Clinical Child Psychology, 7(2),* 113-116.

Finkelstein, J. & Herman, C. (1978). Psychiatric checklist for children. (unpublished). Division of Child Psychiatry, University of Washington Medical School, Seattle, Washington.

Frankenberger, W., & Harper, J. (1987). States' criteria and procedures for identifying learning disabled children: A comparison of 1981/82 and 1985/86 guidelines. *Journal of Learning Disabilities, 20(2),* 118-121.

Fried, P. A. (1990). Personal Communication.

Fried, P. A. & Watkinson, B. (1990). 36- and 48-month neuro-behavioral follow-up of children prenatally exposed to marijuana, cigarettes and alcohol. *Dev Behav Ped, 11,* 49-50.

Fried, P. A., Watkinson, B. & Gray, R. (1992). A follow-up study of attentional behavior in 6-year-old children exposed prenatally to marijuana, cegarettes, and alcohol. *Neurotoxicol Teratology, 14::*299-311.

Friedman, J. H. (1984). *A variable span smoother.* Technical Report No. 5. Palo Alto, CA: Laboratory for Computational Statistics, Department of Statistics, Stanford University.

Furlong, M. J. (1981). Torque: An at-risk indicator of reading or behavior problems? *Journal of Clinical Child Psychology, 10(3),* 165-167.

Galtung, J. (1967). *Theory and methods in social research.* Oslo: Universitetsforlaget; New York: Columbia University Press.

Golden, N. L., Sokol, R. J., Kuhnert, B. R., & Bottoms, S. (1982). Maternal alcohol use and infant development. *Pediatrics, 70*(6), 931-934.

Goodglass, H., & Kaplan, E. (1972). *The assessment of aphasia and related disorders.* Philadelphia: Lea and Febiger.

Goodlett, C. R., Bonthius, D. J., Wasserman, E. A., West, J. R. (1992). An animal model of CNS dysfunction associated with fetal alcohol exposure: Behavioral and neuroanatomical correlates. In Gormezano, I., Wasserman, E.A. (Eds). *Learning and Memory: The Behavioral and Biological Substrates* (pp. 183-208). Inglewood, NJ, Lawrence Erlbaum Associates.

Goodlett, C. R., Marcussen, B. L., & West, J. R. (1990). A single day of alcohol exposure during the brain growth spurt induces brain weight restriction and cerebellar Purkinje cell loss. *Alcohol, 7(2),* 107-114.

Goodlett, C. R. & West, J. R. (1992). Fetal alcohol effects: Rat model of alcohol exposure during the brain growth spurt. In I. S. Zagon & T. A. Slotkin (Eds.), *Maternal substance abuse and the developing nervous system (45-75). San Diego: Academic Press, Inc.*

Goyette, C. H., Connors, C. K., & Ulrich, R. F. (1978). Normative data on revised Connors Parent and Teacher Rating Scales. *Journal of Abnormal Child Psychology,* 6(2), 221-236.

Greene, T., Ernhart, C. B., Ager, J., Sokol, R., Martier, S. & Boyd, T. (1991). Prenatal alcohol exposure and cognitive development in the preschool years. *Neurotoxicol Teratology, 13,* 57-68.

Greene, T., Ernhart, C.B., Martier, S., Sokol, R. & Ager, J. (1990). Prenatal alcohol exposure and language development. *Alcohol Clin Exp Res, 14,* 937-945.

Greenacre, M. J. (1984). *Theory and application of correspondence analysis.* London; Orlando: Academic Press.

Gross, M. D., & Wilson, W. C. (1974). *Minimal brain dysfunction.* New York: Brunner/ Mazel.

284 en Literature Cited ...

Gusella, J. L., & Fried, P. A. (1984). Effects of maternal social drinking and smoking on offspring at 13 months. *Neurobehavioral Toxicology & Teratology, 6*, 13-17.

Hastie, T. J., & Tibshirani, R. J. (1990). *Generalized additive models.* London; New York: Chapman and Hall.

Hollingshead, A. B. & Redlich, F. C. (1958). *Social class and mental illness, a community study.* New York: John Wiley.

Horowitz, S. H. (1984). Fetal alcohol effects in children: Cognitive, educational and behavioral considerations. Unpublished Dissertation, Teachers College, Columbia University, New York, 1-100.

Hutchings, D. E. (1980). Neurobehavioral effects of prenatal origin: Drugs of use and abuse. In R. H. Schwartz & S. J. Yaffe (Eds.), *Drug and chemical risks to the fetus and newborn: Progress in clinical & biological research, vol. 36* (pp. 109-114). New York: Alan R. Liss, Inc.

Ioffe, S. & Chernick, V. (1988). Development of the EEG between 30 and 40 weeks gestation in normal and alcohol-exposed infants. *Developmental Medicine and Child Neurology, 30,* 797-807.

Jastak, J. F., & Jastak, S. (1978). *The wide range achievement test, revised.* Wilmington, DE: Jastak Associates.

Jessor, R., Graves, T. D., Hanson, R. C., & Jessor, S. L. (1968). *Society, personality and deviant behavior: A study of a tri-ethnic community.* New York: Holt, Rinehart & Winston.

Johnson, D., & Blalock, J. (1987). Sentence building task. *Adults with learning disabilities: Clinical studies.* Orlando: Grune & Stratton.

Jones, K. L., & Smith, D. W. (1973). Recognition of the Fetal Alcohol Syndrome in early infancy. *Lancet, 2,* 999-1001.

Jones, K. L., Smith, D. W., Streissguth, A. P., & Myrianthopoulos, N. C. (1974). Outcome in offspring of chronic alcoholic women. *Lancet, 1,* 1076-1078.

Jones, K. L., Smith, D. W., Ulleland, C. N., & Streissguth, A. P. (1973). Pattern of malformation in offspring of chronic alcoholic mothers. *Lancet, 1:*1267-1271.

Jöreskog, K. G., & Sörböm, D. (1984). *LISREL VI: Analysis of linear structural relationships by maximum likelihood, instrumental variables, and least squares method, 3rd Ed.* Mooresville, IN: Scientific Software.

Jöreskog, K. G., & Wold, H. (Eds.) (1982). *Systems under indirect observation: Causality-structure-prediction, Parts I and II.* Amsterdam: North Holland Publishing Company.

Kaminski, M., Rumeau-Rouquette, C., & Schwartz, D. (1976). Consummation d'alcool chez les femmes enceintes et issue de la grossesse. *La Revue d'Epidemiologie, Medecine Sociale Sante Publique, 24,* 27-40.

Kirk, S. A. (1962). *Educating exceptional children.* Boston: Houghton Mifflin.

Koppitz, E. (1964). *The Bender gestalt test for young children.* New York: Grune and Stratton.

Kron, R. E., Litt, M., Phoenix, M. D., & Finnegan, L. P. (1976) Neonatal narcotic abstinence: Effects of pharmaco-therapeutic agent and maternal drug usage on nutritive sucking behavior. *Journal of Pediatrics, 88(4),* 637-641.

Kyllerman M, Aronson M, Sabel KG, Karlberg E, Sandin B, Olegård R. (1985). Children of alcoholic mothers: Growth and motor performance compared to matched controls. *Acta Paediatrica Scand, 74(1),* 20-26.

Landesman-Dwyer, S., Ragozin, A. S., & Little, R. E. (1981). Behavioral correlates of prenatal alcohol exposure: A four-year follow-up study. *Neurobehavioral Toxicology & Teratology, 3(2),* 187-193.

Lee, L. (1984). Developmental sentence analysis. Evanston, IL: Northwestern University Press.

Lemoine, P., Harousseau, H., Borteyru, J. P., & Menuet, J. C. (1968). Les enfants de parents alcooliques. Anomalies observees. A propos de 127 cas. (Children of alcoholic parents: Abnormalities observed in 127 cases.) *Paris, Ouest Medical, 21,* 476-482.

Lemoine P., Lemoine, Ph. (1992) Avenir des enfants de mères alcooliques (Étude de 105 cas retrouvés à l'âge adulte) et queloques constatations d'intérêt prophylactique. *Ann Pediatr* (Paris) *39,* 226-235.

Lewis, M., (1975). The development of attention and perception in the infant and young child. In W. M. Cruickshank & D. P. Hallahan (Eds.), *Perceptual and learning disabilities in children* (pp 137-162). Syracuse, NY: Syracuse University Press.

Little, R.E., Anderson, K.W., Ervin, C.H., Worthington-Roberts, B., Clarren, S.K.. (1989). Maternal alcohol use during breast-feeding and infant mental and motor development at one year. *New England Journal of Medicine, 321(7),* 425-430.

Little, R. E. (1977). Moderate alcohol use during pregnancy and decreased infant birth weight. *American Journal of Public Health, 67(12),* 1154-1156.

Little, R. E., Schultz, F. E., & Mandell, W. (1976). Drinking during pregnancy. *Journal of Studies on Alcohol, 37(3),* 375-379.

Little, R. E., Schultz, F., & Mandell, W. (1977). Describing alcohol consumption: A comparison of three methods and a new approach. *Journal of Studies on Alcohol, 38*(3), 554-562.

Lohmöller, J. B. (1984). LVPLS program manual: Latent variables path analysis with partial least-square estimation. Koln: Zentralarchiv fur Empirische Sozialforschung, Universitat zu Koln. (Available in the USA from Dr. J. J. McArdle, 1929 Lewis Mountain Rd., Charlottesville, VA 22901.)

Majewski, F. (1981). Alcohol embryopathy: Some facts and speculations about pathogenesis. *Neurobehavioral Toxicology & Teratology, 3(2),* 129-144.

Marcus, J. (1984). *Neurological findings in Fetal Alcohol Syndrome.* Paper presented at the Academy of Neurology meeting.

Mardia, K. V., Kent, J. T., & Bibby, J. M. (1979). *Multivariate analysis.* New York: Academic Press.

Matthews, C. G., & Klove, H. (1978). Wisconsin motor steadiness battery. *Administration manual for child neuropsychology battery.* Madison: University of Wisconsin Medical School, Neuro-psychology Laboratory,.

Mattson, S. N., Riley, E. P., Jernigan, T. L., Ehlers, C. L., Delis, D. C., Jones, K. L., Stern, C., Johnson, K. A., Hesseling, J. R., Bellugi, U. (1992). Fetal Alcohol Syndrome: A case report of neuropsychological, MRI, and EEG assessment of two children. *Alcoholism: Clinical & Experimental Research, 16*(5), 1001-1003.

McGivern, R.F., Berka, C., Languis, M.L., & Chapman, S. (1991). Detection of deficits in temporal pattern discrimination using the Seashore Rhythm Test in young children with reading impairments. *Journal of Learning Disabilities, 24*(1), 58-62.

Meyer, L. S. & Riley, E. P. (1986). Behavioral teratology of alcohol. In E. P. Riley & C. V. Voorhees (Eds). *Handbook of Behavioral Teratology* (pp. 101-140). New York: Plenum Press.

Miller, M.W. (1992). Effects of prenatal exposure to ethanol on cell proliferation and neuronal migration. In Miller, M. W. (Ed). *Development of the Central Nervous System: Effects of Alcohol and Opiates* (pp. 47-69). New York, Wiley-Liss Inc.

Milner, B. (1968). Visual recognition and recall after right temporal-lobe excision in man. *Neuropsychologia, 6,* 191-209.

Mosteller, F., & Moynihan, D. P. (Eds.) (1972). *On equality of educational opportunity.* New York: Random House.

Mulford, H. A., & Miller, D. E. (1960). Drinking in Iowa: Part IV. Preoccupation with alcohol and definitions of alcohol, heavy drinking and trouble due to drinking. *Quarterly Journal of Studies on Alcohol, 21,* 26-39.

Myklebust, H. R. (1981). *The pupil rating scale revised: Screening for learning disabilities.* New York: Grune & Stratton.

Nanson, J.L., Hiscock, M. (1990). Attention deficits in children exposed to alcohol prenatally. *Alcoholism: Clinical, Experimental Resarch, 14*(5), 656-661.

National Institute on Alcohol Abuse and Alcoholism. U.S. Dept. of Health & Human Services. (1990, January) Seventh Special Report to the U.S. Congress on *Alcohol & Health.* From the Secretary of Health & Human Services.

National Joint Committee for Learning Disabilities. (1981). *Learning disabilities: Issues on definition.* Position Paper. (Available from The NJCLD c/o Orton Dyslexia Society, Chester Bldg. #382, 8600 LaSalle Road, Baltimore MD 21286).

Porter, R., O'Connor, M. J., & Whelan, J. (1984). *Mechanisms of Alcohol Damage in Utero.* CIBA Foundation Symposium, 105. London: Pitman; Newark, N.J.; Distributed in North America by CIBA Pharmaceutical Company (Medical Education Division).

O'Connor, M. J., Brill, N., Sigman, M. (1986). Alcohol use in primiparous women older than 30 years of age: Relation to infant development. *Pediatrics, 78*(3), 444-450.

Olegård, R., Sabel, K. G., Aronson, M., Sandin, B., Johansson, P. R., Carlsson, C., Kyllerman, M., Iversen, K., Hrbek, A. (1979). Effects on the child of alcohol abuse during pregnancy. *Acta Paediatrica Scandinavica,* Supplement (Stockholm) *275,* 112-121.

Ouellette, E. M., Rosett, H. L., Rosman, N. P., & Weiner, L. (1977). Adverse effects on offspring of maternal alcohol abuse during pregnancy. *New England Journal of Medicine, 297*(10), 528-530.

Parker, E. L., & Noble, E. P. (1977). Alcohol consumption and cognitive functioning in social drinkers. *Journal of Studies on Alcohol, 38(7),* 1224-1232.

Pentney, R. J. & Miller, M.W. (1992). Effects of ethanol on neuronal morphogenesis. In M. W. Miller (Ed). *Development of the Central Nervous System: Effects of Alcohol and Opiates* (pp. 71-107). New York, Wiley-Liss.

Phillips, D. E. (1992). Effects of alcohol on the development of glial cells and myelin. In Watson, R.R. (Ed). *Alcohol and Neurobiology: Brain Development and Hormone Regulation* (pp. 83-108). Boca Raton, Florida, CRC Press, Inc.

Randall, C., & Taylor, W. J. (1979). Prenatal ethanol exposure in mice: Teratogenic effects. *Teratology, 19,* 305-312.

Reitan, R. M., & Davison, L. A. (1974). *Clinical neuropsychology: Current status and applications.* New York: John Wiley.

Reyment, R. A. & Jöreskog, K. G. (1993) *Applied factor analysis in the natural sciences.* Cambridge; New York: Cambridge University Press.

Richardson, G. A., Day, N. L., & Taylor, P. M. (1989). The effect of prenatal alcohol, marijuana, and tobacco exposure on neonatal behavior. *Infant Behavior & Development, 12(2),* 199-209.

Riley, E. P. (1990). The long-term behavioral effects of prenatal alcohol exposure in rats. *Alcoholism: Clinical, Experimental Research,* 14(5), 670-673.

Riley, E. P., Lochry, E. A., & Shapiro, N. R. (1979). Lack of response inhibition in rats prenatally exposed to alcohol. *Psychopharmacology, 62,* 47-52.

Riley, E. P., & Vorhees, C. V. (1986). *Handbook of behavioral teratology.* New York: Plenum Press.

Rimmer, J., Pitts, F. N., Reich, T., & Winokur, G. (1971). Alcoholism: Part II. Sex, socioeconomic status and race in two hospitalized samples. *Quarterly Journal of Studies on Alcohol, 32(4, Pt.A),* 942-952.

Robinson, E. A., Eyberg, S. M., & Ross, A. W. (1980). The standardization of an inventory of child conduct problem behaviors. *Journal of Clinical Child Psychology, 9(1),* 22-29.

Room, R. (1970). Asking about amount of drinking. *The Drinking and Drug Practices Surveyor, 1,* 16.

Rosett, H. L., Snyder, P., Sander, L. W., Lee, A., Cook, P., Weiner, L., & Gould, J. (1979). Effects of maternal drinking on neonatal state regulation. *Developmental Medicine and Child Neurology, 21(4),* 464-473.

Rosvold, H. E., Mirsky, A. F., Sarason, I., Bransome Jr., E. D., & Beck, L. N. (1956). A continuous performance test of brain damage. *Journal of Consulting Psychology, 20(5),* 343-350.

Rouquette, J. (1957). *Influence of parental alcoholic toxicomania on the psychic development of young children.* Unpublished medical thesis, University of Paris, Paris, France.

Russell, M., Czarnecki, D. M., Cowan, R., McPherson, E. & Mudar, P. J. (1991). Measures of maternal alcohol use as predictors of development in early childhood. *Alcohol Clin Exp Res, 15,* 991-1000.

Sabatino, D. A. (1983). The house that Jack built. *Journal of Learning Disabilities, 16(1),* 26-27.

Savage, D. D. , Montano, C. Y., Paxton, L. L., Kasarskis, E. J. (1989). Prenatal ethanol exposure decreases hippocampal mossy fiber zinc in 45-day-old rats. *Alcoholism: Clinical, Experimental Research, 13(4),* 588-593.

Scher, M. S., Richardson, G. A., Coble, P. A., Day, N. L., & Stoffer, D. S. (1988). The effects of prenatal alcohol and marijuana exposure: Disturbances in neonatal sleep cycling and arousal. *Pediatric Research, 24(1)*, 101-105.

Seashore, C. E., Lewis, D., & Saetveit, D. L. (1960). *Seashore measures of musical talent: Manual. (revised)* San Antonio, Texas: Psychological Corporation.

Seidenberg, J., & Majewski, F. (1978). Zur haeufigkeit der alkoholembryopathie in den Verschjedenen phasen der muetterlichen alkoholkrankheit. (Frequency of alcohol embryopathy in the different phases of maternal alcoholism, STIAR #26, English translation available from the National Clearinghouse for Alcohol and Drug Information, P. O. Box 2345, Rockville, MD   20852.) *Suchtgefahren, 24*, 63-75.

Shaywitz, S. E., Cohen, D. J., & Shaywitz, B. A. (1980). Behavior and learning difficulties in children of normal intelligence born to alcoholic mothers. *Journal of Pediatrics, 96(6)*, 978-982.

Smith, D. W. (1980). Alcohol effects on the fetus. In Schwarz, R. H. and Taffe, S.J. (Eds). *Drug and Chemical Risks to the Fetus and Newborn* (pp. 73-82). New York: Alan R. Liss, Inc.

Smith, D.W. (1979).   Fetal drug syndromes: Effects of ethanol and hydantoins. *Pediatrics in Review, 1(6)*, 165-172.

Smith, D. W. (1970, 1976, 1982). *Recognizable patterns of human malformation; genetic, embruyologic, and clinical aspects, 1st, second and 3rd Editions.* Philadelphia: W. B. Saunders Company.

Smith, M., Delves, T., Lansdown, R., Clayton, B., & Graham, P. (1983). The effects of lead exposure on urban children: The institute of child health/Southhampton study. *Developmental Medicine and Child Neurology, Supplement 47,* 1-54.

Sokol, R. J., Miller, S. I., & Reed, G. (1980). Alcohol abuse during pregnancy: An epidemiologic study. *Alcoholism: Clinical and Experimental Research, 4(2),* 135-145.

Statistical Sciences, Inc. (1991). *S-PLUS user's manual.* Version 3.0. Seattle, WA.

Steinhausen, H. C., Nestler, V., & Spohr, H. L. (1982). Development and psychopathology of children with the fetal alcohol syndrome. *Journal of Developmental and Behavioral Pediatrics, 3(2)*, 49-54.

Stevenson, H. W., & Stigler, J. W. (1992). *The learning gap: Why our schools are failing and what we can learn from Japanese and Chinese education.* New York: Summit Books.

Stoffer, D. S., Scher, M. S., Richardson, C. A., Day, N. L. & Coble, P. (1988). A Walsh-Fourier analysis of the effects of moderate maternal alcohol consumption on neonatal sleep-state cycling. *Journal of the American Statistical Association, 83,* 954-963.

Strauss, A. A., & Lehtinen, L. (1947). *Psychopathology and education of the brain injured child.* New York: Grune & Stratton.

Strauss, A. A., & Kephart, N. (1955). *Psychopathology and education of the brain injured child, Vol 2.* New York: Grune & Stratton.

Szatmari, P., & Taylor, D.C. (1984). Overflow movements and behavior problems: Scoring and using a modification of Fogs' test. *Developmental Medicine and Child Neurology, 26(3),* 297-310.

Trites, R. L., & Price, M. A. (1979). *Assessment of readiness for primary French immersion: Kindergarten follow-up assessment.* Ottawa: University of Ottawa Press.

Vorhees, C. V. (1986). Principles of behavioral teratology. In E. P. Riley & Vorhees, C. V. (Eds.), *Handbook of Behavioral Teratology* (pp. 23-48). New York: Plenum.

Vorhees, C. V., & Butcher, R. E. (1982). Behavioral teratogenicity. In K.Snell (Ed.), *Developmental toxicology* (pp. 247-298). London: Croom Helm Press.

Vorhees, C.V., & Mollnow, E. (1987). Behavioral teratogenesis: Long term influences on behavior from early exposure to environmental agents. In J. D. Osofsky (Ed.), *Handbook of Infant Development.* 2nd ed. (pp. 913-971). New York: Wiley.

Wahlsten, D. (1990). Insensitivity of the analysis of variance to heredity-environment interaction. *Behavioral and Brain Sciences, 13(1),* 109-161.

Warner, R. H., & Rosett, H. L. (1975). The effects of drinking on offspring: An historical survey of the American and British literature. *Journal of Studies on Alcohol, 36*(11), 1395-1420.

Wechsler, D. (1974). *WISC-R Wechsler intelligence scale for children, revised.* New York: The Psychological Corporation.

Wechsler, D. (1976). *The Wechsler preschool and primary test of intelligence.* New York: The Psychological Corporation.

West, J. R. (1986). *Alcohol and brain development.* New York: Oxford University Press.

West , J. R., Goodlett, C. R., Bonthius, D. J., Pierce, D. R. (1989). Manipulating peak blood alcohol concentrations in neonatal rats: Review of an animal model for alcohol-related developmental effects. *Neurotoxicology,* 10, 347-365.

Wilson, J. G. (1973). *Environment and Birth Defects.* New York: Academic Press.

Wilson, J. G. (1977). Current status of teratology: General principles and mechanisms derived from animal studies. In J. G. Wilson & F. C. Fraser. (Eds.), *Handbook of teratology Vol 1: General principles and etiology,* (pp. 47-74). New York & London: Plenum.

Wold, H. (1959). Ends and means in econometric model building. In U. Grenander (ed.), *Probability and Statistics; The Harald Cramér Volume* (pp. 355-434). Stokholm: Almqvist & Wiksell, New York: John Wiley & Sons.

Wold, H. (1975). Path models with latent variables: The NIPALS approach. In H. M. Blalock et al. (Eds.), *Quantitative sociology: International perspectives on mathematical and statistical modeling* (pp. 307-357). New York: Academic Press.

Wold, H. (1982). Soft modeling: The basic design and some extensions. In Jöreskog, K.G. & Herman, O.A. (Eds.) *Systems under indirect observation: Causality-structure-prediction, part 2.* (pp. 1-54). New York & Amsterdam: North Holland Publishing Company.

Wright, S. (1968). Evolution and the genetics of populations; a treatise. Chicago: University of Chicago Press.

Index

References are to pages. All references, whether words or acronyms, are in one single alphabetized listing. Embedded digits come after letters. t, table; f, figure. Abbreviations: LV, latent variable; PLS, Partial Least Squares; WISC-R, Wechsler Intelligence Scale for Children–Revised; WPPSI, Wechsler Preschool and Primary Scale of Intelligence; WRAT–R, Wide Range Achievement Test–Revised.